CAREERS

IN EDUCATION

VGM Professional Careers Series

CAREERS
IN EDUCATION

ROY A. EDELFELT

VGM Career Horizons
NTC/Contemporary Publishing Company

Library of Congress Cataloging-in-Publication Data

Edelfelt, Roy A.
      Careers in education / Roy A. Edelfelt. — 3rd ed.
            p.   cm. — (VGM professional careers series)
      Includes bibliographical references (p.   ).
      ISBN 0-8442-4511-9 (hard). — ISBN 0-8442-4512-7 (soft)
      1. Education—Vocational guidance—United States.   2. Teaching—
Vocational guidance—United States.   I. Title.   II. Series.
      LB1775.E29   1997
      370'.23'73—dc21
                                                                                            97-25118
                                                                                                  CIP

Cover photo courtesy of International Business Machines Corporation.
Unauthorized use not permitted.

Published by VGM Career Horizons
An imprint of NTC/Contemporary Publishing Company
4255 West Touhy Avenue, Lincolnwood (Chicago), Illinois 60646-1975 U.S.A.
Manufactured in the United States of America
International Standard Book Number: 0-8442-4511-9 (cloth)
                                                            0-8442-4512-7 (paper)
15   14   13   12   11   10   9   8   7   6   5   4   3   2   1

CONTENTS

ABOUT THE AUTHOR

Roy A. Edelfelt has had several careers in education. After graduating from the Crane School of Music, State University of New York (SUNY) at Potsdam, and after a stint in the U.S. Navy, he taught instrumental music in the public schools of Kingston, New York. While he was employed in Kingston, Mr. Edelfelt earned a master's degree at New York University. He then took a position at SUNY at Oneonta as an instructor and a consultant in the College of Education's laboratory school, a demonstration facility for K–9 teaching.

Experiences in the Oneonta job soon led Mr. Edelfelt to apply for admission to Teachers College, Columbia University. Once enrolled, he pursued a doctorate in curriculum and instruction. On graduation, he began a career in higher education, first as an assistant professor at Saint Cloud State College (Minnesota) and later as an associate professor at Michigan State University.

In 1962, Dr. Edelfelt left higher education for the first of several leadership roles in the National Education Association (NEA). He was initially an associate executive secretary and then the executive secretary of the NEA's National Commission on Teacher Education and Professional Standards. Later he served as a senior associate in the organization's Division of Instruction and Professional Development.

In the early 1980s, Dr. Edelfelt became a freelance education consultant. Since 1987 he also has been a clinical professor at the University of North Carolina at Chapel Hill, and since 1989, an adjunct professor at North Carolina State University as well. He has authored, coauthored, and edited more than ten books and has published articles in many professional journals. Further, he has reported on numerous studies in the United States and overseas.

CAREERS

IN EDUCATION

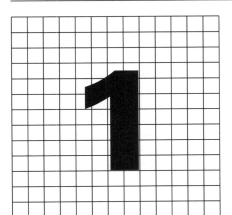

INTRODUCTION

Education in the United States is the underpinning of the culture, the basis of the quality of life. Now more than ever, it is one of the country's top priorities. In 1997, for the first time in a State of the Union address to the Congress, President Bill Clinton gave top billing to the improvement of education. Universal and free public education to age eighteen is a foundation of American democracy. An informed, literate, thinking population is essential to maintaining and improving the condition of the American people and to assisting other nations in raising their standards of living. Those convictions have long been commitments of educators, but now the public and businesspeople, as well as political leaders, concur.

In a country of more than 265 million people, public education alone is an immense undertaking, and public and private education together are a gigantic enterprise. The total expenditure for public and private education in schools, colleges, and universities is more than $500 billion per year. Data from a 1995 study show expenditures on training and development in business and industry to be $55.3 billion. However, some experts think that expenditures in this area are five to six times those figures. Federal government agencies spend an estimated $1.2 billion to $1.8 billion annually on training (direct and indirect costs). The precise outlay for adult and continuing education is unknown because of the many and diverse ways in which this component is delivered, but the amount is substantial. A 1991 study (the most recent available) reported that 69 million people had enrolled in adult education courses over the preceding three years. (There is no doubt some duplication in that figure; some people registered for more than one course.)

Formal education institutions employ more than 3.8 million people in professional (teaching) roles in elementary, secondary, and higher education. They employ another 4.3 million in administrative, other professional, and support staff roles. The number of instructors and teachers involved in adult and continuing education in business, industry, government, and other entities is enormous but elusive. In these fields, part-time and short-term use of people are frequent. An estimate for business and industry alone is 50,000. It is not clear whether that figure represents full-time equivalents or actual numbers, nor whether it overlaps with those for educators in traditional institutions.

A career in education was once exclusively a career in teaching, usually in an elementary or secondary school or in a college or university, or, to a lesser extent, in a church, a synagogue, or another religious institution. Today education is a much broader enterprise. Most educators are still teachers, but many specialty areas have developed. Some involve teaching, but others do not. Reading teachers, guidance counselors, librarians and media specialists, nurses, physical therapists, social workers, business managers, computer experts, deans of student affairs, and public relations officers are just a few of the many education professionals. Of course, there are also administrators for all levels and units of education, from preschool to higher education, building to district, department to institution, university to system, and local plant to corporate headquarters.

Developments in society have created a number of new areas in which education is needed. Some of these developments represent progress. Others present challenges. Still others reflect problems. All three kinds of developments demand new opportunities for learning and for attacking ignorance. They are creating new careers in education as schools, colleges, and other agencies begin to offer types of instruction that will provide enlightenment. Among the developments that represent progress are computers, robotics, and computer-video instruction, which are subjects to be studied and technologies to be applied in education. Among the challenges are learning to live with instant news, the radical reduction of distance, longer life and more elderly people, the continued presence of parochialism in a world that is international, and a new admixture of work and leisure. Among the problems that education must address are the spread of AIDS, drug and alcohol abuse, the special needs of minorities and non-English-speaking youngsters and adults, latchkey children, resegregation, teenage unemployment, and poverty. New and continued attention is being given to education for parenthood, intervention at preschool ages, career changes, dropout prevention and reentry, and prisoner rehabilitation.

Changes in some fields are swift. Teachers in computer literacy and technology became a reality in less than a decade. But agreement on what computer literacy and technology involve and what can and should be taught in schools is still elusive.

There is also the ever-developing phenomenon of adult and continuing education, conducted either for the benefit of the individual or the profit of the organization, but reflecting in either case the persistent need for people to acquire new knowledge and skills to remain effective in a changing society. The boundaries of education have expanded way beyond the school and the college or university. Education is part of almost every institution, agency, and organization in American society—business, industry, government, the military, professional associations, and all types of cultural and service agencies. Knowledge and technology are developing at such a rapid pace that continuing education for almost all citizens is essential.

All such education requires people to deliver it, including teachers, administrators, managers, and counselors. Hence, more people are now engaged in education of one sort or another than in any other occupation in the society.

It is reasonable to say, then, that education is a dominant career in the United States. It is also one that is rising in importance and status. Long a second-fiddle profession that did not offer adequate prestige or good pay, education is finally coming to the fore.

In thirty-two states, schooling is compulsory for children, starting variously at ages five, six, seven, and eight, but continuing until age sixteen. In the remaining states, the starting ages are similar, but the leaving age is seventeen years in nine states and the District of Columbia, and eighteen years in nine other states. Almost all other education is voluntary except that which an employer requires as a condition of continuing employment, or a government agency or a professional group mandates for continuing certification or licensure.

Institutions and agencies offering education include preschools; K–12 schools; vocational-technical schools; two- and four-year colleges and universities; graduate and professional schools; institutes; business and industry; federal government colleges, academies, and universities; the military; schools with programs for adult and continuing education; and arts and crafts schools. This book gives attention to almost all of these except schools that are strictly for vocational-technical, religious, or military training, or largely devoted to preparing artists, musicians, and craftspeople (for example, the Rhode Island School of Design, the Juilliard School, and the Cranbrook Academy of Art).

Teaching is the central career in education; all other educators exist to support teachers in one way or another. Teaching is also the usual entry point to other careers in education. This book therefore gives special attention to teaching at various levels and in various types of educational institutions. Further, it emphasizes public school teaching in kindergarten through grade 12 because that is by far the largest educational enterprise. However, the book does not ignore school administration, private K–12 teaching, higher education, and other careers in education.

Jobs that entail teaching vary so widely that generalizing about this activity as a single phenomenon is not reasonable. Some characteristics, however, apply to teaching anywhere and in any mode:

1. It involves a teacher and a learner.
2. The teacher has a special expertise: part of it is in-depth knowledge of subject matter, part a knowledge of teaching itself, and part a knowledge of the learner.
3. Teachers, even in proprietary institutions, are committed to enlightenment. They want their students to learn.
4. Teachers feel a responsibility to contribute to the welfare of society.
5. Teachers have ethics and standards of scholarship, which include considering the available data, treating data and issues objectively, reporting findings fairly, and respecting the privacy of students.

WHY CHOOSE A CAREER IN EDUCATION?

Education offers a number of career opportunities and entails some major responsibilities. In the best circumstances a career in education can be challenging, satisfying, and rewarding. Whether or not it becomes so depends on what an individual expects or wants from such a career and how deliberately he or she sets out to find employment that will satisfy those desires. This book is designed to help individuals explore various professions in education by providing information, opinions, and other sources of data that will promote a deliberate process of weighing and choosing.

Teaching

Many people choose teaching (and remain teachers) because they are especially interested in a particular subject such as English, chemistry, or engineering. Teaching is one way to pursue an intellectual attraction to a field. College professors, in particular, are committed to study and research in their discipline. The job of any teacher, any educator, requires study throughout a career.

Another reason people are drawn to teaching is that they like working with young people. They find the mind of the child, the adolescent, or the young adult fresh and comparatively unspoiled. They find nurturing the growth and development of the young to be one of life's greatest challenges. Although young people are naive at times, even frustrating and taxing, most are straightforward and trusting, and most are eager to learn. They display a candor and genuineness that often are absent or hidden in adults.

Teaching is a constant learning process. One learns any subject better and in greater depth by teaching it. The fascination of thinking and discovering, which involves probing the dimensions of knowing, is still another attraction of teaching. When a person is keen on a subject, intrigued with the thinking and learning process, and partial to young or uninformed people, there is a good chance that teaching will prove a satisfying career.

Associating with students stimulates some teachers, challenges most, and requires all to examine the current styles and tastes of young (and different) people. The experience keeps teachers with a sufficiently receptive attitude on the forefront of the developing world. Many find that the association helps them stay youthful.

Teachers tend to be altruistic about contributing to the development of the next generation. Some are driven by a desire to help others take advantage of the opportunities that they themselves missed.

Many nonteaching careers in education begin with teaching in an elementary or secondary school, or a college or university. This is true of virtually all public school administrators, from assistant principal to superintendent, and of specialists and supervisors whose entry-level function involves instruction (as opposed, say, to diagnosis and treatment). It is also true of many private school administrators, specialists, and supervisors and many higher education administrators.

On the practical side, people often choose teaching because it has job security, once tenure (and for public school teachers, a regular teaching credential) has been earned. Some are attracted by what appears to be an easy work schedule—for example, for teachers in elementary and secondary schools, a five-and-a-half-hour workday with students, a work year of forty weeks, and time off at Christmas or Hanukkah, in the spring, and on all legal holidays. Appearances are deceiving, however. A recent survey by the National Education Association revealed that public school teachers spend an average of 46.7 hours a week on all teaching duties. Further, on average, they spend 10.3 hours per week on such noncompensated school-related activities as preparing lessons and grading papers and 6.2 hours on such compensated noninstructional activities as serving bus duty, monitoring the lunchroom, and advising clubs.

Public school teachers get little time for lunch at any level of school. Elementary school teachers, who typically teach the same children for the entire day, average thirty-two minutes for lunch, in some cases while supervising students. Secondary school teachers average thirty-one minutes for lunch. Around that daily break, in a week's time secondary school teachers teach a mean of twenty-three periods (usually fifty-two minutes long) and spend a mean of five periods preparing to teach.

That summers are free is a myth for many teachers. The off-season is often occupied with advanced study, fulfillment of local or state inservice education requirements, or travel to enlarge perspective. Data like these refute the popular notion that teachers have an easy work schedule.

Teachers in higher education are drawn to the profession for many of the reasons stated for K–12 teachers, and for others as well. They value the intellectual freedom and interaction, the opportunity continually to seek greater depth of knowledge in a major field, and the chance to do research. And the work schedule, though rigorous, is appealing: professors must be present for classes, for a certain number of office hours with students, and for various meetings, but within those constraints they may come and go as they please, doing their preparations, research, reading, and related activities wherever they wish.

Special Services

Because of the great diversity of specialists and their wide deployment, it is difficult to generalize about why people do or should choose careers as specialists. Specialists are personnel in public schools and colleges who are not regular classroom teachers but who have expertise in an area critical to schooling, such as reading, speech-language pathology and audiology, and psychology. Although they may teach, they also consult and engage in a number of other activities. School specialists have latitude beyond that of most school personnel, particularly if they are itinerant teachers, and that is one reason why the career is appealing. Specialists in higher education may have less freedom of activity than their academic colleagues. A psychologist serving as a counselor to college students, for example, may have full-day office hours on most or all days.

Music, art, and physical education specialists are similar to other school specialists in regard to latitude and thus offer a good example. They have or can have unique work schedules. Most regular classroom teachers (and even administrators) are tied to a building. Classes come one after another, at the same time of day, day in and day out, for forty weeks per year. But many music and art teachers travel from one building to another and thus have a different schedule almost every day. They get out into the air between assignments. They interact with a wide variety of teachers. They eat in a variety of lunchrooms. They teach children in different grades, K–4, K–6, even K–12. The students with whom they work are not merely passive listeners and observers but active participants.

Physical education teachers can work outdoors, weather permitting. Music teachers can teach classes and work with performance groups as well. Art teachers can work with accomplished high school students in a studio situation and still teach beginners in general art in the elementary school.

Art, music, and physical education teachers often receive greater acclaim than other teachers. They are more visible. For example, they have an opportunity to display publicly the accomplishments of their students in exhibitions, concerts, and athletic events.

Administration or Supervision

Most people become educators because they want to help young people grow and develop and because they want to participate in the academic life. They are committed to the intellectual process, to the importance of thinking and reasoning, to discovery and advancement of knowledge. Educators think first about what they can do to meet those commitments.

Administrators or supervisors attempt to facilitate groups of teachers in reaching such goals. The possibility of exercising leadership that motivates others to improve their performance in helping students learn is the attraction. The word *facilitate* is key. Administrators who see themselves as riding a white horse and leading a charge are usually reined in by those whom they are leading, who are often as able and insightful as they are. Further, and particularly in higher education, the protocols of academic life ensure freedom to challenge and contest, the right to voice diverse theories and rationales, and protection for those who take issue with or resist administrative decrees.

People who choose to be administrators and supervisors in public schools share many of the motivations of teachers. One bit of evidence to support this was revealed in a study by the National Association of Secondary School Principals (NASSP). In a random sampling, principals were asked to indicate the degree to which their job *actually* yielded the following rewards: prestige, opportunity for independent thought and action, self-fulfillment, job security, and opportunity to be helpful to other people. They rated the last choice much higher by far than any of the other four. A separate and unrelated study of principals in middle-level schools (which include both middle and junior high schools) produced the same results. Both senior high and middle-level school principals rated prestige and self-fulfillment second and third as both *actual* and *ideal* job characteristics that proved most satisfying.

One hope of those who become principals is that as the people in charge, they will have greater influence on a school than they have as one of many teachers. Two types of influence are obvious: what they can contribute to others and what they can achieve for themselves. Contributions to others can be expressed in terms of purposes. In the surveys of middle-level and senior high school principals, the NASSP found concurrence on four of eleven possible purposes of American schools; that is, that students should:

1. Acquire basic skills
2. Develop positive self-concepts and good human relations
3. Develop skills and practice in critical intellectual inquiry and problem solving
4. Develop moral and spiritual values

It seems reasonable to assume that having identified these four goals as top priorities of American schools, principals hold them among the purposes of their own schools.

CAREER PATTERNS IN EDUCATION

The common characteristics of the many professional jobs in education make it comparatively easy to move from one job to another. Certain vertical moves are typical: college professors, government and organization bureaucrats, superintendents of schools, and other top figures in education typically began as teachers and proceeded through several steps and up successive rungs of a ladder in the education hierarchy.

Horizontal moves are also evident. A reading teacher may for a time teach youngsters who are gifted and talented and later shift to teaching youngsters who are mentally retarded; or a middle school teacher may after a number of years switch to a high school. On other rungs of the ladder, a director of an instructional materials center may become the head of professional development for a district or the director of a media center.

Careers in education, then, can involve vertical and horizontal moves. There is no need to fear becoming stagnant or getting in a rut. Numerous job shifts are possible, provided that the economy and supply and demand remain as they are or improve.

THE SCOPE OF THIS BOOK

This chapter provides an introduction to careers in education and is important as background to the whole enterprise. The person interested in any career in education should read it before reading about a particular career.

He or she also should read Chapter 2 in its entirety, or at least the part that focuses on the act of teaching, regardless of context. Teaching is both a science and an art. Fundamental competencies have been identified and can be taught to prospective teachers. However, some aspects of teaching behavior may be a function of personality type or of intuition. Also, teaching styles may differ according to the practitioner's philosophy of education. Teaching itself calls for the performance of many roles and the orchestration of many methods. But outcomes are not entirely within the practitioner's control. These and similar considerations are addressed in Chapter 2.

Chapter 2 also treats the subject of teaching in the K–12 domain, in public or private schools. Regular teachers at these levels typically work in classrooms, although they function in other contexts as well. The schedule and the organization of work vary by level (elementary, middle, and secondary) but are fairly well defined and similar across institutions within a given level.

Chapter 3 moves the context from the classroom to the school building and then to the school district, examining careers as leaders of these units, that is, as principals and superintendents. Research indicates that principals are key figures in public schooling and often the catalysts for quality and improvement at the building level. Superintendents are the chief executive officers, the top managers of school systems. They link the school to the local community and the state education agency.

In Chapter 4, attention turns to the superintendent's support staff. These are often behind-the-scenes people in instruction, finance and business, personnel, public relations, and other areas who keep the schools open, operating, and, ideally, advancing. Some, such as supervisors of science or home economics, oversee the content and the methods components of schooling. Others manage such responsibilities as the school district's payroll, purchasing, budgeting, and accounting; its hiring, promotion, evaluation, and other personnel matters; its relations with the state and federal governments; or its relations with the local community. Still others focus on services and logistics, like plant maintenance, transportation, and food.

Chapter 5 examines the roles of the professionals who address particular aspects of young people's growth and development, such as reading skills, expressiveness, appreciation of the arts and humanities, social and psychological development, mental health, physical functioning, general welfare, educational future, and speech and hearing abilities. Examples of this type of personnel are art, music, and special education teachers; guidance counselors and psychologists; librarians and media specialists; nurses; occupational and physical therapists; and social workers. These specialists may work with students directly, but they also may help students indirectly, by consulting with teachers, principals, parents, and other school personnel.

Careers in two- and four-year colleges and universities are discussed in Chapter 6. In all three types of institutions, the roles of teacher and administrator are prominent. At the four-year college and university level, the roles of teacher-researcher and researcher emerge. These roles are not wholly absent in elementary and secondary schools or two-year colleges; they are simply rarities in those contexts. Roles analogous to some of the specialist positions described in Chapter 5 also are treated—for example, various student affairs officers, whose responsibilities resemble those of guidance counselors.

Chapter 7 transports the reader from the subject of careers in traditional education to that of careers in the nontraditional realm. The focus is education that is intended to benefit the individual, be it work- or leisure-related. Some educators in this domain are employed in traditional institutions, and some in new delivery systems, but all are teaching, administering, or counseling in nontraditional ways—for example, in independent study and distance learning.

Chapter 8 explores careers in continuing education that are job oriented and profit motivated. Attention here is on training and development in the private sector, including efforts to keep employees abreast of technological advances, to boost their morale, and to increase their productivity. Education in this sector has long existed in the guise of on-the-job training, but it has mushroomed as the country has been transformed from an industrial society to a postindustrial one grounded in information and service.

Chapter 9 focuses on the agencies, the councils, and the professional associations that monitor and provide technical assistance to the professionals, the institutions, and the organizations discussed in Chapters 2 through 7. They influence, and in some cases mandate, standards for training and, to a lesser extent, standards for practice. Many of them also have formulated ethical principles. Virtually all are involved in the accreditation of programs that prepare candidates for their field, in the recognition or approval of programs, or in the credentialing of individual practitioners.

The data in this book are the most up-to-date that were available at the time of writing. Indeed, some information was supplied to the author in pre-publication form. Nevertheless, certain kinds of data—such as those on salaries—are frequently two or three years old by the time they are published. Hence, the reader is advised to explore the various sources and resources that are identified in the two appendixes. These contain information about relevant print materials and organizations.

Obviously, this volume does not cover every conceivable job in education. For example, it omits discussion of positions in proprietary schools at the elementary and secondary levels. It does not address short-term teaching and administration, such as overseas assignments in the Peace Corps or the Department of Defense Schools, and stints in colleges operated by private corporations. It makes little mention of religious education. Also, there is no attention to work in radio and television instruction or distance learning, or to the administrative and other positions attendant on those activities. The book does not treat private tutoring or lessons, camp work, and athletic coaching, all of which are kinds of teaching, nor does it address preschool teaching and work in daycare centers, which are becoming prominent—and controversial—areas of education.

Neglected too are education careers in the government (except in education agencies) and the military. Chapter 7 does include a brief discussion of major military and government programs in adult and continuing education—DANTES and the USDA Graduate School, respectively. Many more programs of these kinds exist. Furthermore, both the government and the military invest vast sums in training and development of civil servants and service members, analogous to the business and industry effort described in Chapter 8. These omissions may be perceived as mistaken, but they were deliberate. Boundaries must be drawn somewhere.

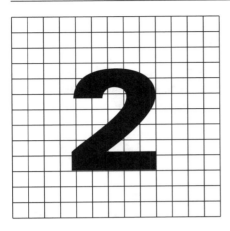

TEACHING IN K–12 SCHOOLS

People interested in a career in teaching are approaching it differently these days than they did in the past. They are giving greater consideration to its benefits and shortcomings, and taking steps to discover what it involves, what it requires, and whether work in schools will be satisfying. These changes have been brought on primarily by four conditions.

First, the realities of teaching have been exposed in the extensive public attention given to education. Those exploring teaching seem to have discovered that teaching is no simple endeavor. Jobs vary greatly. Some, particularly in urban and rural areas, can be very difficult. A few are only for those who truly want to help disadvantaged, abused, neglected, or disillusioned youngsters, and who have the temperament, ingenuity, and disposition to deal with the situation. In rural schools, particularly those in remote locales or poverty zones, materials and facilities are often meager, the exposures available to students are minimal, and a teacher's personal life and privacy are limited. Teachers in such schools must have strong social commitments. They must be equipped emotionally and intellectually with the skills, the tenacity, and the personality to handle the special problems that may arise.

Even jobs in affluent suburbs may be hard to manage. Some youths have everything money can buy, but little depth or self-discipline.

Most teaching jobs, although difficult and stressful, are not that challenging to one's values. Teaching can yield great satisfaction for the serious professional, but an individual must carefully explore the type of school and context in which he or she accepts employment.

A second reason that people are now looking differently at teaching is that employment prospects are better. In a number of places, in some specialties, and at some levels, the supply of teachers is not sufficient to meet the demand.

Slight improvements in salaries constitute the third reason for more people considering teaching as a career. Although pay is still not equal to that in other fields requiring college degrees, progress has been made in the last few years. Also, teaching provides job security and fringe benefits that are much better than average.

Finally, teaching is attracting a number of older candidates. About one-third of those in training are twenty-five years of age and over, and many of them are entering teaching from another career. More mature people tend to look at career choices with greater seriousness. They bring broader experience and greater wisdom to the profession.

The more-considered exploration of teaching is a welcome change from the approach of the last half century, which relied heavily on high school and college recruitment programs. The vigor of such programs declined in the early 1970s when an oversupply of teachers developed. Surprisingly, institutions preparing teachers had little effect on reducing that oversupply. When job prospects became almost nonexistent, young people simply decided not to enter teaching. Simultaneously, new and promising careers began to open to women. The opportunity to pursue careers other than teaching was one reason that a number of women opted not to teach.

The prospect of more people choosing teaching with their eyes wide open augurs well for the profession. Schools should become better places to work if they are staffed by people who select teaching as a career after comparing it with other possibilities and taking a careful look at what it involves. The goal of this chapter is to help people make such examinations. Most of the chapter deals with teaching in public schools. At the end, some characteristics that differentiate private school teaching from public school teaching are discussed.

PUBLIC SCHOOL TEACHING

Teaching is different from work in industry and business. Its method, purpose, and process are distinctive in several ways. Teaching, for instance, has no clear cause-and-effect relationships. No one claims with assurance that a given lesson will result in a precise outcome. Research confirms that children who go to school learn more than children who do not. But whether learning can be attributed directly to one or several teachers, or whether it is a result of such other factors as the student's socioeconomic status and the school context, is often uncertain. Also problematic is whether learning can be verified immediately or whether it can be determined only over weeks, months, and years. Many variables intervene and learners themselves are quite different.

Teachers, however, are not absolved of accountability. Parents and other citizens want assurance that teachers are doing their job.

Teaching as a Science In the last several years, educators have begun to define more precisely what is meant by teaching and what a competent teacher should know and be able to do. The elements of teaching have been drawn from experience and research, and they have begun to constitute a science, or technology, of teaching. In this context, *technology* is defined as "the means of getting a job done." Although the development of a technology of teaching has not conclusively demonstrated that one technique is more effective than another or that good teachers can be clearly distinguished from other teachers, it has given the profession more respectability.

The problem, however, has not been so much codifying the elements of teaching as ascertaining whether a given teacher has mastered the essential competencies. The situation is further complicated because there are no guarantees that teachers who have demonstrated competence will exercise it day in and day out.

The elements of teaching represent what has long been taught, at least theoretically, in good teacher education programs. Lately those elements have been made more explicit in terms of teacher behavior. Some have become the basis of state evaluation systems—for example, in Connecticut, Florida, Georgia, and North Carolina. For people exploring teaching, such systems illustrate the essential elements of teaching, the legal expectations, and the official standards against which performance is evaluated for a regular teaching license and probably for tenure.

The North Carolina Teacher Performance Appraisal System, for example, identifies eight behaviors that a teacher must be able to demonstrate:

1. Manage instructional time
2. Manage student behavior
3. Present instruction
4. Monitor student performance
5. Provide instructional feedback
6. Facilitate instruction
7. Communicate within the educational environment
8. Perform noninstructional duties

During the first two years of teaching, the adequacy of a North Carolina teacher for a standard license is measured against these standards.

The National Teacher Examination, created by the Educational Testing Service, had wide use in the country for many years. The Praxis System, initiated in 1994, has now superseded it. It is administered in three phases corresponding to phases of teacher education: during preservice education, on graduation, and after initial induction. The latter phase is still in development. The Praxis System relies on an outside evaluator, who ostensibly provides an objective view.

But there is more to teaching. It is imprecise work. Standard techniques to ensure that it produces learning for every student in all situations do not exist. Learning develops over time. It is seldom all or nothing. Usually it is a matter of degree. How adequately a student learns knowledge and skills in school depends on many factors, among them how well a teacher diagnoses motivation, ability, and attitude and how effectively he or she translates that diagnosis into teaching.

Context is also a major influence on achievement in teaching and learning. Context is the social and psychological climate of the school, the teaching resources available, the way time is used, the quality of management, the physical environment, the lifestyle of the student body, the school setting, and the quality of school life.

The students' life outside school is another great influence on what is learned. Isolating what is learned in school from what is learned elsewhere is usually next to impossible.

Teaching as an Art

Artistry, the exercise of almost mystical talents or intuition, is also a part of teaching. Teacher behavior is idiosyncratic—that is, highly individualistic. People can learn to teach, but some personality types are more adept at teaching than others. The degree to which a personality suited to teaching can be cultivated, or intuition can be acquired, is not known. For example, why a teacher has a certain spark, projects enthusiasm, probes a question, reiterates a particular point, opts to use a personal illustration, changes pace in the middle of a lesson, compliments a particular student, discusses rather than lectures, changes an assignment, or reads to a class, is not always explainable. Part of such teaching is intuitive. But making teaching decisions amid hundreds of cues is not merely innate talent exercised automatically. It involves perception and processing, inspiration and reflection, improvisation and studied action. A teacher may *sense* that a particular action is the right move to make, but in choosing that action, he or she is drawing on a repertoire of *learned* techniques. Artistic teaching is more than talking. It is a performance. It is body language, facial expression, voice modulation, intellectual gymnastics, timing and pacing, rhythm and tone, humor and empathy, harmony and chemistry—all falling appropriately into place.

Teachers are probably best challenged when they realize how little or how much they may contribute to student growth and development. Teaching is a mind-boggling job. A teacher often does not know that he or she helped a particular student until the student returns years later to say so. Moreover, the learning that students gain may not be knowledge of subject matter. Instead, it may be skills in thinking, the inspiration to excel, or a model to emulate. Consequently, teachers are constantly faced with deciding what is most important in their teaching.

Concepts of Teaching

The most obvious part of teaching is instruction of students. That means different things to different teachers, depending on how they conceive of teaching. A teacher's concept of teaching influences his or her approach and activities in the classroom. In *Beyond Surface Curriculum,* a trio of researchers, after spending hundreds of hours in schools observing and interviewing teachers, characterized teaching in three ways. In the most conservative characterization, the teacher concentrated mainly on transmitting the basic skills and facts that students were expected to learn at particular grade levels. Politeness, hard work, and minimal disruptions were emphasized. A major concern was socializing the student "into an adult stereotype, with little regard for the student's internal experience."

The middle-range teacher was described as striving to get children "to assume responsibility for their own learning, to become more self-directed" and thus to need "less and less guidance from the teacher." The teacher's social priorities were helping students to "feel good about themselves and their abilities" and to be "happy and content in learning, and experience some sense of accomplishment."

At a third level the teacher was concerned that children know "what they are about and why," think that through, understand it, and "interject their own purposes into an activity." In the process the teacher tried to help students develop an awareness and an acceptance of self. That is, the teacher tried to help students "recognize and differentiate their feelings and abilities and accept them as legitimate and worthwhile,…knowing self and experiencing self-respect in order to cope better with life."

There are many concepts of teaching because people have different philosophies of education, different beliefs about how learning takes place. Teachers should recognize what they believe teaching to be, and, for the greatest contentment, they should seek employment in a school system where they can practice what they believe.

The Many Roles of Teachers

Although instructing is the most obvious part of teaching, it is not all of what teachers do. Few people who explore teaching realize fully the many tasks and duties that teachers must assume in an effective school. In a small number of well-supported schools that have enlightened leadership, action to recognize and support the multiple roles that teachers play has begun. These roles may be categorized as follows:

- Individual professional
- Teacher of students
- Member of a faculty
- Member of a staff hierarchy
- Liaison with parents and the public

- Colleague of other professional educators
- Member of a teacher organization
- Member of the teaching profession

Clearly, teaching is more than what goes on for five or six hours in a single classroom. As the multiple tasks of teaching are recognized, there is a better chance that more adequate time will be allocated to all the roles that contribute to a fully functioning professional teacher.

Other Factors Influencing Teaching

Teaching practice also varies greatly in terms of the students, be they talented, disabled, disadvantaged, urban, bilingual, or a mixture of these. School climate and the community in which the school is located are other influences on the nature of teaching.

The way in which a school is organized also shapes teaching. For example, in schools where teachers are assigned classes of students with whom they work alone, they are solo performers. For long periods they do not interact with other adults. However, the value of more interchange with colleagues is gaining recognition in educational thinking. The prospects are good that as teachers are empowered with greater authority in decision making, there will be more collaborating and sharing among them, much to the advantage of students. Teachers know that one and one can add up to more than two when teachers work together.

An example of a school structure in which there is collaborative action and sharing is a comparatively new organization in some middle schools. Teachers in language arts, social studies, mathematics, and science work as a team with the same group of students. They have a common planning period each day to share teaching experiences and to exchange information on student progress across fields of study.

Method or technique—how a teacher teaches—is still another variable in teaching. A number of factors influence method: facilities, equipment, the teacher's concept of teaching, the teacher's view of the purpose of education and the process of learning, the quality of administrative leadership, and the school district's goals. Making a subject come alive so that the student engages in serious thought about a problem or a phenomenon is constantly a challenge. Teachers are often constrained to cover certain content in a course. Textbooks adopted by school districts establish basic subject matter to be learned. Standardized tests also set some parameters of content and knowledge. In some schools the emphasis on testing has substantially influenced what is taught. Under pressure for students to perform well on tests, teachers sometimes must emphasize content that they know will be tested.

Variety in Teaching

Variety in teaching is considerable. There are different age groups, different subjects, and different types of students. The first two distinctions are the ones most often recognized.

Table 2–1   Types of Teachers, Types of Schools in Which They Teach, and Licenses They Need to Teach

Type of Teacher	Type of School	License Required
Preschool	Prekindergarten and nursery school	Usually not licensed
Elementary school	Kindergarten Grades 1–6	Early childhood license *or*
Middle school	Grades 4–8, Grades 5–7, Grades 6–8, Grades 6–9	K–6 license *or* K–8 license *or* Secondary school teacher license[1]
Special area (music, art, physical education, special education)	K–6, K–8, and K–12	K–6, K–8, *or* K–12 license
High school		
Junior high school	Grades 7–9, Grades 6–8 Grades 8–9	K–8 license *or* Secondary school teacher license[1]
Special area (music, art, physical education, special education, home economics, industrial arts, foreign languages)	K–8 and K–12	K–8 *or* K–12 license
Combined junior and senior high school, core subjects	Grades 7–12	Secondary school teacher license[1]
Special area (music, art, physical education, special education, home economics, industrial arts, foreign languages)	Grades 7–12	K–12 *or* 7–12 license, endorsed in the field of specialization
Senior high school, core subjects	Grades 9–12, Grades 10–12	Secondary school teacher license[1]
Special area (music, art, physical education, special education, home economics, industrial arts, foreign languages)	Grades 9–12, Grades 10–12	K–12, 7–12, *or* 9–12 license, endorsed in the field of specialization

[1]Almost always with a major in a subject or an area; sometimes also with a minor in a subject or an area.

Clear differentiations are made among kindergarten, elementary school, middle and junior high school, high school, and special-area teachers. However, training programs and licensure exist in all states only for elementary school, secondary school, and special-area teachers.

Some colleges and universities prepare prekindergarten and nursery school teachers, but in most states a license is not required or available to teach in either kind of school. As recognition of the importance of teaching young children has grown, more attention has been given to requiring a level of competence and licensure of preschool teachers. The result is the beginning of official recognition by state departments of education that standards and licensure for preschool teachers are needed. A few states now license early childhood (preschool) teachers.

Middle schools are a comparatively new invention in American public education; they have not yet become a universal fixture. Consequently, there is no long-standing tradition in the preparation and the licensure of middle school teachers. Several colleges and universities have preparation programs for middle school teachers, but in practice, middle schools have been staffed largely by teachers trained as elementary or secondary school teachers.

Table 2–1 lists the most common categories of teachers, the types of schools in which they teach, and the kinds of teaching licenses that they must hold.

Most special-area teachers—that is, teachers who work in fields other than the core subjects—are included in Table 2–1. Special education teachers, who serve *exceptional children* (children who are disabled or gifted), are also included. Some of these teachers work all day in special rooms with children who are severely disabled. Often these children are not graded into levels. Others teach students with disabilities for part of the day, with students rotating between regular classrooms and special education. The practice of *inclusion,* which means placing exceptional children in regular classrooms, is changing the role of special education teachers. They are becoming consultants to, or co-teachers with, regular classroom teachers. Special education teachers and such other types of special-area teachers as specialists in reading and speech correction are discussed in Chapter 5, along with guidance counselors, school psychologists, nurses, social workers, and other special service personnel.

The Size of the Enterprise

The size of the public school teaching enterprise just described is enormous. It consists of more than 45 million students and more than 2.6 million teachers. Each grade in public schools enrolls over 3 million students except for grades 11 and 12, which enroll about 2.5 million each. In fall 1995 there were 32.3 million children in grades K–8 (plus about .5 million children at the elementary school level unclassified), taught by 1.5 million teachers; and 12.7 million youngsters in grades 9–12 (plus about .25 million youngsters at the secondary school level unclassified), taught by 1.1 million teachers. More than 5 million students (newborn to twenty-one years of age) are served by programs for persons who are disabled, funded by the Individuals with Disabilities Education Act and Chapter 1 of the Education Consolidation and Improvement Act.

Enrollment in elementary schools (K–8) is projected to reach 38 million by the year 2006. Enrollment in secondary schools, which began rising in 1991 after fifteen years of decline, is projected to reach 16.5 million by 2006. Teaching jobs, as a consequence, are becoming more numerous. Between 1994 and 1996, they increased by 109,000. Federal officials estimate that by 2006, 360,000–476,000 additional teachers will be needed (158,000–230,000 elementary school teachers and 202,000–246,000 secondary school teachers). In most states the annual rate of increase from 1994 to 2006 is expected to range from .9 to 1.6 percent, for a total increase of 16 percent over the period. However, there will be considerable differences in demand by state and region. By the year 2000, Mountain and Pacific states are projected to increase enrollment by at least 20 percent and some by more than 50 percent.

The Work Schedule

The school day is five to five-and-a-half hours long each day, five days a week. In some other countries, schools are in session on Saturdays. Several national commissions and committees studying American education have recently recommended longer school days and more school days per year in the United States. Kindergarten students usually spend only half a day in school. Students in grades 1–6 (elementary schools) attend school all day and are most frequently taught by one teacher. Teachers of music, art, and physical education in the elementary school often teach their subject in all grades two or three times a week, either in the students' regular classroom or in a room especially designed for their field—a music room, an art room, or a gymnasium. In some schools, classroom teachers teach all the subjects, and special-area teachers serve as consultants to, or team-teach with, classroom teachers.

Middle schools (encompassing grades 4–6, 6–8, or 8–9) are organized in several ways. One arrangement schedules students with a teacher for each subject, departmentalizing the school structure. A popular model for such an organization orchestrates faculty into teams consisting of one teacher from each of the core subjects (language arts, social studies, mathematics, and science). Each team works with a cadre of about 100 students. Team members have a common period each day for planning. Although students may move from class to class, they are often in their own wing of a building for core subjects. For other subjects, such as art, music, physical education, home economics, or industrial arts, students go to special teachers.

Another kind of middle school structure keeps students together for part of the day and uses special teachers for such subjects as math, science, and language arts. Still another kind of middle school arrangement organizes teachers and students in the same way that elementary schools do.

Junior high schools are almost always departmentalized. Teachers remain in the same classroom throughout the day, and students come to them in groups, or sections. They teach five or six sections each day, a new one every forty-five to fifty-five minutes. In addition, they manage a homeroom, where students assemble each morning and return in the afternoon. To an extent, the homeroom provides a guidance function: the teacher gets to know students individually and remains with them for a full school year.

Some junior high schools use large blocks of time for English and social studies. Some block programs are labeled *core curriculum*—that is, English and social studies are taught in an integrated mode, with the teacher serving in a guidance capacity similar to that of a homeroom teacher. The integrated curriculum seems to ebb and flow in popularity. Where public school programs have become more conservative in philosophy, the focus is more on a separate course for each subject.

Special-area teachers in such fields as home economics, health, industrial arts, computer science, and foreign language are joined with those in music, art, and physical education to provide a broader program of studies in many junior high schools. In some junior high schools, though, the arts have become less important and are sometimes almost nonexistent. Guidance counselors, assistant principals, attendance officers, and coaches fill out the instructional staff. Some teach and some do not, but all have contact with both teachers and students.

Almost all senior high schools are organized into departments by subject. The exceptions are alternative and progressive high schools, where both teachers and subjects may be integrated, and magnet schools, where a particular area of study, such as science and technology or music and art, is the emphasis. Departments in the typical high school vary in size. English, mathematics, science, and social studies departments (in that order) are the largest because the subjects they offer are most frequently required.

The Organization of Work

Teaching in K–12 schools most often takes place in classes. Often the teacher instructs the entire class. Students also work independently and in small groups, critiquing one another's work, debating, doing hands-on projects and experiments, participating in learning games and mock situations, and engaging in discussion and problem solving. The teacher is centrally involved in planning and managing such activities. The multitude of organizational schemes that teachers devise are designed to help students learn. Thus, teachers must provide for different interests, motivations, and abilities. This creates tension, as a noted educational sociologist points out in *Perspectives on Organizations:*

> Because students are normally in groups, the particular immaturities of some children may force procedures on all that prove alienating; for example, to maintain order, teachers may be forced to become more austere than they wish to be. This tension between "discipline" and instilling confidence and enthusiasm among students is one of the fundamental issues of working with energetic young people.

The elementary school teacher must find ways to individualize instruction while faced with twenty-three to twenty-five children in a day-long schedule. Junior and senior high school teachers must try to attend to individual differences as they teach five classes and more than a hundred students a day.

Current Reform Efforts

Current reforms include various efforts to reduce such overloads and excesses. The goals are to help teachers increase the quantity and improve the quality of learning and to serve the individual student better. Unfortunately, there is a long way to go to reach these goals. New teachers join an army of educators who want tomorrow to be better than yesterday but are not always sure how to make that happen in a large bureaucracy. Contemporary recommendations that teachers be empowered with greater authority to make instructional decisions could improve both teaching and the life of students.

More Personnel in the Classroom.

The use of more than one adult to work with a class of students has been a gradual but pervasive development.

As yet, only a few schools embrace the practice, but it will grow as teachers become more comfortable with it and as parents and teachers recognize how much more can be accomplished by it.

Teacher aides are one type of personnel being added, albeit slowly. Evidence indicates that instruction improves if a person is available to free the teacher from some of the paperwork and other day-to-day details of the job. The total load is then not carried by one person. Teacher aides assist in preparation and use of instructional materials, preparation of the classroom (for example, setting up desks and chairs and creating bulletin boards), creation of the classroom environment (for example, arranging learning centers and supporting cooperative learning), instruction, and taking lunchroom and playground duty.

In 1991, 31.0 percent of all teachers received some assistance from a teacher aide. There was variation by level and by region. Among elementary school teachers, 44.6 percent had aides; among middle and junior high school teachers, 20.9 percent; and among senior high school teachers, 14.8 percent. In the elementary school, teacher aides were most numerous in the primary grades. Schools in the West (38.1 percent) and the Northeast (32.9 percent) provided the most aides, schools in the Southeast (29 percent) and the middle region (24.9 percent) the least.

Sixty percent of elementary school teachers and 78 percent of secondary school teachers receive secretarial assistance. Aid to senior high school teachers in grading papers went up from 38 percent in 1981 to 61 percent in 1986, then dropped to 42 percent in 1991.

Another approach that employs more than one adult in a class is team teaching or cooperative teaching. Two or more teachers in a class work together or in turns. When more than one professional is present to work with a class and with individuals, the range of perception, understanding, and knowledge put into teaching is at least doubled. Conferring regularly with another professional provides teachers with relief and support in a job that, up to now, has literally inundated them. The presence of more personnel also makes additional guidance available to students and provides them with more options regarding whom they might consult. Students can then choose to work with the teacher with whom they feel more comfortable.

More Kinds of Personnel Involved in Schools.   Two kinds of innovative programs underway around the country assemble even more professionals to address the growth and development of children, youth, and families. The *professional development school,* a collaboration between a school and a school of education, expands the school staff to include college professors, interns and student teachers, researchers, teacher aides, volunteers, parents, and others. This kind of school, often compared with a teaching hospital, is designed to serve K–12 students, to provide internships for prospective teachers, to support research and experimentation, and to demonstrate promising practices.

An extension of the professional development school is the *interprofessional development school,* which uses not only educators but personnel from other human services—social workers, psychologists, child care workers, nurses, physicians and other health professionals, tutors, mentors from business and industry, adult literacy specialists, and more—to serve the multiple needs of children and families. Some herald the interprofessional development school as the successor to the school—a family-centered, community-based collaborative that integrates various components of human service. At least 100 interprofessional development schools are in existence today. (See Chapter 6 of *Teachers for the New Millennium.*)

Mentoring.   To help new teachers, a number of schools have begun mentor programs, many financed by the state. Selected experienced teachers, many of them with special training, assist beginners in the first year or two. Often called *mentors,* these teachers serve in an advisory role rather than a supervisory one. They do not evaluate beginners for job retention. Rather, they help new teachers with such problems as managing discipline, organizing time, preparing lessons, finding materials, and individualizing instruction. They also provide confidential feedback on teaching performance.

Help for the career teacher has been slower to develop and more difficult to bring about because experience often establishes habits and routines that are hard to break. Also, seasoned professionals often have difficulty admitting that long-used practices and procedures might be outdated or could be improved. Too often, they perceive making changes as admitting inadequacy. Assisting career teachers is more effective when it happens at the request of the veteran. That has happened in a few instances when the work of mentors with beginning teachers has been so successful that regular teachers have sought out mentors for help.

Reduction of Class Size.   Progress has been made in reducing class size, which tends to improve student learning. On the average, from 1966 to 1991, classes in elementary schools decreased from 30 to 24 pupils in large school systems and from 26 to 22 in small ones. In secondary schools (and in departmentalized elementary schools, which are few in number) during the same period, teachers' average student load each day declined from 132 to 93.

Change of Assignment.   Another approach to stimulating and revitalizing teachers is encouraging them to change assignments. For example, a third-grade teacher might switch to fifth grade, or a teacher of senior English might teach sophomores instead. The idea seems to work well only when the change develops with the teacher's concurrence or on the teacher's volition.

Other Approaches.   Career ladder programs and novel staffing patterns such as the lead teacher are among other efforts to break with tradition and seek new, more effective ways to teach. In a growing number of school districts, teachers have been empowered with latitude in decision making—for example, a voice in hiring and promotions, and more say over curriculum, budgets, and other areas. Being in greater control of their own destiny has been a goal of teachers for many years. Recent recommendations to that effect by national panels and commissions seem to hold new promise of implementation, at least in some places.

Adequate Budget.   Few of these ideas and goals are new, but there is a fresh commitment to implement them. An adequate budget is essential to progress. The U.S. Congress appropriated $26.3 billion for the U.S. Department of Education for fiscal year 1997—$.7 billion more than President Bill Clinton had requested. Some states increased their appropriations for education before Congress acted; others have followed Congress's lead.

National Education Goals.   Other actions by political leaders since the late 1980s include the establishment of national goals for education. In 1989, at the invitation of President George Bush, the governors of the fifty states met to discuss the condition of American education. They agreed on six goals to guide improvement. Subsequently discussed across the country, the six goals became widely accepted as targets for the revitalization of schooling. Through a national goals panel, the public, state legislators, and boards of education have become more active in promoting education. In 1994, with support from the Clinton administration, the original six goals and two more received the sanction of law in Goals 2000: The Educate America Act. The targets for progress by the year 2000 are as follows:

Goal 1: All children will start school ready to learn.

Goal 2: The high school graduation rate will increase to at least 90 percent.

Goal 3: All students will leave grades 4, 8, and 12 having demonstrated competency over challenging subject matter including English, mathematics, science, foreign languages, civics and government, economics, arts, history, and geography, and every school in America will ensure that all students learn to use their minds well, so they may be prepared for responsible citizenship, further learning, and productive employment in our Nation's economy.

Goal 4: The Nation's teaching force will have access to programs for the continued improvement of professional skills and the opportunity to acquire the knowledge and skills needed to instruct and prepare all American students for the next century.

Goal 5: United States students will be first in the world in mathematics and science achievement.

Goal 6: Every adult American will be literate and will possess the knowledge and skills necessary to compete in a global economy and exercise the rights and responsibilities of citizenship.

Goal 7: Every school in the United States will be free of drugs, violence, and the unauthorized presence of firearms and alcohol and will offer a disciplined environment conducive to learning.

Goal 8: Every school will promote partnerships that will increase parental involvement and participation in promoting the social, emotional, and academic growth of children.

If freedom for teachers to change and improve is added to those goals, the prospect of making teaching more manageable and desirable seems attainable.

Preparation

States have been regulating entry into the teaching profession for well over a hundred years, initially through the issuance of certificates to teach in the public schools and subsequently through the approval of programs for teacher preparation as well. Since the turn of the century, requirements for teacher preparation and licensure have been steadily upgraded, with those for secondary education setting the pace (see Table 2–2). All fifty states now require public school teachers to hold a valid license issued by the state's office of teacher education and certification. In most cases a state issues an *initial license* based on a recommendation from the college at which the candidate earned his or her degree (in a program approved by the state, as described later). The bachelor's degree is universally required for the initial license, as is a stint as a student teacher, supervised by a university professor and an experienced schoolteacher. Forty-one states offer a second-stage license, although only twenty-seven of them require it. The trend is toward more states requiring this *regular license* or *standard license.* Teachers usually must earn it within a few years of receiving their initial license. Requirements vary, including such achievements as a master's degree, a specified number of hours of graduate study or units of continuing education, three or more years of experience, and a performance assessment. Some states require teachers to extend or renew the standard license periodically, usually by completing a certain number of credit hours or professional development units.

In some states, licenses are generic for teaching but endorsed for a certain level (such as elementary or secondary school) or a special area (such as special education, home economics, or industrial arts). In other states, licenses are for elementary or secondary school teaching or certain special areas, and there may be endorsements for subjects (such as social studies and English) and other special areas (such as music, art, and physical education). The license for middle school teaching is separate in a few states, bunched with a junior high school license in most other states.

All the teacher education programs that a college or university offers must be approved by the state. On the strength of such approval, many state departments of education now issue licenses to graduates of approved programs, provided that the college recommends the graduates.

Table 2–2 Growth of the United States, Education, and Teacher Education, 1869–1995

Year	Number of States	U.S. Population	Public School Enrollment		Number of Public School Teachers	Number of Institutions Preparing Teachers			Number of States Requiring Bachelor's Degree for Certification	
			Elementary School	Secondary School		Normal Schools	Teachers Colleges	Total Institutions Preparing Teachers	Elementary School Teachers	Secondary School Teachers
1869–1870	37	39,818,000	6,792,000	80,000	201,000	69	0	78	0	0
1879–1880	38	50,156,000	9,757,000	110,000	287,000	ND	0	ND	0	0
1889–1890	44	62,948,000	12,520,000	203,000	364,000	204	0	234	0	0
1899–1900	45	75,995,000	14,984,000	519,000	423,000	289	2	ND	0	2
1909–1910	46	90,492,000	16,899,000	915,000	523,000	247	12	379	0	3
1919–1920	48	104,512,000	19,378,000	2,200,000	657,000	326	46	ND	0	10[1]
1929–1930	48	121,770,000	21,279,000	4,399,000	843,000	212	134	839	2[1]	23
1939–1940	48	130,880,000	18,833,000	6,601,000	875,000	103	186	ND	11	40
1949–1950	48	148,665,000	19,387,000	5,725,000	914,000	5	138	1,005	21	42[2]
1959–1960	50	179,323,000	27,602,000	8,485,000	1,387,000	0	55[c]	1,150[3]	39	51
1969–1970	50	201,385,000	32,597,000	13,022,000	2,131,000	0	16	1,246	47	52
1979–1980	50	224,567,000	27,931,000	13,714,000	2,300,000	0	10*	1,365*	52[2]	52
1989–1990	50	246,819,000	29,152,000	11,390,000	2,860,000	0	0	ND	52	52
1994–1995	50	262,000,000	36,814,000	13,962,000	3,017,000[4]	0	0	1,332[5]	52	52

ND = No data.

Sources: From *Digest of Education Statistics 1995*, by T. D. Snyder, Washington, DC: National Center for Education Statistics, 1995; *A Manual on Standards Affecting School Personnel in the United States*, edited by T. M. Stinnett, Washington, DC: National Education Association, 1974; *The NASDTEC Manual 1996–97: Manual on Certification and Preparation of Educational Personnel in the United States and Canada*, edited by T. E. Andrews, L. Andrews, & C. Pape, Dubuque, IA: Kendall/Hunt, 1996; *National Survey of the Education of Teachers*, Vol. 6, *Special Survey Studies*, by B. W. Frazier, G. L. Betts, W. J. Greenleaf, D. Waples, N. H. Dearborn, M. Carney, & T. Alexander, Washington, DC: U.S. Government Printing Office, 1935; *Projections of Education Statistics to 2006* (25th ed.), edited by W. J. Hussar & D. E. Gerald, Washington, DC: National Center for Education Statistics, 1996; and *A Study of Teacher Education Institutions as Innovators, Knowledge Producers, and Change Agents*, by D. L. Clark & E. G. Guba, Bloomington, IN: Indiana University, 1977.

*Estimated

[1]The District of Columbia is included in this figure and the following figures in this column.

[2]Puerto Rico is included in this figure and the following figures in this column.

[3]This is a 1961 figure.

[4]This is a projected figure.

[5]This is a 1995–96 figure.

Two other ways in which teacher education programs are assessed are (1) regional and (2) national accreditation. Both of these processes are voluntary; that is, institutions choose whether or not to be reviewed. Across the country there are six regional accrediting associations. Their focus is the general quality of a college or university. At the national level there is the National Council for Accreditation of Teacher Education (NCATE). Its focus is the preparation of teachers and other education personnel. Accreditation involves site visits by educators from outside the state. Before applying to an institution, the prospective student of education should check the accreditation status of its colleges and programs.

Preparation programs vary somewhat for elementary, secondary, and special education teachers, but all candidates must take courses in the psychology of learning and the social foundations of education. They also must study human growth and development, with an emphasis on children or adolescents, depending on the level at which they expect to teach. In thirty-eight states, programs require students to have clinical experiences in schools before student teaching. In all states, programs require student teaching full time for eight to eighteen weeks, supervised by both schoolteachers and college professors. A recent report by the National Commission on Teaching & America's Future recommends year-long internships in professional development schools to "allow extended practice in teaching in schools tightly tied to relevant coursework."

Secondary school teacher education programs require a major in the projected teaching field and instruction in techniques and methods of teaching that subject. In some states candidates also must have a minor teaching field.

Prospective elementary school teachers are prepared to teach all the subjects of the curriculum. They are usually required to complete a program of liberal studies; in some states that means taking a major in a subject field. They also must receive instruction in methods of teaching the subjects of the elementary school.

Special education, art, music, and physical education teachers focus on their specialty. They may even have a concentration within it. For example, a special education teacher might concentrate on teaching children who are hearing impaired, an art teacher on painting or sculpting, a music teacher on instrumental or vocal music, and a physical education teacher on sports or dance. In some specialties, teachers receive preparation to teach students from kindergarten through grade 12.

Career Patterns

There are few good measures of the length of a typical teaching career. In fact, there may not be a typical teaching career. Some people enter teaching and stay a short time. Highly publicized data suggest that half of new teachers leave their initial position by the fifth year.

In a 1991–92 study (the latest available), the National Center for Education Statistics found 87.6 percent of public school teachers to be stayers (teachers who stayed in the same school from the 1990–91 school year to the 1991–92 school year), 7.3 percent to be movers (teachers who changed schools during that period), and 5.1 percent to be leavers (teachers who left the profession). Among the leavers, only 13.5 percent were working in an occupation outside elementary or secondary education at the time of the survey.

Because few studies have tracked teachers' employment nationally or longitudinally, little is known about where teachers go when they leave a job. The 1991–92 study sheds some light. The largest group of leavers in this study, 30.4 percent, retired. The next-largest group, a distant 10.9 percent, left because of pregnancy or childrearing, and 10.0 percent left because of a family or personal move. Frequently, leavers in both the latter groups return to teaching, those in the first group after their youngsters reach school age, those in the second after they have settled in at their new location. Another 9.8 percent departed because of school staffing actions, and 8.4 percent left to continue their education—to take courses to improve their opportunities in education or to take a sabbatical. Family and personal reasons accounted for 5.7 percent, health for 3.7 percent, better salaries and benefits for 3.6 percent, and enrollment in courses to improve opportunities for employment outside education 1.5 percent. Only 8.3 percent left because they were dissatisfied with teaching and 7.8 percent because they wanted to pursue another career. The study is helpful in understanding attrition in teaching, but there is no assurance that these patterns will continue. Retirement, for example, will be variable depending on the age spread of the teaching force.

Teaching can be a prelude to more lucrative jobs in education and in other professions. In fact, teaching is a profession that fosters upward social-class mobility. Many people become middle class by virtue of the college education they receive to become teachers. For some, that acculturation stimulates a desire to remain in teaching, to stay where there is continuous opportunity to learn and grow. Teaching exposes a person to a wide variety of new occupations and professions. Because teaching is focused on working with people, it provides training that is appropriate, with only slight additions and modifications, for many of the service occupations.

Teaching has recently become a popular second career. Many colleges report that one-third of their preservice students in teacher education are older than the usual eighteen to twenty-four-year-old (college) age group. People entering teaching at an older age tend to have stronger convictions about working with youngsters, often from experience as parents. The work schedule and the lifestyle of teaching also attract second-career people.

Data on the teaching experience of full-time teachers give some indication of career length (see Table 2–3). More teachers are making a career of teaching. There is little generalizable evidence regarding why. In 1991, 52.9 percent of all teachers had fifteen or more years of experience, compared with 37.3 percent in 1981, 28.0 percent in 1971, and 38.0 percent in 1961. Among male teachers, 78.9 percent reported no break in service during their career, whereas among female teachers, 58.1 percent reported no break. By far the largest percentage of breaks in service for women, 23.0, was for maternity or childrearing.

Finding Employment

Both new and experienced teachers can usually find assistance in job placement through the college or university from which they graduated. Most

Table 2–3   Percentages of the Teaching Force at Different Levels of Experience, 1961–1991

Teaching Experience	1961	1966	1971	1976	1981	1986	1991
1 year	8.0%	9.1%	9.1%	5.5%	1.6%	2.5%	2.8%
2 years	6.3	9.3	7.7	5.8	3.7	2.1	3.9
3–4 years	13.2	14.4	15.6	16.0	8.2	4.8	7.0
5–9 years	19.4	21.7	24.0	28.9	26.2	17.7	16.3
10–14 years	15.1	14.2	15.8	17.3	23.0	22.3	17.2
15–19 years	10.4	9.8	9.7	12.5	15.4	23.1	18.2
20 or more years	27.6	21.4	18.3	14.1	21.9	27.7	34.7

Source: *Status of the American Public School Teacher 1990–1991*, by National Education Association, Research Division, Washington, DC: Author, 1992, p. 27. © 1992 by the National Education Association. Reprinted by permission.

teacher education institutions have placement offices where vacancies are listed. The more advanced the placement service, the broader is the geographical spread of the jobs listed. Teachers seeking employment through a placement office must take the initiative in opening a placement file. The cost of the service is minimal. Placement officers provide information and counsel without charge to teachers who seek their advice.

Candidates for positions must complete information for their placement folder and secure recommendations for their file. The usual procedure is for the candidate to seek several professional recommendations and a few character references. These should be from people who know the candidate well. Candidates quite naturally select people who will make positive comments about them. However, the most desirable recommendations are objective and candid, not effusively complimentary. They describe the teacher's abilities, traits, temperament, and character in straightforward language and may identify a few areas of needed growth. Helpful too is the recommendation that gives an opinion about the kind of situation in which the candidate will be most successful. The candidate is well advised to recommend to those who will write letters of support that they be candid and explicit. Most often the teacher does not see the written recommendation he or she has solicited. That encourages frank and honest opinions.

Some teacher education programs now require prospective teachers to maintain a portfolio, particularly during the professional part of their college work. Portfolios are used for both documentation and assessment. They include specimens of work, descriptions of experience, photographs, videotapes of teaching episodes, units taught during student teaching, a statement of philosophy, critiques by college supervisors and cooperating teachers, and so forth. Such documentation conveys more—and more comprehensive—information to a potential employer than the standard résumé does.

Teachers also find employment by direct contact with prospective employers and through placement services offered by state education departments, teachers' unions, and private agencies. The latter charge a fee, usually a percentage of the first-year salary. Often the employing district will cover that fee if the candidate negotiates coverage before signing a contract. Placement services operated by state education departments and teachers' unions are typically low-cost or free. References, once acquired, can be used for any and all of these placement files, as can other professional data.

During the oversupply of teachers in the 1970s and 1980s, private placement agencies suffered because they could not supply lists of job openings to the many teachers who registered with them. Meanwhile, teachers learned to exercise greater initiative in contacting employers on their own. Their initiative took a number of forms. Most teachers mailed copies of their résumé to several school districts where positions might be open and they might like to teach. More enterprising job-seekers found positions as substitutes or teacher aides, giving school administrators a chance to see them in action, irrespective of title.

Student teaching provides another such entrée. The extended period that a student teacher spends in a school provides school district administrators, particularly principals, with opportunities to observe the novice firsthand in the classroom and to seek the opinion of cooperating teachers and the college supervisor on his or her potential. With student teaching now a full-time stint of eight to eighteen weeks, the principal also can observe how the student teacher relates to other faculty and parents. Naturally, when jobs open, former student teachers, substitute teachers, and teacher aides (with teaching credentials) of proven ability have an advantage over other applicants.

Whichever approach a teacher uses, a placement file at the college or university from which he or she graduated is advisable. It provides a central point of information for prospective employers, no matter how they may discover a candidate.

Intangible Rewards

Teachers do not make a lot of money when compared with other people who have a similar level of education. The profession offers other kinds of rewards, however, and many teachers find satisfactions that money cannot buy. One is public esteem. Parents, for example, think quite well of schools and, by implication, of teachers. In the latest (1996) Phi Delta Kappa/Gallup poll of the public's attitudes toward the public schools, a random sample of adults was interviewed and asked to grade the schools locally and nationally. The choices were A, B, C, D, or FAIL. Parents with children in school were specifically asked to grade the school their oldest child attended. Twenty-three percent of them gave the school an A, 43 percent a B, 22 percent a C, 6 percent a D, and 5 percent a FAIL; 1 percent did not know what grade to give. When asked to rate public schools in the nation as a whole, 2 percent of parents with children in school gave the schools an A, 24 percent a B, 43 percent a C, 14 percent a D, and 7 percent a FAIL; 10 percent did not know what grade to give. Citizens with no children in school did not rate schools quite so highly.

It is characteristic of teachers to value other rewards at least as highly as money. In a recent exhaustive study of teacher incentives and rewards, an educational sociologist concluded that teachers viewed a wide range of incentives and rewards as reasons to choose and remain in teaching, money being only one and not necessarily the most important. In a 1990–91 study by the National Education Association, teachers were polled on the reasons they entered teaching and continue to teach. Responses to both questions yielded three top reasons: a desire to work with young people, the value or the significance of education in society, and job security, in that order.

Salary and Fringe Benefits

Salary and other material rewards for teaching are important, however, if teachers are to live in the manner to which they have become educated and to enjoy a life-style that enables them to remain current, vital, and conversant with the culture they are charged to reflect, understand, and transmit. Table 2–4 presents teachers' salaries in constant dollars over a twenty-five-year period. Recent trends are encouraging.

Table 2–5 compares average starting salaries in teaching with those in selected other professions whose members are college graduates.

Table 2–4   Estimated Average Annual Salaries of Public School Teachers, 1960–95 (in 1995 constant dollars)

Year	All Teachers	Elementary School Teachers	Secondary School Teachers	Beginning Teachers[1]
1960	$25,959	$25,023	$27,419	ND
1964	29,682	28,740	31,024	ND
1968	33,330	32,365	34,538	ND
1972	36,014	34,971	37,223	$25,462
1976	34,694	33,813	35,622	23,109
1980	31,412	30,624	32,374	19,749
1984	32,908	32,236	33,837	20,984
1988	36,954	36,274	37,961	24,082
1992	37,635	36,989	38,476	24,717
1995	37,436	36,874	38,249	24,463

ND = No data.

Source: From *The Condition of Education 1996*, National Center for Education Statistics, Washington, DC: U.S. Government Printing Office, 1995, p. 296.

[1]Salary for beginning teachers is for the calendar year.

Table 2–5   Average Starting Salaries of Bachelor's Degree Holders, 1993

Field	Annual Income
Engineering	$35,004
Computer science	31,164
Mathematics/statistics	30,756
Chemistry	30,456
Economics/finance	28,584
Sales/marketing	28,536
Accounting	28,020
Business administration	27,564
Liberal arts[1]	27,216
Teaching	22,505

Salaries represent what corporations (a sample of 200) planned to offer persons graduating in 1993 with bachelor's degrees.

Source: *Statistical Abstract of the United States: 1996*, Washington, DC: U.S. Bureau of the Census, 116th ed., 1996, p. 167.

[1]Excludes chemistry, mathematics, economics, and computer science.

Teachers are among the best-educated people in the nation, despite the criticisms leveled at them. Virtually 100 percent have at least four years of college, compared with just over 20 percent of the U.S. population twenty-five to sixty-four years of age. In 1991, 52 percent held at least a bachelor's degree, 42 percent a master's degree, 4 percent an education specialist certificate, and 7 percent a doctorate.

Teachers receive compensations other than cash. Chief among them are support for professional development and graduate study, various types of insurance, contributions toward their retirement, and leave.

Support for Professional Development and Graduate Study. Teachers are encouraged to participate in professional development and graduate study, and they sometimes receive financial support to do so. According to figures from the National Education Association and the Educational Research Service, in 1991, 74 percent of all teachers attended workshops sponsored by their school district during the school year. In the 1994–95 academic year, 37 percent of a stratified sample of the nation's school districts reported provisions for reimbursement of all or part of tuition costs for graduate study.

Fifty percent of all teachers in 1991 had earned some college credit in the preceding three years. With more teachers holding master's degrees or six-year diplomas—up from 23 percent in 1961 to 42 percent in 1994—fewer teachers over the age of forty are electing formal graduate study. Teachers

Table 2–6   Insurance Benefits Provided for Teachers by School Districts, 1994–95

Type	Districts Providing	Premiums Fully Paid for Employee	Premiums Fully Paid for Family
Hospitalization coverage	96.5%	84.2%	29.3%
Medical/surgical coverage	95.2	84.1	29.4
Major medical coverage	95.6	84.5	28.9
Dental care coverage	80.9	85.7	36.4
Vision care coverage	48.3	82.1	41.0
Prescription drugs coverage	84.6	83.2	29.4
Group life insurance	73.3	————(varies greatly)————	
Professional liability insurance	64.5	ND	NA

ND = No data.

NA = Not applicable.

Source: From *Fringe Benefits for Teachers in Public Schools, 1994–95,* by Educational Research Service, Arlington, VA, 1995, pp. 49–51.

holding master's degrees have all the academic credentials required by state certification offices. Many therefore undertake a wide variety of other growth activities beyond the master's degree, including travel, conference and workshop attendance, sabbatical leaves, and special projects.

Insurance Benefits.   School districts provide various types of insurance for teachers. Almost all offer hospitalization, medical/surgical, and major medical insurance. Among the districts providing insurance of any kind, over three-fourths pay all the premiums for coverage of the employee, whereas less than one-third pay all the premiums for coverage of the whole family. Table 2–6 presents data for 1994–95.

Liability suits, still largely a phenomenon in medicine, nonetheless have a few precedents in education, and these have caused school districts to insure against unfavorable accountability judgments. In 1994–95, 64.5 percent of districts provided professional liability insurance, and 58.4 percent offered Errors and Omissions coverage for teachers. In more than 90 percent of the latter districts, this coverage was under blanket provision of school board policy.

The insurance benefits of teachers have continued to improve, and they are much better than those of American employees across all jobs. For example, in 1994 essentially all public school teachers had health insurance, compared with approximately 85 percent of the general population (under government or private coverage). In 1995, nearly 81 percent of teachers had dental care coverage, whereas only 46 percent of all employees had such insurance.

A critical shortcoming in some insurance benefits, such as hospitalization and major medical insurance, is that they are not transferable from one state to another. Teachers who are looking at possible employment outside their current state should inquire about the effective beginning date of hospitalization and major medical coverage. Often they can more easily negotiate such coverage before signing a contract than afterward.

Retirement Programs.   Participation in a retirement system is obligatory for almost all American public school teachers, whereas only about 49 percent of the total workforce has a retirement provision. In 1994–95, 76 percent of American school districts provided teacher retirement benefits under a statewide teachers' retirement system, and 26 percent offered the benefits through a state public employees' retirement system. (The two percentages add up to more than 100 because some districts reported more than one type of retirement provision.) No teachers were outside any system.

In many instances both the teacher and the school district contribute to retirement. The respective percentages of contribution vary by state and school district. Some state retirement systems are quite good, providing for a substantial contribution by the employer that becomes the employee's property, or is *vested,* after a relatively short period (for example, five years).

Like some insurance benefits, teacher retirement provisions do not transfer from state to state. Something similar to the plan developed for higher education, the Teachers Insurance and Annuity Association–College Retirement Equities Fund (TIAA–CREF), has been advocated for public school teachers. Action is bound to be a long time in coming because there are so many teachers and they do not function in a national market as professors do. A better alternative for teachers, and one that operates in many states, is that of transferring years of service or buying in to a state retirement plan on the basis of experience elsewhere. Even when transfers or buy-ins are possible, though, the number of years teachers can purchase is limited. Teachers moving to new employment in another state should investigate the number of years that can be credited toward retirement. As with hospitalization and medical coverage, retirement credit is often easier for teachers to negotiate before signing a contract than afterward.

Leave Provisions.   Leave policies are usually determined by local school systems. According to data from the Educational Research Service, considerable variation exists in the extent of coverage and the percentage of districts granting various types of leave. For example, sick leave is granted by 99 percent of districts, but differences exist in the number of days provided, the number of days credited per year, and the number of days that can be accumulated. Family, personal/emergency, bereavement, and jury leaves are granted almost universally—by 97, 97, 96, and 97 percent of districts, respectively. Substantial percentages of districts allow for professional (91 percent), military (89 percent), religious (69 percent), and sabbatical (69 percent) leaves. Unfortunately, no data have been collected on the number of teachers who have availed themselves of these benefits.

PRIVATE SCHOOL TEACHING

About 356,300 teachers (301,880 full-time equivalents) teach roughly 4.7 million students (10.4 percent of American schoolchildren) in about 24,700 private or independent schools. Among the full-time equivalent teachers, 43 percent are employed in Catholic schools, 34 percent in other religious schools, and 23 percent in nonsectarian schools.

Across all types of private schools, 77 percent of the teachers are women and 23 percent men. These proportions vary somewhat by a school's orientation. Among the religious schools, they range from 81 and 19 percent, respectively, in Catholic schools, to 57 and 43 percent in Lutheran schools of the Wisconsin Synod. Among nonsectarian schools they range from 91 and 9 percent in Montessori schools, to 34 and 68 percent in military schools.

In ethnic and racial makeup, 92.2 percent of private school teachers are white, 3.3 percent Hispanic, 2.7 percent black, 1.5 percent Asian, and 0.4 percent Native American.

Sixty-two percent of private school teachers hold a bachelor's degree, 32 percent a master's degree or higher. Six percent have less than a bachelor's degree.

Great diversity exists among private schools, but most have the following characteristics in common:

1. They are not controlled by the government.
2. They are primarily supported by private funds.
3. Most employ some requirements for admission. (Of those that include grades 10, 11, or 12, 64.4 percent require an interview.)
4. Attendance is voluntary.
5. They are smaller than most public schools. Only 19 percent enroll 300 or more students, compared with 69 percent of public schools.
6. They are nonprofit and tax-exempt.
7. They welcome gifts and grants, and many seek such funds.
8. They select their own teachers and administrators.
9. Tuition is often their main source of revenue.
10. Except for some parochial schools, they are controlled by a local board and establish their own curriculum.

Ninety-five percent of private schools charge tuition. The average tuition in private elementary schools is $1,780, the range $1,243 to $6,377. The average tuition in secondary schools is $4,395, the range $2,831 to over $9,067. These figures do not include boarding fees.

Approximately 1,500 private schools are members of the National Association of Independent Schools (NAIS). This organization is highly regarded for its attention to standards of private school education. Some 340 NAIS schools are residential (boarding); the balance are day schools. Median tuition is $5,066 at NAIS elementary schools, $7,306 at NAIS secondary schools, and $7,317 at NAIS combined elementary and secondary schools. For the residential schools, there are also room and board costs.

Church-sponsored schools (mostly day schools) constitute the largest proportion of private schools—82 percent. Of these, about 8,700 are Catholic. They enroll 86 percent of all students attending religiously oriented schools, 55 percent of all students attending private schools. Nonsectarian schools, numbering about 4,500, make up the balance of private schools.

There was a net loss of more than 850 Catholic schools between 1987–88 and 1990–91, and over the same period, the number of students attending private schools decreased by about half a million. Most of this decrease was in elementary school enrollments.

About half of the private schools operating today have developed in the last thirty-five years. These include most Hebrew schools, evangelical Lutheran schools, member schools of the Association of Christian Schools International, special education schools, and Montessori schools. For such young institutions, establishing a track record is difficult. In fact, some last only a short time.

Individuals interested in teaching in private schools are advised to explore the accreditation status and the membership affiliation of the school that advertises employment. The accreditation status, in particular, will provide an indicator of quality. Inquiries at NAIS, the Council for American Private Education, the Association of Christian Schools International, and the American Association of Christian Schools will yield reliable information. Further, checking whether accreditation by the latter two organizations is recognized by the appropriate regional accrediting association would be worthwhile.

In many church-related day schools, teaching conditions and approaches are much the same as in public schools. The main difference is the inclusion of religion in the curriculum. However, in a number of private schools, usually nonsectarian ones, the schedule of the school day is different, with classes in core subjects in the morning and the early afternoon, and extended periods in the mid to late afternoon for activities and study that require more than the usual one-hour class.

According to an NAIS publication on careers in independent school teaching, independent schools support a philosophy that, for teachers, "coursework in a particular discipline is more desirable than education courses." Yet they espouse a liberal, humanistic philosophy of education that is not unlike the progressive credo of public school teachers. That is, they advocate building a sense of community in school, providing teachers with an opportunity "to develop and shape courses and curriculum," and giving teachers "the chance to have an effect on the total development of young people." They subscribe to having teachers be "role models, advisors, and counselors." Further, they seek teachers who "have a genuine interest in and commitment to all aspects of children's growth." In boarding schools, teachers often live in the same buildings as students, serving as surrogate parents, and thus have the opportunity, if not the responsibility, to shape the social, personal, and academic values of their charges.

Preparation

Preparation for private school teaching is similar to that for public school teaching, except that private schools do not uniformly require teachers to have training in the field of education. A very few do not require even a bachelor's degree. A look at the educational backgrounds of private school teachers in 1991 confirms those statements: Overall, 64 percent were licensed in the field of their main assignment. There were many variations, however. About three-fourths of teachers in Catholic schools and special education schools were licensed in their main field, compared with just a little more than half of teachers in all other private schools. However, about 94 percent had at least a bachelor's degree.

Private school teachers in most states are not subject to state licensure requirements. The few exceptions are Hawaii, Idaho, Iowa, Michigan, and North Dakota, which require all private school teachers to be licensed.

Finding Employment

All the approaches to finding employment followed by public school teachers are appropriate for private school teachers. Placement services are often an event at national conferences of private school associations. For example, NAIS runs an employment information exchange at its national conference, at which both prospective teachers and interested employers register and candidates and school representatives have interviews. In addition, school-based induction programs, often called internships, teaching fellowships, or apprentice programs, are available in a number of private schools. Many pay participants, some charge participants a fee (which may be in addition to pay), and several offer possibilities for earning college credit toward licensure or a degree. The NAIS maintains a roster of such opportunities in its member schools.

Salary and Fringe Benefits

The intangible rewards of private school teachers are much the same as those of public school teachers. In addition, teachers with strong religious commitment may gain satisfaction from the moral and spiritual environment and guidance they provide. Some teachers would argue that the intellectual climate and the stimulating interaction with well-educated colleagues are incentives. Testimonials of independent school teachers laud the rewards of working with young people.

Salaries typically are lower in private schools than in public schools. The average base salary in all private schools (1993–94 data) is $21,968. Secondary schools, on the average, have the highest base salary, $24,770–$26,869 depending on the type of community, elementary schools the lowest, $17,446–$20,760.

The median of salaries in NAIS independent day schools is $31,815, the range from $8,588 to $63,075. Salaries in the top 10 percent range from $41,666 to $63,075, salaries in the middle 50 percent from $27,489 to $37,061.

More private school teachers than public school teachers receive in-kind benefits. Teachers in boarding schools, for example, may be provided with housing and board, often for their whole family. Many schools offer tuition waivers for faculty children, and some make grants for college tuition. Some also give grants to teachers for graduate study and support participation in professional associations and societies. Teachers in non-Catholic religious schools and in nonsectarian schools are more likely to receive in-kind benefits than teachers in Catholic schools.

A few private schools belong to the TIAA–CREF retirement program (described in Chapter 6) and to other TIAA insurance programs. Other schools provide similar benefits, usually health and hospitalization insurance and retirement. Fringe benefits are so diverse that individuals interested in private school teaching should inquire at each school at which they are considering employment.

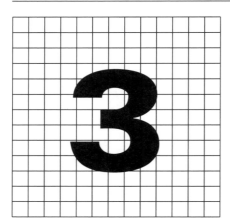

SCHOOL ADMINISTRATION

In the last half century, as schooling in the United States has become more universal and the population has doubled, the need for school management and administration has grown tremendously. There have been increases in the number and the kinds of school administrators, and changes and expansions in school administration have occurred for various reasons.

School systems that serve essentially all young people from kindergarten through high school are a recent development. With the country's population exploding from 92 million in 1910 to over 265 million in 1996, and with a much larger percentage of school-age youngsters staying in school than ever before, it goes unrecognized that education is better, curriculum offerings are broader, and management and administration are vastly improved. In 1950, only about 35 percent of the U.S. population twenty-five years of age and over had completed twelve years of school; by 1994 that figure had risen to 86 percent.

The recency of extended schooling and the increase in the number of students are but two factors influencing school administration today. School districts have become larger and more complex as a consequence of legal mandates to provide education for all children to at least age sixteen, and to ensure equality of educational opportunity. Also, good roads and greater ease of transportation have made schools farther from home more accessible.

Further, the public, business, and government have demanded richer and more varied curriculum offerings to meet the needs of young people for life in a rapidly changing cosmopolitan society. Such demands require more extensive facilities and resources as well as a consolidation of efforts in educational planning and management. Particularly since World War II, a massive effort to reduce the excessive number of small school districts has created greater management challenges and bigger administrative jobs. Consolidation reduced the number of school districts from 127,531 in 1931 to 14,931 in 1994–95.

Today the leading player in schools is the superintendent, who is the administrative head of a school district. As might be expected, the greater the responsibility of new and larger school districts, the more powerful and the more political the position of superintendent has become. The superintendent is the "point person," the individual on whom both praise and criticism settle. Even though the days of the publicly elected superintendent are gone (in most districts), local boards of education control selection of superintendents and terms of office. The political vulnerability of today's superintendent in the continuing controversy over the quality and the direction of education has made the longevity of employment extremely tenuous. Terms of office in large cities are particularly short.

The superintendent's supporting administrative cast varies in size. In large systems it may include deputy, associate, and assistant superintendents; principals; and assistant principals. The latter two players are building-level leaders, administrative heads and subheads of elementary, middle, junior high, and high schools. Other players include central or regional office administrators and supervisors and building specialists.

This chapter discusses careers as superintendents or principals and their deputies, associates, or assistants. Chapter 4 addresses careers as middle-level administrators and supervisors. Roles at the middle level have expanded, proliferated, and become more specialized as school districts have grown. Often part of a central or regional office staff, these are the superintendent's high-level professionals—experts in curriculum, supervision, guidance and psychological services, testing, social work, computers, budgeting, transportation, technology, and maintenance. The same people are the servants, so to speak, of principals and teachers at the building level, helping them improve curriculum and instruction and stay current in content, teaching techniques, and materials. Middle-level managers also provide professional and logistical support, which includes planning and evaluating, ordering and distributing equipment and supplies, maintaining and repairing the school plant and grounds, keeping accounts and budgets, and keeping records. Chapter 5 turns to careers as specialists, personnel in individual buildings who offer special services to children directly, or indirectly through consultation with, and education of, teachers, principals, and parents. These specialists include art and music teachers, school librarians and media people, guidance counselors, school social workers, computer experts, occupational and physical therapists, and speech-language pathologists.

PRINCIPALS

There are four levels of principals: elementary, middle, junior high, and high school. However, there are as yet few preparation programs for principals at levels other than elementary and secondary school (the latter of which includes junior high and high school). Most state licensure regulations provide only for elementary and secondary school principals. In fact, two-thirds of middle school principals hold a secondary school principal's license. Fewer than 10 percent hold middle school licensure; almost as many have an elementary school principal's license.

The basic administrative job in a school district remains the management of the individual school. Principals and, in larger schools, assistant principals are charged with leadership and management at the building level. National studies and reviews of education affirm the importance of dynamic, effective, inspired leadership of the building unit. The result has been greater recognition and more attention to the role of the principal.

The principal is the key person in a school. He or she is the setter of tone and the catalyst for success—or in some cases the reason for mediocrity. Principals work with, and have administrative responsibility for, teachers, specialists, students, support staff, and nonlicensed employees. They deal with parents, the public, and the community, and they serve as the link between the staff and the students of a school building and the school district's central office.

Chapter 2 points out the difficulty of generalizing about the job of the teacher. The job of the principal almost defies generalization. There is no typical principal because there are such a variety of principalships. The principal's job depends on the enrollment of a school; the nature of the student body; the size of the school district; the district's per pupil expenditures; the community, regional, and state context; and more.

The principal is a school's chief administrative officer. He or she is the leader, the head of the faculty. The label *principal* probably grows out of the British term *head teacher* or *principal teacher*. When all principals taught in addition to managing their school (this is still the case in some small schools), they were the principal teacher.

Assistant principals are just that, assistants to the principal. Their duties are determined by the principal or in consultation with the principal. Student discipline and attendance are most often among the duties of assistant principals.

Principals and assistant principals are appointed to their jobs, usually by the superintendent of schools with the advice and the consent of the school board. In school districts that have moved to site-based management, teachers often have a voice in selection of the principal. Most principals and assistant principals do not have tenure.

What Being a Principal Is Like

Describing the length of the typical workweek or the usual duties of a principal is far easier than painting a picture of what being a principal is like. There is hardly a typical day in the life of a principal. There are so many different schools and principalships, and the job has so much diversity. Yet a few aspects of the job can be generalized.

A principal's day can be full of excitement, pressure, conflict, intensity, pathos, joy, sadness, confusion, and order. To keep on an even keel, principals must know who they are, what they believe, and what the limits and the license of their job are. Whether alone or with one or more assistants, the principal is responsible for the various aspects of managing a school: planning; scheduling; developing programs and curriculum; supervising personnel, student activities, food services, and student behavior; providing instructional leadership; and fostering professional development.

The foregoing duties are responsibilities within the building. Principals also must maintain relationships with parents and citizens in the community and with the school district's central office. Relationships with parents and citizens vary greatly, just as communities and traditions of home-school interaction differ. In locations where the concept of a *community school* is operational, schools are the center of education and social activities for parents and citizens as well as for students. Recently some schools have broadened their offerings to include health and social services as well, the idea being that there should be a one-stop location to serve the many needs of children and families. These places, sometimes called *community learning centers,* sometimes *interprofessional centers,* attempt to coordinate a number of services that contribute to the growth and development of children and families. Obviously, in such settings the principal has many additional roles beyond those expected in conventional schools. Fifteen states have already passed legislation fostering collaboration across state agencies and local communities. Interprofessional centers are part of the future for principals who now have responsibility only for education.

In the realm of central office relationships and responsibilities, the principal must deal with matters of budget, personnel evaluation, selection of new staff, attendance, student testing, school board decisions, legislative mandates, legal and court actions, and public relations. Many of the foregoing have ramifications or corresponding responsibilities at the building level, no matter how broad or restricted the services of the school.

In two surveys conducted by the National Association of Secondary School Principals (NASSP), middle-level and high school principals ranked their responsibilities in terms of the time that they gave to those responsibilities. Management was first, personnel second, and student behavior and student activities third. The vignettes that follow give further evidence of the way in which principals across the nation allocate their time on the job. The vignettes do not present a comprehensive picture of what principals do. They are just slices of life of three individuals who head different schools in very different situations.

Vignette 1
A Day in the Life of a Big-City Elementary School Principal
(Male principal, twenty years of experience)

Student body: 700 students, grades K–6.

Ethnic makeup of student body: 49 percent Hispanic, 41 percent black, 8 percent white. (Ten years earlier the student body was 44 percent Hispanic, 27 percent black, 26 percent white, and 2 percent Asian.)

Academic capacity of students: A good range of abilities.

Staff: A total of 50 teachers: 25 classroom teachers; 7 special education teachers; 6 cluster teachers; 11 additional teachers for reading, language, and the resource room; and 1 dual-language program coordinator. No assistant principals.

Ethnic makeup of faculty: Teachers—8 Hispanics (bilingual, regular classroom teachers), 6 blacks, 1 East Indian, and 35 whites. A number of minority paraprofessionals.

An after-school program in conjunction with the neighborhood "Y" runs from 3:00 to 6:00. The program serves families in which both parents work or there is a single parent. The school also offers a preschool program, largely for children of neighborhood people and school staff.

The community of the school goes beyond those who live around the school. Students from other parts of the city are admitted. Among the parents are lawyers, physicians, and specialists, but the vast majority are working-class people. Some parents are very poor. A few children live in hotels. Children who are not walkers are entitled to public transportation.

The school's bilingual program is a dual-language program; that is, English and Spanish are taught to all students.

The principal feels that although he does not have autonomy officially, he has considerable autonomy unofficially. He has learned to use the system to his advantage and can exercise much initiative. In general, he can organize the school the way he wants, without interference from the central office. However, policies on curriculum and finance sometimes make that difficult.

There are citywide policies on testing, but they are not necessarily followed. The curriculum guides and materials issued from the central office, though, are useful, for the most part.

I came in at 7:30 a.m. I had some parents in the office first thing. It was a situation from yesterday, a fight between two girls. I called the parents in the afternoon, and they came in with the girls immediately this morning. We talked about what had happened and why and so on, and we resolved it. In this case they were not kids who get in trouble a lot, but I told them why they were here and that we cannot tolerate fighting. The kids left with their parents, and it looks like that is settled.

Then I set up the day. One of my people (a teacher) who does some of my administrative work was absent. She takes care of lunch period, among other things. I had to contact the office that handles substitutes. We needed two subs (another teacher was also out), but we could only get one, leaving one class uncovered. That meant we had to do some rescheduling.

After getting all that and some other details set up, I was off to a conference of principals with the superintendent. I got there about 9:30 a.m. That lasted until noon. The topic was libraries. A person from the central office talked about ways to help get the library set up. Some specific references to put in a library were recommended, and there were some very helpful hints on publications about libraries that the central office is putting out. The only problem is that none of us has a librarian. We have different arrangements. Many schools use cluster teachers in the library. Those are the positions that are there to give preparation time to the classroom teachers. So most of us use a cluster teacher with her class to cover the library; by doing that she can at least be there to help other kids with research things. That's not by any means a full-time librarian.

When I got back to the building, I had to take part of the lunch recess because of that absent administrative person—till 12:45—then I had an observation to do till 1:30. We have several formal observations of new teachers each year. Of course, I visit classrooms a lot on an informal basis, which gives me a pretty good idea of how well a teacher is doing. These formal evaluations are part of administrative policy so that there is formal evidence of teacher performance, and interaction between the principal and the teacher on each observation. That means a formal conference after the observation. We keep a file on each teacher that includes evaluations, letters, reprimands, etc.

Then I grabbed a bit of lunch at my desk while I went over some paperwork.

After lunch I had an auditorium plan (kids from several classes are brought to the auditorium, usually to see a film) so that we could cover students for several teachers. Today we showed them a nice film, keeping them occupied with something of interest that was educational. That was at 2:00. It made possible bringing together seven early childhood teachers for a grade-level meeting. Grade-level meetings take place regularly. Ours is a Chapter I school [serving low-income families], and teachers are given one preparation period a day. Some of that time can be used for things that I plan. One period a week, each grade level has a common released time. We often use that for grade-level or other faculty meetings, usually on curriculum or something like that.

At 3:00 p.m. I had a meeting with several teachers that dealt with problems we are having with young children. The early childhood group this year is larger than usual, and the children are very immature. There had been a problem in the play yard. The kids seem unable to stay with one activity, and we do not have enough help, especially at times like that, to supervise every activity adequately. So we end up with accidents, and we had to deal with that.

Next I had to remind some teachers about the importance of getting down to assembly on time to pick up their kids. These are extremely conscientious teachers—I am not concerned about them generally—but they don't see the whole picture sometimes. If they don't get their kids from the assembly on time, the kids get unruly.

After that I had a meeting with the school-based support team. That's one of the special education department's efforts. Two parents came in immediately after the support team meeting was over and said their children hadn't come home yet and it was already after 3:30 p.m. Most of our children live nearby. Generally they get home by 10 minutes after 3:00. I went upstairs to find the teacher. The teacher had kept the kids in. She was a new teacher. She didn't know or remember that keeping kids after school is against school policy. I had to let the kids out.

Today actually was not a complicated kind of day.

Vignette 2
A Day in the Life of a Middle School Principal
(Female principal, thirty years of experience)

Student body: 700 students, grades 6–8.

Ethnic/socioeconomic makeup of student body: children from lower income families, 44 percent minority.

Staff: One full-time assistant principal; 55 teachers (including itinerant teachers); 2 art teachers, 3 teachers of children with learning disabilities; 2 full-time counselors; shared social workers and school psychologists; services of a curriculum coordinator one day a week. Parent volunteers provide 2,200 hours of help annually. Businesses provide people to tutor on company time. There is one special education room.

The school is on the same campus as the high school, and that makes sharing of facilities possible.

The program is organized around a language arts block with the rest of the programs departmentalized. The students have good test scores. There are strong orchestra, band, and art programs during school hours, and strong intramural and club programs after school (a second bus serves those who stay).

The principal is known as tough but fair. She has the prerogative to hire new teachers and is allotted a budget.

> My day began at 6:30 a.m. when I arrived at school. Three youngsters were already here, one with a McDonald's breakfast. I had to remind him to dispose of his trash. So I started by baby-sitting. About 7:00 parents started calling in absences. Somebody comes in at 7:15 a.m. to take those calls. Then I called maintenance. Today I had to get someone to wire the computer room. I find that if I get on the phone early, I can get the maintenance I need done the same day.
>
> When I got back to the office, three children were sitting around. I had to lay on the line what's going to happen in this school. We have very strict rules for discipline here. I don't have two sets of standards; we have the same rules for everyone. I sent three children home on suspension.
>
> A couple of teachers came in for advice about what to do with certain kids, what to do with the curriculum. Then I dealt with the curriculum coordinator for about fifteen minutes. Afterward I talked with two kids for about three minutes and then visited three classrooms.
>
> Next I taught two French classes. As a principal, I do that twice a week because it gives me direct contact with about seventy-five students.
>
> Then it was lunchtime, and I had to check the lunchroom, after which I returned calls to a couple of parents and the superintendent.
>
> I have authorization to hire a new teacher, so I called the state university to see if they could recommend some certified candidates for middle-grades language arts.
>
> By then it was 4:30 p.m., and we began to prepare for the girls' ball game that's going on right now. I'll be here till after the boys' game.

Vignette 3
A Day in the Life of a High School Principal
(Male principal, first year in this assignment,
fifteen years of administrative experience)

Student body: 1,150 students, grades 9–12.

Ethnic makeup of student body: 92 percent white, 8 percent black.

Staff: Two assistant principals; 70 teachers (including 1 half-time and 3 full-time special education teachers, 1 half-time athletic director, 1 half-time band teacher, and 1 half-time choral teacher); 3 guidance counselors.

Geographically the district is long. One-half of the student body lives in sub-urbs spread out around a small town; the other half is from surrounding rural areas. Thirty buses are needed to transport students to and from school. The high school's dropout rate is 25 percent. Thirty percent of the graduates attend some kind of postsecondary institution.

A lot of time and energy goes into the sports program, which includes inter-scholastic teams in tennis, volleyball, football, basketball, track, and golf.

According to the principal, administration in the district is becoming more centralized, and fewer and fewer decisions are being made at the building level. Principals used to be more involved in the selection of teachers. There is a policy for everything now. They are striving for consistency in the state.

> I arrived at 7:30 a.m. At 8:00 I met with a parent concerning a discipline prob-lem. The student had gotten into some trouble on the bus and apparently was a little upset.

> Then I walked around the building. I didn't make a complete tour, but I did take about thirty to forty minutes to see what was going on.

> We have a dance coming up tonight, so I met with the student council faculty advisor to make sure everything was in order.

> Following that, I did a formal observation of a teacher in her classroom. And I met with a teacher about an observation I'd done the day before.

> We have had a problem with one of our bus routes on a turnaround. I've got an assistant principal in charge of buses, but he's new and doesn't know the area that well. I know it better than he does. So he and I went out to the area where we had the complaint about the bus turning around—it's about 20 miles from here—and tried to come up with a decision on what to do. But we couldn't come up with a solution that was satisfactory to everyone. There wasn't much of an alternative.

> The supervisor for maintenance came by. There was a problem in our agricul-ture building. Steam was coming up through a leak into an electrical box, and we went down and had a look at that. Also, we went out to the parking lot where some work is being done marking off spaces. We needed some gravel in the area, and I showed the maintenance supervisor where we wanted it. The two of us also went into another wing of the building where we had some leaks, because they're working on the roof. The damage from the leaks had caused the floor tile to buckle up, and there was also damage to the ceiling. I probably spent close to an hour with the maintenance supervisor.

Sixth period, some students needed help with moving tables and getting everything ready for the Christmas dance. The teacher who is responsible for that was in class, so I supervised.

After school I helped get the buses out. I do that daily. The principal has got to have some help on that. A teacher and an assistant principal and I—we all go out and help when the buses are leaving.

We've had a visitor on the campus every morning and afternoon, and I found out that one of our students has been going out to the vehicles to meet with him. So I called her in and got the name of the individual. This young man was a dropout a couple of years ago. I called him and gave my feelings about what he could do from here on out, that he was not to come visiting our campus. I'd had this reported before but had been unable to catch him or identify him. I hope I got that one stopped. Non-school-age visitors are a constant problem. We need to watch the traffic coming in and out. A lot of mornings I spend the first thirty minutes in my vehicle patrolling the campus. We have a rather large campus. Kids stay out in the cars, or we get visitors wanting to come in.

We also get some visitors during the lunch period, which is an hour-and-a-half long, so I spend some time in the lunchroom and out in the break areas and on the parking lot. I do a little police duty on that. It should be a daily occurrence, but I can't do it that often.

After school I went to tryouts for cheerleaders. A couple of cheerleaders quit—one got injured in an auto accident. So we had tryouts again yesterday.

I got away from the school about 4:30. I went home because I had to be back about 6:30 p.m. for the dance. This is my first year as principal here. It's been traditional for the administration to take care of the gate because we do charge for it. The dance is a fund-raiser for the student council. They sponsor it. The assistant principal and the athletic director and I took turns manning the gate. And, of course, I stayed for the dance and supervised wherever I could. We had a great dance. I left here about 10:45 p.m. The dance was over at 10:00, but there are always students who don't have rides. It takes a while to see that they are taken care of.

Elementary School Principals.   There are nearly 63,000 elementary schools in the United States. All have a principal of some kind, and some have assistant principals. Very small schools have teaching principals or one principal who is responsible for more than one school. The grades typically included in elementary schools are K–6. Sometimes there is a prekindergarten as well. Elementary schools vary as to the grades they include, however. The U.S. Department of Education's National Center for Education Statistics divides public elementary schools into five categories:

From	*Through*
Prekindergarten, kindergarten, or grade 1	Grade 3 or 4
Prekindergarten, kindergarten, or grade 1	Grade 5
Prekindergarten, kindergarten, or grade 1	Grade 6
Prekindergarten, kindergarten, or grade 1	Grade 8
Grade 4, 5, or 6	Grade 6, 7, or 8

Each configuration, as well as size, setting, geographical locale, type of student body, and financial support, dictates differences in administrative responsibility. As a consequence, there are many types of elementary school principalships.

The size of an elementary school is a major determinant of the scope and the complexity of the job. Administrative responsibility, a principal's relationships with teachers and students, and the number of duties that are delegated to assistant principals and teachers vary greatly depending on the size of a school. Nearly 44 percent of all public elementary schools (which serve about 22 percent of the students) enroll 399 students or less (see Table 3–1). About 28 percent enroll fewer than 300 students. At the other extreme, more than 36 percent (almost 22,000 schools) are medium to large, enrolling from 500 to 999 students.

About two-thirds of the nation's public school principals head elementary schools. For about 2 percent, the bachelor's is the highest degree earned; for 64 percent, the master's; for 26 percent, the education specialist's certificate; and for 9 percent, the doctor's. The average elementary school principal has had at least eleven years of teaching experience before becoming a principal.

Most elementary school principals are responsible for one school only; a few manage two schools. About 41 percent work in rural/small-town schools, about 30 percent in urban-fringe/large-town schools, and about 29 percent in central-city schools. The principal's contract may be for ten to twelve months of work. Increasingly, principals are on eleven- or twelve-month contracts.

Middle and Junior High School Principals. The middle school and the junior high school have been labeled *middle-level* schools. The grades in middle-level schools are usually in one of four configurations: 4–6, 5–8, 6–8, or 7–8. Sometimes the configuration is grades 7–9. Together these describe a *senior* elementary school and a *junior* high school. The middle-level school mostly serves children who are preadolescents. The grade 7–9 configuration includes preadolescents and adolescents. One of the reasons for the creation of the middle school was to group students so as to avoid the combination of seventh and ninth graders. The striking difference between the grade 5–8 school and the grade 7–9 school makes clear that middle-level principals have even more varied jobs than elementary and high school principals do.

Table 3–1   Public Elementary Schools and Students, by Size of Enrollment, 1993–94

Enrollment	% of Schools	Number of Schools	% of Students	Number of Students	Number of Students/School
Under 100	5.85	3,513	0.62	174,194	50
100–199	9.32	5,597	3.02	848,494	152
200–299	12.50	7,507	6.77	1,902,088	253
300–399	15.94	9,572	11.91	3,346,214	349
400–499	16.07	9,650	15.44	4,337,996	449
500–599	13.63	8,185	15.96	4,484,095	548
600–699	9.79	5,879	13.52	3,798,556	646
700–799	6.42	3,855	10.24	2,877,013	746
800–999	6.59	3,957	12.47	3,503,550	885
1,000–1,499	3.52	2,114	8.70	2,444,337	1,156
1,500–1,999	0.32	192	1.15	323,102	1,683
2,000–2,999	0.03	18	0.17	47,763	2,654
3,000 +	0.00	0	0.04	11,238	—
	100.00	60,039[1]	100.00	28,098,640[1]	468

Source: From *Digest of Education Statistics 1995*, by T. D. Snyder, Washington, DC: National Center for Education Statistics, 1995, p. 104.

[1]These figures are the totals of the addends shown. The addends were derived from totals and percentages given in the source. The actual totals given in the source were 60,052 and 28,095,832.

Typical principals in these types of schools are white males. Most were assistant principals, teachers, or elementary school principals before their appointment to a middle school principalship.

Middle-level school principals have annual contracts similar to elementary school principals: ten to twelve months. Only about one-third have tenure. Principals at this level like their jobs. Sixty-eight percent would select administration if they could choose again.

Middle-level school principals report that they work more than fifty hours per week. The workload includes: managing the school, administering the personnel component, dealing with student behavior problems, developing programs, supervising teachers, evaluating teachers, supervising student activities, maintaining liaison with the district office, meeting with parents, keeping up community relations, planning, and fostering professional development. Very few middle-level school principals teach.

The age of the student body and the curriculum for the students present unique challenges for the middle-level school principal. The principal must have a deep understanding of this age group. Middle-level schools serve many children who are going through that mystifying growth period, puberty, with all its accompanying emotional, social, physical, and intellectual manifestations. Anyone who has worked in a junior high school knows that these youngsters can be among the most exciting students. At the same time, they can be among the most difficult.

The middle-level school is also an institution of transition. In the elementary school, usually one teacher teaches a given class for the entire day. In the middle-level school, departmentalization (a different teacher for each subject, students moving from classroom to classroom) begins either gradually or abruptly, depending on how the school is organized. The principal must orient students and their parents to the new organization. More responsibility is put on the student. How to help the student accept it is the worry of every middle-level school principal.

Help in exploring the middle-level school principalship is available from publications by the National Middle Schools Association, the National Association of Elementary School Principals (NAESP), NASSP, and other authors listed in Appendix A.

High School Principals. About 60 percent of high school principals administer three- or four-year high schools, grades 10–12 or 9–12. The four-year unit is by far the most common (54 percent). About 18 percent of high schools are five- or six-year institutions (grades 8–12 or 7–12). The size of the schools varies greatly. About 15 percent of principals manage schools enrolling 499 students or fewer. At the other extreme, 15 percent administer schools that enroll over 2,000 students. Thirty-seven percent of principals head schools in the middle-size range, 800–1,499 students.

The gender and the ethnicity of public high school principals vary with the location of the school. In the central city, 74 percent of principals are male, and 70 percent are white, 22 percent African-American, and 8 percent Hispanic. In urban-fringe/large towns, 83 percent are male, and 89 percent are white, 8 percent African-American, and 2 percent Hispanic. In rural/small-town areas, 91 percent are male, and 94 percent are white, 3 percent African-American, and 2 percent Hispanic.

Overall, the average public high school principal is about forty-seven or forty-eight years old and has had nearly eleven years of teaching experience before becoming a principal. Ninety-nine percent of high school principals have earned at least a master's degree, 11 percent a doctorate.

Most principals work forty-five hours or more a week. The majority are on contracts calling for twelve months of work per year, about a quarter on contracts calling for eleven or eleven-and-one-half months, and a small percentage on contracts calling for ten or ten-and-one-half months. Most have one-year, renewable contracts with the school system, but more than 30 percent have two- or three-year contracts. In one study, 41 percent reported that they planned to remain in their present position, whereas 27 percent said that they aspired to a central office position or a superintendency.

Most high schools are comprehensive schools. A small percentage are magnet schools. Even fewer are alternative schools. Two percent are commercial, vocational, and so forth.

The high school principal administers an institution with unique functions and problems. High school is the time when students are in essence screened in relation to their future. Students select a curriculum from those offered. Academic, general, business, and vocational are the usual options. Some students are college-bound, others terminate formal education with graduation, and still others drop out before completing school.

Principals spend their time in a variety of ways to provide all students with the best education that the school can offer. An NASSP survey offered insight into what that means in actual practice. Principals indicated the amount of time they spent in nine types of responsibilities in a typical workweek. From the most time spent to the least, the responsibilities were ranked as follows:

Management (calendar, office, budget, memos, etc.)
Personnel (evaluating, advising, conferring, recruiting, etc.)
Student activities (meetings, supervision, planning, etc.)
Program development (curriculum, instructional leadership, etc.)
Student behavior (discipline, attendance, meetings, etc.)
District office (meetings, task forces, reports, etc.)
Community (PTA, advisory groups, parent conferences, etc.)
Planning (annual, long-range, etc.)
Professional development (reading, conferences, etc.).

The five major obstacles that principals identified, from a list of twenty-six, were (1) time taken by administrative detail, (2) lack of time, (3) variation in the ability of teachers, (4) inability to obtain funding, and (5) apathetic or irresponsible parents.

Other concerns voiced by principals included problem students, insufficient space and physical facilities, inability to provide teachers with time for professional development, resistance to change by staff, and defective communications.

Preparation

Table 3–2 lists the areas of study often required of prospective high school principals by university school-administration programs. These areas of study are not necessarily separate courses. Curriculum is put together in different ways at different institutions.

People who aspire to administrative leadership in schools are well advised to think about more than the study that they need to qualify for a position. In the early stages of considering a career as a principal, it is wise to make an assessment of one's aptitude for the job and potential for success. Teachers have a unique and privileged vantage point from which to observe the job of principal. They are on the inside of the school. They can get a view of the principal in all kinds of situations, even if they never see the whole picture or feel the full responsibility.

Table 3–2   University Requirements for School Administration

Study Required by Most Universities

Administrative theory
Adolescent development
Community relations
Curriculum and program development
History of education
Human relations
Leadership
Personnel administration
Philosophy of education
Secondary school principalship
School finance and budgeting
School law
School management
Supervision of instruction

Study Required by Some Universities

Comparative education
Counseling and guidance
Internship and field experience
Collective bargaining
Politics of education
Psychology of learning
Research methodology
Social and economic context of contemporary education
Tests and measurements
Vocational education

Source: Adapted from a list produced by the National Association of Secondary School Principals, Reston, VA.

There are at least four ways in which a person might learn about the preparation required to be a principal. They are not mutually exclusive. One is to consult university catalogs and discover the training necessary to complete a program in school administration with either an elementary, middle, junior high, or high school emphasis. A second is to review the areas of study and the courses that principals have found most useful on the job (for example, as reported by many principals in a survey or by individual principals anecdotally). A third approach is to inquire at a state department of education about licensure requirements. A fourth way is to think through the kind of principal one wants to be and decide how to prepare oneself to be that kind of principal, within legal and academic requirements.

Preparation for a principalship requires graduate study. Virtually all practicing principals have at least a master's degree, and a high percentage have graduate work beyond that credential. All states require a person to have a license in school administration to be employed as a principal at any level.

Most principals were teachers before they started graduate study. For a prospective principal, graduate study often parallels work as a teacher. Taking courses in the evening, on Saturdays, and during the summer makes graduate study affordable. However, it often contributes to less than the best performance as either graduate student or teacher and may prove costly sooner or later. In the short run, students suffer when a teacher is not well prepared, and in the long run, a new principal will find it difficult to recover on the job from neglecting depth of study in the knowledge and the skills needed to be successful.

Some universities require an internship as a part of graduate study in administration. The prospective principal must dedicate time and effort in concentrated work-study on the firing line under the supervision of an experienced principal and a university professor. The internship gives prospective principals and their supervisors an opportunity to examine potential and to test ability and aptitude in a real situation. Most principals who have served internships rate them highly useful or essential.

If an internship is not required, candidates must wait for their test until they are actually on the job. Often that happens in the role of assistant principal. Many principals have served as assistant principals before assuming the head position, even though the assistant role is usually quite different from the top spot. Being an assistant to an able school executive can substitute for an internship. However, most principals expect their assistants to be self-sufficient; there is not much time to play mentor, even if one is so disposed.

Career Patterns

Nearly all principals have been teachers first. Experience in the classroom is considered by most educators to be essential for that career. NAESP, NASSP, and the American Association of School Administrators (AASA) all officially endorse successful classroom teaching in schools as a requirement for a principalship. The dominant persuasion is that to be sensitive to and understand what teaching involves and requires, a person must have participated directly in that role. A small number of educators and people outside education contend that a good manager, irrespective of background, should qualify as a school administrator. That viewpoint is illustrated in Chicago and Washington, D.C., where managers (in D.C., a retired army general) have been hired to bring solutions to the problems of inner-city schools. Nevertheless, most states require principals to have teaching experience and advanced study, usually a master's degree in educational administration. There is, therefore, a hierarchy and a career ladder for those who choose educational leadership as a career.

A pattern within the principalship is advancement from small elementary schools to large ones, or small secondary schools to large ones. Occasionally a principal changes levels.

Finding Employment

Principals find employment in much the same way that teachers do. They register with the placement office at the university at which they completed advanced preparation, either a master's degree or other appropriate graduate training, and they solicit recommendations from professors and other educators who know their work. When a prospective principal has completed an internship as a part of graduate training, the recommendations of the cooperating principal and the university supervisor can be telling. There is also an informal network through which information and recommendations pass by word-of-mouth. Data on which process is better are unknown. A wise aspirant will keep both alternatives operating.

The track record of a prospective principal in a teaching role or assistant position, if it is solid and strong, is also an asset. In fact, many principals begin graduate study in administration on the encouragement of principals or superintendents for whom they have worked.

The assistant principal position is often a stepping stone to a principalship at the high school level. Many high school principals were assistant principals in high schools just before taking the top building-level job. A substantial percentage were assistant principals or principals in elementary or middle-level schools immediately before becoming a high school principal. High school principals most frequently attribute their first appointment as principal to success as an assistant principal and to a successful job interview.

Salary and Fringe Benefits

Salaries, like almost everything else about principals, are difficult to generalize. Averages miss all the distinctions caused by size of school, wealth of school district, years of experience, and level of principal's education. Several ways of presenting salary figures help to tell the story. Table 3–3 presents figures on the salaries of principals and assistant principals by the student enrollment in the district.

The hierarchy in school administration is apparent in the salaries paid principals in the lower schools compared with those paid principals in the upper schools. However, an elementary school principal can earn more than a junior or senior high school principal. The factor of size makes a difference.

Per-pupil expenditure in a district—that is, the average amount that a district spends per student on education—provides another perspective on salaries. The wealth of a district usually determines the salary paid to school personnel, including principals. (Wealth is almost always directly related to the socioeconomic level of residents.) District wealth is so important a factor

Table 3–3   Mean of Average Salaries Paid to Principals and Assistant Principals, by School District Enrollment, 1995–96

	Systems of 25,000 or More Students	Systems of 10,000–24,999 Students	Systems of 2,500–9,999 Students	Systems of 300–2,499 Students
Principals				
Elementary school	$60,284	$60,938	$63,038	$58,008
Junior high/middle school	63,375	64,719	67,521	59,125
Senior high school	69,852	70,191	72,845	62,173
Assistant Principals				
Elementary school	49,470	49,392	52,953	51,521
Junior high/middle school	51,451	53,536	56,992	50,672
Senior high school	55,089	57,629	59,953	54,027

Source: From *Measuring Changes in Salaries and Wages in Public Schools*, Arlington, VA: Educational Research Service, 1996, pp. 16–19.

Table 3–4   Mean of Mean Salaries Paid to Principals and Assistant Principals, by Per-Pupil Expenditure, 1995–96

	Per-Pupil Expenditure					All Systems
	$7,000 or more	$6,000–$6,999	$5,000–$5,999	$4,500–$4,999	Less than $4,500	
Principals						
Elementary school	$71,436	$61,561	$57,267	$56,699	$57,258	$60,922
Junior high/middle school	75,443	65,116	61,268	60,445	60,136	64,452
Senior high school	79,507	69,329	66,329	65,930	64,632	69,277
Assistant Principals						
Elementary school	62,469	53,948	47,832	47,098	46,899	50,537
Junior high/middle school	65,152	56,237	51,479	49,181	50,614	54,355
Senior high school	67,782	58,887	54,925	51,461	53,291	57,555

Source: From *Salaries Paid Professional Personnel in Public Schools, 1995–96*, Arlington, VA: Educational Research Service, 1996, Part 2, p. 12.

that a smaller school in a wealthier district will often pay its principal more than a larger school in a poorer district. Table 3-4 reports mean salaries of principals and assistant principals in 1995–96, by per-pupil expenditure.

Salaries also vary by state. This is related to per-pupil expenditure and district wealth. It may be a function of cost of living as well. Additional kinds of salary information of value are salary ranges and state and regional breakouts. The Educational Research Service in Arlington, Virginia, conducts periodic salary studies that specify salary range.

Support for Professional Development and Graduate Study. Tuition reimbursements for graduate study, like so many other benefits, varies by size of district. In districts with 300 to 9,999 students, more than 40 percent of school districts pay tuition; in districts with 10,000 to 24,999 students, 30 percent; and in districts with 25,000 or more students, 17 percent. Reimbursement also varies by wealth, with affluent districts paying more, and more often.

One important way for administrators and supervisors to stay abreast of developments is by attendance at meetings and conventions. Seventy-eight percent of school districts pay at least some of the expenses of travel to and participation in professional gatherings. Of those, 64 percent pay actual expenses, with no limit set. In most cases, reimbursement is for travel, registration fees (which have become substantial), lodging, and meals. In 74 percent of all school districts, paid professional leave is granted for attendance at meetings and conventions. This means that leave time is not charged against the employee's accumulation. Professional association membership dues are paid by 63 percent of school districts.

Insurance Benefits. Insurance benefits for administrators and supervisors (except superintendents) are grouped together because they are usually the same. They are at least comparable to, and normally better than, those provided for teachers. Typical benefits and the percentage of districts providing them are listed in Table 3–5. The percentage of districts that pay the full cost of a particular benefit is also noted.

Not reported is the percentage of districts offering family coverage for each of the health benefits. It too varies by the district's per pupil expenditure. Overall, 78 to 87 percent of school districts provide family coverage, depending on the benefit.

Among districts providing health benefits, more than four-fifths fully pay the premiums for individual administrators and supervisors, but only about one-third fully pay them for families. Married candidates for an administrative position will want to ask about coverage of dependents.

About 78 percent of districts report providing group life insurance for administrators and supervisors. The range of policy amounts is $2,000–$500,000 depending on several factors, including salary, the availability of options to increase the policy's value, and enrollment in the school district. The mean face value of the group life insurance policy is $65,401.

Whether principals and central office staff are more vulnerable than teachers in liability suits is uncertain. However, there is sufficient concern to cause school districts to insure against judgments. About 67 percent of school districts cover administrators and supervisors with professional liabil-

Table 3–5   Insurance Benefits Provided for Administrators and Supervisors (Except Superintendents) by School Districts, 1994–95

Type	Districts Providing	Premiums Fully Paid for Employee
Hospitalization coverage	97.1%	85.0%
Medical/surgical coverage	95.8	84.9
Major medical coverage	96.2	85.3
Physical examination	32.0	26.3
Dental care coverage	81.4	86.6
Vision care coverage	50.0	82.7
Prescription drugs coverage	85.3	84.4
Group life insurance	77.5	76.9
Accidental death and dismemberment	44.4	ND
Professional liability insurance	67.2	ND

ND = No data

Source: From *Fringe Benefits for Administrators and Supervisors in Public Schools, 1994–95*, Arlington, VA: Educational Research Service, 1995, pp. 41, 51–53, 56, 58–60.

ity insurance. Sixty-two percent cover them for Errors and Omissions liability, 90 percent of those under a blanket provision of board policy.

Some school districts provide administrators and supervisors with at least part of the cost of periodic physical examinations. Among districts with per pupil expenditures of $6,000 or more, more than 41 percent pay at least part of the cost.

As with teachers' insurance benefits, those for administrators and supervisors have improved over the last two decades and are now much better than average when compared with those of employed people in general. For example, essentially all administrators and supervisors have health insurance, whereas only 85 percent of the general population have. About 74 percent of administrators and supervisors have dental care coverage, compared with 46 percent of all employees.

Retirement Programs.   All administrators and supervisors participate in a retirement system of some kind, compared with about 49 percent of the total workforce. About 76 percent of all districts provide for retirement through a state teachers' retirement system, about 31 percent through a state public employees' system, and about 5 percent through a local system. (Percentages add up to more than 100 because some districts reported offering more than one type of retirement provision.)

In almost all retirement systems, both the employee (the administrator or the supervisor) and the school district contribute. The percentage of contribution varies by state and school district, as does the period necessary for *vesting* (that is, for the employer's contribution to become the property of the employee). Some retirement systems require a substantial contribution by the employer; others prescribe that both employer and employee pay a share.

Another kind of retirement income is Social Security. Because public education personnel are government employees of sorts, some states have not made administrators, supervisors, or other school personnel eligible for Social Security. Only a little more than half of administrators and supervisors are covered by Social Security.

Severance Pay.   Many administrators and central office personnel do not have tenure, and terminations may be abrupt. As a consequence, severance pay is more important for them than for teachers. Severance pay can be helpful in a number of instances: when an administrator or a supervisor resigns, when a superintendent leaves and the school board wants a new administrative team, when a board wants to encourage early retirement, or when regular retirement comes. Some type of severance pay as such is reported by about 36 percent of school districts, but the practice of paying a departing administrator a sum of money on leaving, for whatever reason, varies widely. Some districts pay the monetary equivalent of all or some of unused leave days earned. About 52 percent pay the monetary equivalent of unused sick leave. Other factors influencing payments (usually in a lump sum) to departing administrators are years of service, age at severance, early retirement incentives, and retirement provisions.

Leave Provisions.   Leave policies are determined by local school systems. Vacation leave is usually provided for administrators who have a twelve-month contract. Seventy-three percent of districts (probably the percentage that have year-round contracts with administrators) provide a set number of days. Twenty days is a common figure for vacation leave for twelve-month people.

For other types of leave, there is considerable variation both in the extent of coverage and in the percentage of districts granting them, according to the Educational Research Service's figures. For example, sick leave is granted by about 98 percent of districts, but differences exist in the number of days provided, the number of days credited per year, and the number of days that can be accumulated and applied toward retirement. Family, bereavement, and jury leaves are almost universal. Substantial percentages of districts allow for professional (92 percent), personal/emergency (91 percent), military (87 percent), religious (67 percent), and sabbatical (53 percent) leaves. There are no data on the number of administrators who actually take advantage of these benefits.

Transfer of Health and Retirement Benefits from One State to Another.   Critical fringe benefits—that is, hospital and medical insurance and retirement—are not transferable from one state to another. Some states have buy-in provisions for work experience in another state if official documentation of experience is presented, but the number of years one can purchase is limited. Before signing a contract, administrators or supervisors taking new employment in another state should check the effective beginning date of hospitalization and medical insurance and the years that can be credited toward retirement. Fringe benefits are often easier to negotiate before signing a contract than afterward.

SUPERINTENDENTS

The top-level positions in school administration are those of the superintendent of schools and his or her deputies, associates, and assistants. The job of chief administrative officer of a school system has become particularly difficult and vulnerable in recent years. The rapidly changing world, new expectations of schools, different lifestyles, changes in social and moral values, desegregation, drugs and violence in schools, increases in the variety of ethnic populations, shifts in funding patterns, declining resources, an aging teaching force, and demands for accountability are among the problems that make difficult times, and often short tenure, for top-level school administrators. When situations become strained and conflict in decision making creates turmoil, the top person is the first to be replaced. Superintendents usually work on term contracts and do not have tenure. They are the easiest to fire. Their average tenure (6.5 years) is testimony to their plight.

One way to explore the prospects of becoming a superintendent of schools is to examine the kinds of people who now hold those positions, their routes to the jobs, and the nature of the jobs. Such inquiry is not easy because there is also great diversity among superintendents and wide variety in their circumstances. Geographic location, the size of the school district, the diversity of the district's population, and the level of support provided to the school district are major dimensions of difference. If one keeps those variables in mind, however, it is possible to sketch the superintendency in broad strokes and report some specifics about the job.

Almost 14,900 superintendents of schools manage the school districts in the United States. Almost all of them are white males. Few superintendents are women, and only about 4 percent are members of minority groups (many of them in the nation's largest school districts).

The characteristic that most clearly distinguishes types of superintendents is the size of the school district. In a study sponsored by the American Association of School Administrators (AASA), school districts were grouped by size, as follows:

- Group A—25,000 students or more
- Group B—3,000 to 24,999 students

**Table 3–6   Number of Public School Districts and Percentage of Students
Enrolled, by Size of District, 1993–94**

Enrollment Size of District	Number of School Districts	Percent of Students Enrolled
25,000 or more	206	29.9
10,000 to 24,999	525	18.2
5,000 to 9,999	973	15.6
2,500 to 4,999	2,008	16.3
1,000 to 2,499	3,570	13.5
600 to 999	1,785	3.2
300 to 599	2,162	2.2
1 to 299	3,294	1.0
Size not reported	358	—
Total	14,881	

Source: From *Digest of Education Statistics 1995*, by T. D. Snyder, Washington, DC: National Center for Education Statistics, 1995, p. 96.

- Group C—300 to 2,999 students
- Group D—fewer than 300 students

A fifth group (E) was included to cover a variety of other chief school administrators, those of county and intermediate school districts and other configurations, such as multidistrict vocational schools, cooperative service units, and so on.

The U.S. Department of Education's National Center for Education Statistics presents data on school districts in a slightly different manner. It reports the number of districts and the corresponding percentage of students in each of eight enrollment categories (see Table 3–6). Arranging figures in this manner makes it easy to calculate that a little more than 3,700 of the nation's 14,881 school districts enroll 80.0 percent of the nation's students. At the extreme of schools enrolling 10,000 students or more, 731 (4.9 percent) of the nation's school districts account for 48.1 percent of its students. At the extreme of schools enrolling fewer than 1,000 students, 7,241 (48.7 percent) of the districts enroll 6.4 percent of the students. Clearly, there are some very small school districts in the country in places where the population is very sparse.

Everyone knows that populations are concentrated in cities, and it is often assumed that the cities contain the large school districts. That is true, but some county districts have larger enrollments than city districts. Just a few of the numerous examples are the district serving Prince George's County, Maryland, with about 115,900 students, compared with the districts of Seattle and Omaha, enrolling about 45,200 and 43,600 students, respectively. Jefferson County's district, in suburban Denver, enrolls about 82,800 students, whereas the school system in Rochester, New York, serves about 35,600 students. The district encompassing Montgomery County, Maryland, which includes suburban Washington but extends into rural areas, enrolls almost 113,400 students, compared with Boston's school system, which enrolls only about 63,700. Hence, superintendents of large school districts may as often be suburban-rural administrators as big-city school heads.

Because of these great variations, there obviously is no typical or average school superintendent. A superintendency in a school district with small enrollments may well be no more complicated than the principalship of a school in a large district.

The superintendent is, of course, responsible for all aspects of a school district's operation. He or she either handles directly or delegates the various tasks and duties outlined in Chapter 4: planning, development, operation, evaluation, curriculum and instruction, special education, guidance and psychological services, personnel, library and media, materials and supplies, plant maintenance, business affairs, food services, transportation, communications, community relations, and state and federal programs. In a few very small school districts in rural America, the superintendent is the lone top officer and manages all those responsibilities (some are not even required in very small districts). When many of the tasks are delegated, the superintendent spends much of his or her time on general policy, coordinating the activities of staff, planning and assessing future needs, selecting highly competent people for key administrative positions, supporting those people, and maintaining relationships with state offices of education, the school board, and the community.

Preparation

Preparation for the superintendency is very much like preparation for other school administration positions. The superintendent may have completed all his or her formal training before becoming a superintendent, either during a principalship or in the position of assistant superintendent.

Patterns of preparation vary as much as the superintendency itself. Most superintendents have earned at least a master's degree. One complaint about graduate preparation is the lack of full-time study. However, much of the preparation for such a position consists of on-the-job training and learning from experience. The fact that many superintendents in large school districts got their experience in large districts demonstrates that much is learned on the job.

Career Patterns

Almost all superintendents of schools in the United States today began their careers as teachers. Most entered administration before they were thirty years old. Few gained their first superintendency before age thirty-five, though. Among today's superintendents, the median age for entry into the superintendency was thirty-eight to forty.

Just as there is a career ladder in moving from teacher to superintendent, so is there a series of steps in the hierarchy of superintendents, from small systems to large ones and from central office staff member to assistant superintendent and then to superintendent. By far the majority of superintendents head schools in the AASA's Group C (those with enrollments of 300 to 2,999) or the National Center for Education Statistics' categories 5–8 (those with enrollments of 1 to 2,499).

The men and women who manage the various school districts have a median age of 49.4 years. Seventy percent of them are forty-one through fifty-six years of age. Median age is fairly uniform across districts of different size, except that nearly 40 percent of the superintendents heading very large districts (more than 25,000 students) are under age 50, as are nearly 60 percent of superintendents heading very small districts (fewer than 300 students).

In the past, most superintendents coached athletics as an extracurricular activity before becoming a chief executive. That has changed in the last twenty-five years. Just under half of today's superintendents have a past in coaching.

The career ladder to superintendent has also changed. Formerly most came to the superintendency directly from a principalship and before that a teaching position. Today 36 percent have followed that track, whereas 38 percent of them have climbed from teacher to principal to central office staff to superintendent. One study comparing a sample of exemplary superintendents with a random sample of superintendents found that the exemplary ones more often had taken the route that included a central office staff position.

Seventy-one percent of superintendents today were secondary school teachers at one time. Nineteen percent were social studies teachers, 11 percent science teachers, 9 percent mathematics teachers, and 9 percent English teachers. The rest were from various disciplines—physical education/health, business education, special education, industrial arts, and so on. Their careers as teachers were relatively brief, however: 77 percent taught for ten years or less.

Advancement up the ladder often requires moving to another school system. Only 8 percent of superintendents have spent their entire professional career in one school system, and only 36 percent were hired from inside the system they now serve.

Once they have gained the superintendency, however, these educators tend to stay put or move little. Fifty-six percent have held only one superintendency, 26 percent only two.

Most superintendents are appointed. They serve at the pleasure of their local school board on a contract or a letter of appointment, with a specified term of office. (More than 75 percent of those on contracts or appointments of a fixed length have terms of three years or more.)

Finding Employment

Employing superintendents is usually much more complicated than hiring administrators at lower levels, particularly in larger school districts. Openings are often publicized widely. Candidates sometimes apply on the basis of public advertisements or information from placement offices. More frequently they learn about an opening through the grapevine or through the network to which they belong. Not infrequently candidates are sought out by a school board itself or by a consultant hired by a board. In any case the school board establishes goals, criteria, procedures, and a timeline for selecting a superintendent.

Superintendents often come from within a system. A principal or an assistant superintendent may have been groomed formally or informally for the position. Gaining a superintendency may in part involve being at the right place at the right time. On the other hand, an appointment from inside the school district is probably based more on a school board's observation of the candidate's performance over time.

Salary and Fringe Benefits

Salaries for superintendents are idiosyncratic. Although some generalizations can be made—for example, large districts usually pay more than small districts and wealthy districts pay more than poor districts—there are all kinds of exceptions and caveats.

Table 3–7 provides one way to explore salaries. The 1995–96 contract salary of all superintendents reporting in an Educational Research Service study averaged $94,229. One should also factor in the cost of living in an area, the degree of discretion with budget, support systems, and fringe benefits.

For the top administrative officer, more clearly than for any other administrator in the school district, rewards include certain intangibles that are valuable and satisfying as a part of doing a job. For example, the authority (the legitimate right to exercise power) that goes with the superintendency is valuable, even when used sparingly. A reasonably long contract can be considered another kind of reward, in part for its value in providing time to accomplish goals, but also for its assurance that the expense of a move will not have to be borne again soon.

Fringe benefits for superintendents have improved over the last two decades. They are a significant part of income, and many of them are not taxable. Candidates for superintendencies should examine the provisions carefully. Additional benefits not discussed in this section include transportation (some districts provide cars); expense accounts; paid expenses to

Table 3–7   Mean of Mean Salaries Paid to Superintendents, Deputy or Associate Superintendents, and Assistant Superintendents, by School District Enrollment, 1995–96

	Systems of 25,000 or more Students	Systems of 10,000–24,999 Students	Systems of 2,500–9,999 Students	Systems of 300–2,499 Students
Superintendent	$118,019	$98,151	$92,624	$78,443
Deputy/associate superintendent	88,962	81,967	78,962	79,810
Assistant superintendent	80,203	78,431	77,288	67,253

Source: From *Salaries Paid Professional Personnel in Public Schools, 1995–96*, Arlington, VA: Educational Research Service, 1996, Part 2, p. 9.

Table 3–8   Insurance Benefits Provided for Superintendents by School Districts, 1994–95

Type	Districts Providing	Premiums Fully Paid for Employee
Hospitalization coverage	96.3%	85.9%
Medical/surgical coverage	95.2	85.7
Major medical coverage	96.3	86.3
Physical examination	63.2	65.6
Dental care coverage	82.3	86.5
Vision care coverage	51.7	85.7
Prescription drugs coverage	85.9	85.2
Long-term disability insurance	38.6	ND
Group life insurance	80.7	62.3
Individual life insurance	20.6	ND
Professional liability insurance	77.3	ND

ND = No data.

Source: From *Fringe Benefits for Superintendents in Public Schools, 1994–95*, Arlington, VA: Educational Research Service, 1995, pp. 39–40, 68–69.

conventions; civic, social, and/or health club dues; tuition reimbursements; and dues for association membership. The Educational Research Service is a source of complete details on all these benefits.

Insurance Benefits.   Insurance benefits for superintendents are much the same as those for principals and central office administrators and supervisors except that they include more provisions. The percentages of districts providing various benefits and the percentages paying the full premiums for the superintendent are shown in Table 3–8:

More than 80 percent of districts provide family coverage in the health care areas. About half of those districts fully pay the premiums.

The mean dollar value of group life insurance provided for superintendents is $101,390.

Sixty-three percent of school districts pay at least part of the cost of a regular physical examination. Many districts require a physical examination on an annual basis.

Retirement Programs.   About 98 percent of districts cover their superintendent through a state retirement system, about 3 percent through a local system. Fifty-six percent offer Social Security.

In almost all retirement systems, both the employee and the school district contribute. The percentage of contribution varies by state and school district, as does the period necessary for vesting. Some retirement systems require a substantial contribution by the employer; others prescribe that employer and employee pay equal shares. Within a state a superintendent is, of course, able to change positions without losing continuity in his or her retirement plan.

Twenty-three percent of districts offer a separate annuity plan paid for by the district.

Severance Pay.   Most superintendents serve under a contract, usually for a specified term—most often three years or more. Therefore severance pay is important, particularly when terminations may be abrupt. The mean tenure for superintendents reported in a recent study was 6.5 years. Severance pay is provided by 35 percent of school districts. However, policies for paying a departing superintendent a sum of money on leaving tend to differ. Most districts pay the monetary equivalent of all or some of unused leave days earned. About 31 percent pay the monetary equivalent of unused sick leave days. Other factors that influence lump-sum payments are years of service, age at severance, early retirement incentives, and retirement provisions.

Leave Provisions.   Ninety-two percent of local school systems provide vacation leave. The mean number of leave days per year is twenty-one. About half of the school districts limit the number of days that may be accumulated (the mean number is forty).

Sick leave is granted by 96 percent of districts, but differences exist in the number of days provided. Family and bereavement leaves are almost universal. Substantial percentages of districts allow for jury (89.6 percent), professional (89.6 percent), and personal/emergency (86.1 percent) leaves, according to the Educational Research Service. Sabbatical leaves are offered in 28.3 percent of districts.

Transfer of Health and Retirement Benefits from One State to Another.   Critical fringe benefits such as hospitalization, medical, and surgical insurance and retirement, are not transferable from one state to another. Some states have buy-in provisions for work experience in another state if official documentation of experience is presented. But the number of years one can purchase is limited. Before signing a contract, superintendents taking new employment in another state should check the effective beginning date of hospitalization/medical insurance and the years that can be credited toward retirement. As noted elsewhere, fringe benefits are often easier to negotiate before signing a contract than afterward.

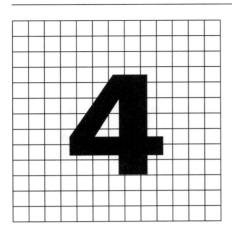

CENTRAL OFFICE ADMINISTRATION AND SUPERVISION

Supervisors and middle-level administrators are found in large school districts, where the job of the superintendent of schools is sufficiently complex to require that responsibilities be delegated and where a single individual cannot oversee and provide leadership and support to all the personnel and programs.

RESPONSIBILITIES OF CENTRAL OFFICE STAFF

The professional personnel who staff a central office ensure that a school district's program is effective, has continuity and coherence, and is efficiently administered. They assist in and monitor planning, development, operation, and evaluation of all the areas that are part of running the school system. The traditional areas that they oversee are curriculum, special education, guidance and psychological services, personnel, library and media, materials and supplies, and plant maintenance. Various support services also are managed from the central office: business affairs, food services, transportation, and communications and community relations. In recent years several new areas have been added to the responsibilities of central office staff, such as labor relations, state and federal programs, legislation, legal and judicial oversight, technological developments, and energy coordination. Whether each of these areas is assigned to one individual, or one person carries the responsibility for several, depends on the expertise required and the size of the district.

Most middle-level administrators and supervisors in this category are housed with the superintendent at a central location, often in the board of education building. Very large districts have subdistrict centers in regional offices. Supervisors, who are responsible to the central administration, have offices at these headquarters, but many spend considerable time in the schools helping personnel at the building level.

Experts currently recommend that greater latitude for decision making be assigned to personnel at the building level. Although the practice is not yet general, it is operational in some school districts and will probably become widespread. Where decision making has been delegated to those closer to the teaching of students, the role of many central office personnel, particularly instructional and curriculum support staff, has changed from managing to coordinating and advising. However, in management and fiscal matters—for example, in accounting for attendance and school expenditures—there remains a central office responsibility for a managing and administrative-monitoring function.

Central office personnel spend much of their time in administrative and coordinating functions, facilitating and executing the policies of the school district as well as the mandates and the regulations of the state and federal governments. They take major responsibility for budgeting, payroll, food service, transportation, requisitions, and maintenance of school plant. Principals and teachers wrestle with many of those matters in their own schools; central office personnel coordinate the matters districtwide and carry out many of the administrative details.

In addition, many central office personnel, particularly in subject areas and general curriculum, plan and facilitate in-service education for teachers and administrators. This role becomes especially important when the school district introduces new content, program innovations, or different organizational structures. For example, many school districts have recently sponsored instruction and workshops on computer literacy, sex education, AIDS prevention, drug and alcohol abuse, school violence, career ladders, and textbook evaluation.

Central office jobs are not always distinct or clearly defined by title. A position under a particular title in one district may entail quite different duties from those included in a position by the same title in another district. For example, depending on the district, a guidance person may be a supervisor of psychological counseling, of career counseling, of standardized testing, or of attendance. Discovering the duties of a central office position is often puzzling to prospective applicants.

A person interested in a vacated position may think that the best way to get candid, firsthand information is to talk with the person who left the job. That is perhaps true, but there is often other or new information available from official sources. The administration, for example, may be taking the occasion of a change in staff to modify the duties associated with the position, or it may be shifting the position to another department to make central office administration more efficient. The best source of information about the particulars of a position is the job description produced by the personnel office, which is made available when an opening is advertised.

Another source of insight is a district's organization chart. The grouping of areas and the arrangement of the lines of authority tell a lot about the power structure and the program emphasis of the central office. A chart may take some reading between the lines, but it does offer a perspective on how people function operationally (see Figures 4–1 and 4–2).

A prospective applicant for a central office position should also explore the conditions of work, or the work climate. Job descriptions and organization charts will not be of much help in this regard. Instead, the person will have to rely mainly on his or her powers of observation during a visit to the office for an interview.

Redefinition and expansion of middle-management and supervisory positions occur frequently. For example, general administrators may be moved to management of state and federal programs, librarians may become library media specialists, math and science supervisors may extend their responsibility to include computer science, and guidance personnel may take charge of drug and alcohol abuse prevention programs. There are a variety of reasons for such shifts in role and responsibility. People may begin in one job and demonstrate a talent, an interest, or a competence that causes them to be drafted into or attracted to a new role. The administration may discover a new problem or area needing attention. Outside influences may suggest or mandate new procedures or regulations.

Central office professional personnel are in either line or staff positions. The distinction is important. Line positions are usually management jobs dealing with the elements of school that support and make possible the instructional program—for example, compliance with school board, state, and federal regulations and mandates; personnel decisions; payroll; supplies; transportation; and food services. Staff positions are leadership roles in instruction that have a teaching flavor; the duties are neither as precise nor as controlling as those of line personnel. The functions of personnel in staff positions are to consult and advise on personnel matters, curriculum, teaching, and materials/media/resources. In other words, staff people generally serve as guides and supporters, whereas line personnel have administrative authority and responsibility.

Some staff personnel do, of course, have line responsibilities. For example, when departments become large, as happens when two or more school districts are consolidated, or when a district adds new staff because of growth in enrollment, the chief of a staff group becomes an administrator (sometimes systemwide). An example is the consolidation of guidance, counseling, testing, and other psychological services into pupil personnel services. Someone from among the staff must administer the specialty area, even though it is composed largely of nonadministrative types.

Preparation

General administrators, the line people, often come from the ranks of administrators at the building level; their jobs are considered promotions in

Figure 4–1   A Traditional Administrative Organizational Chart

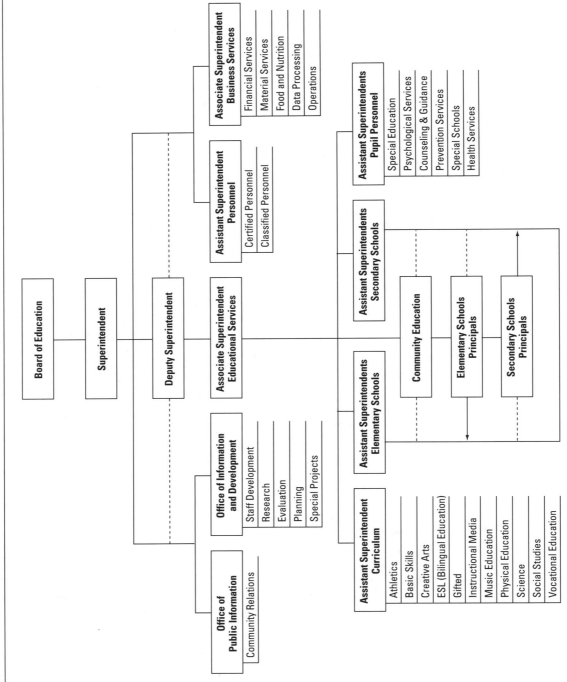

Figure 4-2 A Nontraditional Administrative Organizational Chart

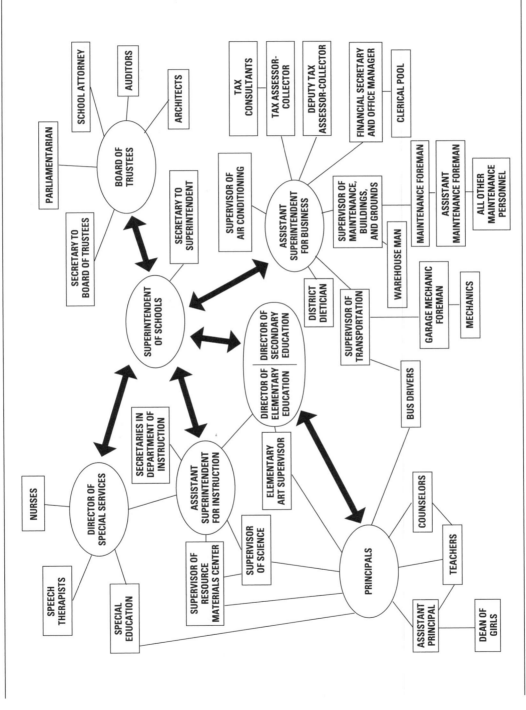

This nontraditional organization chart shows the same traditional organization depicted in Figure 4–1. The sense of hierarchy, however, is diminished. By scattering "line" jobs (indicated by ovals) and by clustering "staff" jobs around them, the idea that certain jobs are at the bottom of the totem pole is eliminated. The emphasis here is on the concept of intercommunication, informal as well as formal relationships, and collegiality among workers.

the administrative hierarchy. Their preparation involves an established sequence of graduate study, and many specialize in the area of their work assignment, often with school district support. The combination of study and experience makes possible a progression of promotions up the steps of a standard system.

Some line areas, such as transportation, food service, and buildings and grounds, are too new for formal college preparation programs to have developed, or they have evolved into something different from earlier definitions. People who hold administrative positions in such line areas have relied on experience and frequent short-study programs to make their way up the ladder. The system is dynamic. It makes possible the development of new specialties as new requirements become apparent. Employees, irrespective of formal training, have a chance to grow and develop and be promoted. Individuals without college degrees may no longer find employment in some of these specialties, but new areas will continue to evolve. In a sense there will always be people who pioneer, who create (or live with the development of) their own specialty.

Specialists in subject areas, guidance, and social and psychological services, who are hired to perform tasks that require advanced training in particular disciplines or areas of knowledge, may come to a central office position from a building assignment or from graduate school. Specialist positions that are not directly related to teaching, such as social workers, school psychologists, and audiologists, may not require prior teaching experience or licensure as a teacher. Other specialists need a comprehensive knowledge of teaching, in both content and procedures. They are usually required to have teaching experience and a license to teach, as well as advanced study and degrees in their specialty. Although there are arguments about whether all central office specialists should have teaching experience, most who occupy such positions today have taught before moving to district headquarters.

Almost all central office professional personnel are required to have advanced graduate study and degrees. Most specialist positions, even those at the entry level, require preparation at the graduate level—for example, curriculum and teaching, guidance and counseling, school psychology, and school administration. Some exceptions, most of them not connected with instruction, include business managers; directors of communications, transportation, food service, and building and grounds; energy coordinators; state and federal program officers; and visiting teachers. Personnel in these positions often begin with less than a graduate degree, but increasingly advanced study is being required. Subject-matter specialists begin specialization at the undergraduate level; however, to qualify for a supervisory position, they must have at least a master's degree.

The literature on central office staff is sparse. The reason lies in the difficulty of generalizing about such a widely diverse category of personnel. Even though many specialists work together in school districts, their professional allegiance tends to be to their individual specialty. In addition, no single organization has interest in, or data on, the general category called central office personnel, and central office personnel themselves do not all belong to the same organization. Instead, they belong to professional groups associated with their own specialty. These groups include the American Association for Counseling and Development (with fifteen subunits), the American Association of School Administrators, the American Association of School Personnel Administrators, the American Home Economics Association, the American Library Association (and one of its subunits, the American Association of School Librarians), the Association for Educational Communication and Technology, the Association for Supervision and Curriculum Development, the Council for Exceptional Children, the National Association of Elementary School Principals, the National Association of Pupil Personnel Administrators, the National Association of Secondary School Principals, the National School Public Relations Association, and others. More information about central office specialties of interest can be secured by writing to the appropriate organizations. Often, special interest groups (SIGs) have formed within such organizations to convene members whose jobs are alike in order to address their unique interests. Committees in many organizations deliberate on the preparation required for the jobs they hold (not infrequently raising standards above those that members have met) and issue standards for entry into their field. Some organizations maintain a list of job openings in their field, but most do not have a placement service. All publish such materials as journals, newsletters, monographs, and books; some produce films and videotapes; and some have sites on the World Wide Web. Print and audiovisual media are designed to help members stay current with developments in their field and for use in training programs. All organizations respond promptly and helpfully to requests for materials on organizational purpose and services. Informational flyers and brochures are provided free of charge.

Salary and Fringe Benefits

Salary data for such central office jobs as directors, managers, coordinators, and supervisors are broken out for the broad areas of finance and business, instructional services, public relations/information, staff personnel services, and subject area supervisors. Data for other areas, including pupil personnel, research, food services, health, transportation, federal programs, media services, and plant operations, are lumped together. Information on salaries for many types of positions within these various categories is lost in the generalizing of data for broad areas. The data are made even more vague by being reported as means. On the positive side, the figures give a clear indication of the salary that can generally be expected for certain categories of personnel.

The scheduled range of means for directors, managers, and coordinators varies according to the size and the per pupil expenditure of the school system. Table 4–1 indicates the mean of salaries paid to various categories of

Table 4–1   Mean of Average Salaries Paid to Central Office Personnel, by School District Enrollment, 1995–96

	Systems of 25,000 or more Students	Systems of 10,000–24,999 Students	Systems of 2,500–9,999 Students	Systems of 300–2,499 Students
Administrators for				
Finance and business	$70,318	$65,731	$65,200	$54,062
Instructional services	71,417	69,985	68,628	58,396
Public relations/information	60,890	53,232	47,933	42,506
Staff personnel services	71,096	68,038	66,703	50,843
Subject area supervisors	54,455	56,186	56,516	58,911

Source: From *Measuring Changes in Salaries and Wages in Public Schools*, Arlington, VA: Educational Research Service, 1996, pp. 16–19.

central office personnel by school district enrollment. More specific data are available from the Educational Research Service in Arlington, Virginia.

Fringe benefits for central office administrators and supervisors, including those at the building level, are the same as those for principals and assistant principals. They are reported in Chapter 3.

SPECIAL SERVICES

In Chapter 4 considerable attention was given to special service personnel, or specialists, who work in a school district's central office or one of its regional offices. This chapter deals with specialists who work at the school-building level with students, teachers, principals, other specialists, and parents. Building-level specialists include teachers and supervisors of art, music, and physical education; school library media specialists; computer specialists; guidance counselors; school psychologists; school social workers; reading teachers; English-as-a-second-language (ESL) teachers; special education teachers; school nurses; occupational and physical therapists; and speech-language pathologists and audiologists. Information included in this chapter often applies also to staff in central office positions who fall into the specialist categories.

Attention to specialists is important because existing programs in most of these positions continue to have openings and because more specialists are being assigned to the building level as mandates and recommendations for school improvement materialize. Three examples of the latter development illustrate why there is a continuous call for specialists:

1. Public Law 94–142, the Education for All Handicapped Children Act of 1975, reenacted in 1990 as the Individuals with Disabilities Education Act (IDEA), mandates that youngsters with disabilities receive a "free, appropriate public education that includes special education and related services to meet their unique needs," and that individualized education programs be planned and provided for them. For this legislation to be implemented, many more specialists are needed in school buildings than were present before, including occupational therapists, physical therapists, and school psychologists.

2. Recent advances in technology, particularly in the personal computer, have required that schools employ computer and other technology experts to instruct both students and teachers. The first need is for teachers to learn how to use computers and other hardware, to become acquainted with software, and, most important, to find effective ways to use technology in enhancing the learning of students. This requires that teachers and administrators develop new attitudes about the instructional process. It also calls for employment of technicians and curriculum specialists with knowledge of technology and its possible uses, and supervisors to assist and support teachers.

3. The recommendation made by several national commissions that teachers be empowered with greater authority for decision making (and thus that more autonomy be delegated to the building level), if implemented, creates a need for additional specialists and support personnel, such as lead teachers, technology experts, and allied health experts, to work on site with teachers and administrators.

A bit of explanation regarding the third example may be helpful here. The rationale for moving decision making closer to the client, the student, is so simple that one might wonder why commitment to such a policy has been so long in coming: teachers and other educators who work directly with children and adolescents are in a better position to recognize their unique characteristics, problems, needs, and interests than administrators and specialists who are more distant.

Before the recommendation was made to empower teachers with more authority for decision making, there was a period of standardizing curriculum (which continues in some places). The goal was to have all schools in a district—all students in similar grades or subjects—cover the same curriculum. But research and experience have proved that such expectations are unrealistic. Children are sufficiently different in ability, interest, background, and attitude to make it impossible for a single curriculum to satisfy or accommodate all. Schools that have recognized and responded to the differences in their students have been more successful than those that have laid down essentially the same expectations for all students.

To implement a program that responds to the students being taught, teachers need to fashion curriculum to their own situation. As a result, curriculum becomes different in each school, though the general goals of education for each school in the district would be the same. Strong support is apparent for such an approach. No less prestigious and influential a group than the Carnegie Task Force on Teaching as a Profession, for example, has recommended that "teachers should be provided with the discretion and autonomy that are the hallmarks of professional work" and that they should have "the ability to make—or at least to strongly influence—decisions concerning such things as the materials and instructional method used." Carrying out such a recommendation would enable teachers to better accommodate each student. In an ideal situation, it would mean that each youngster's curriculum would be individualized.

The latter is probably not possible in present circumstances. The expense would be too great. But there will inevitably be more decision making on curriculum at the building level and in classrooms. Specialists are important in that process. They are essential to teachers, who do not have the time, the perspective, or the expertise to diagnose, plan, teach, remedy, and evaluate all that a responsive school program requires without assistance.

Specialists, as such events materialize, will be used differently. Exactly how their roles will be modified is still not clear, but creating the staffing patterns, collaborative efforts, and instructional approaches needed will involve stimulating and challenging work for specialists and school faculties.

RESPONSIBILITIES OF SPECIALISTS

Each of the specialist categories named in the opening paragraph of this chapter is examined separately in this section, but first, some common characteristics are described. For example, most specialists are both teachers and supervisors: They teach or counsel students directly, and they consult with and advise teachers in their area of expertise. For music, art, and physical education specialists in elementary schools, that double duty takes the form of actually teaching classes of children as well as helping the elementary school teacher teach the subject. For counselors—guidance personnel, school psychologists, or social workers—it involves working with students and consulting with teachers, parents, and other school personnel who deal with students.

A few illustrations will help show what specialists contribute. Teachers in the lower school often try to integrate subjects. A social studies lesson, for example, may include not only the history and the geography of a country, but also the country's culture—its literature, music, art, and dance. One or more specialists may serve as consultants in helping the classroom teacher create such a unit of work, advising on content, materials, and teaching techniques.

Another example is developing an individualized education program (IEP) for a youngster with disabilities at either the elementary or the secondary school level. In such an activity, special educators, school social workers, school psychologists, occupational and physical therapists, and speech-language pathologists may consult with teachers and the parent to plan a program that seems appropriate for that youngster. The issue in special education is determining what should be expected of a student and how various teachers and specialists (and parents) can contribute to achieving the goals on which they agree.

Other situations, particularly in small and medium-sized school districts, find the specialist teaching his or her subject at several levels. For example, specialists in art, music, physical education, and sometimes foreign language may teach classes in the elementary, junior high, and high school. In many instances that requires serving several schools and relating to the program and the teachers in each school.

Special education teachers often have their own classroom in a school. Reading specialists and speech-language pathologists frequently use smaller rooms for tutoring, remedial work, and coaching. In either situation, children may not be in the special room all day. Practice since the enactment of Public Law 94–142 has been to *mainstream* children who are disabled—that is, to integrate them with children who are not disabled as much as possible, at least for part of the day. More recently, the approach in some schools has been to include students with disabilities in regular classrooms. This practice, dubbed *inclusion*, creates other problems. It also challenges teachers to individualize more, even for students without disabilities.

Often in the case of children with reading or speech difficulties, students are pulled out of the regular classroom for short periods, and diagnosis and remedial instruction take place in the specialist's space. In schools that use group counseling, the guidance specialists bring together in a separate space students who need or can benefit from therapy. In all these types of assistance by specialists, the teacher is consulted and advised so that there is coherence and consistency in each student's learning program.

Teachers and principals have a number of reservations about these scheduling arrangements. School personnel are particularly critical of mainstreaming and "pull-out" practices because they disrupt the students' concentration and the rhythm of learning in regular classrooms. A challenge for specialists, teachers, and administrators in the years ahead will be creating better ways to schedule time and treat students with special needs. The practice of inclusion is one attempt to schedule so that disruption is minimized while the needs of all students are met.

Guidance counselors, school library media specialists, school psychologists, school social workers, school nurses, occupational and physical therapists, speech-language pathologists, and audiologists act in still other capacities. Guidance counselors, who are present in greater numbers than the other specialists just mentioned, serve in a mode that illustrates the kind of service all these specialists provide.

Guidance and student personnel work involves counseling students and consulting with teachers, administrators, and parents. Most high school counselors confer with students on an individual basis. Recently they have begun to consult more with teachers and principals, encouraging them to take a greater responsibility in guiding the personal-social adjustment of youngsters and to assume a more prominent role in advising. In the elementary school, counselors do some individual counseling, but they have long spent more time helping teachers create a better environment in which children can learn and develop.

School guidance counseling is mainly educational and vocational, with some personal-social (or adjustment) counseling. A few counselors are involved in mental health counseling.

A problem for counselors (and teachers) in junior and senior high schools is confidentiality. Personal-social counseling is probably their most delicate activity. It involves developing trust. Students frequently reveal facts and feelings that cannot be shared. Yet counselors and teachers often consult with parents and other teachers about the students they counsel. Discretion and good judgment are therefore important qualifications for counselors.

In large schools, several professional and support staff usually share the many duties carried on by student personnel and guidance specialists. In smaller schools, often elementary schools, one counselor or a person who serves as both a teacher and a counselor may perform only the most important guidance functions. The trend recently has been to encourage teachers to take on an advisor's role. In some schools, guidance counselors have assisted teachers in preparing for a teacher-advisor role.

Increasingly, counselors are working with single parents, who in many cases are looking for solutions to problems that married couples might be able to solve for themselves in their discussions with each other. Group counseling or support groups for youngsters of recently divorced parents is another comparatively new task for guidance personnel.

All the foregoing services may not be available from counselors actually located in a school building, but many school districts have a full-time staff of specialists at their central office. In smaller school districts or where a single district cannot afford full-time personnel in a particular specialty, such specialists are provided by cooperative service boards, intermediate school districts, or both. Many variations exist in the types of employment for specialists, but all must have basically the same level of training and competence.

TYPES OF SPECIALISTS

Art Teachers and Supervisors

Data on the number of certified art teachers in the country are sketchy. On the basis of a 1997 survey, the National Art Education Association (NAEA) estimates that there are about 70,000 full-time art teachers employed in the public schools. However, precise data are not available from NAEA. The U.S. Department of Education's National Center for Education Statistics reports the 1991 count of art teachers in secondary schools to be about 26,300.

In the elementary school, forty-eight states require licensure for art teachers, so it can be assumed that art is taught at that level in those states. Licensure is not required in two states (Alaska and Hawaii). Art education is required in most middle/junior high schools. In grades above the sixth, it is taught by a specialist, an art teacher. Twenty-five states require art or fine arts for high school graduation.

Teachers and supervisors of art are difficult to distinguish from one another, possibly because art educators themselves do not see much of a difference. There are comparatively few art teachers or supervisors in the elementary school, perhaps 10,000 to 15,000. In the high school, teachers of art far outnumber supervisors. District art administrators (supervisors and directors) clearly are specialists.

Preparation for teaching art can be accomplished in four years, culminating in a bachelor's degree. An art supervisor usually must have a master's degree. In many states a master's degree or the equivalent is required for continuing certification.

The publication *Status of the States: Art Education Reports* indicates the requirements for art teacher licensure as of September 1996. Art, like music, is so much a matter of experience and proficiency that subjecting all prospective art teachers to the same training makes little sense. NAEA champions this point: "Not all prospective art teachers need the same amount or even the same sequence of class work, general studies, content in the special art area, teaching and learning theory, observation/participation and practicum experience, and professional studies." NAEA's Standards for Art Teacher Preparation Programs are consistent with those of the National Council for Accreditation of Teacher Education. There is no guarantee, however, that all colleges and universities abide by NAEA's plea for flexibility in program, so this is an important point to check in exploring a place to study.

Music Teachers and Supervisors

There are about 80,000 teachers of music in American public schools. This figure includes vocal and instrumental music teachers and music supervisors. Usually music is required at the elementary, middle, and junior high school levels and is elective in the senior high school. A number of music specialists teach at more than one level.

In the lower schools, the focus for all students is general music. Instrumental and vocal music programs are part of many elementary and junior high/middle school programs. Whether they are curricular or extracurricular is a local option. Some schools build vocal and instrumental music into the school day. Others offer only instrumental music during school hours. Choirs, bands, and orchestras usually meet before or after school or during lunch, but in schools with a strong commitment to music, any of these activities might be a part of the regular schedule.

Music in senior high school is most often elective and includes courses and performance groups. Courses may include general music, theory, music history, and literature. A few schools offer classes in voice training. Performance groups include band, orchestra, chorus, and music theater. Some high schools have extensive offerings. Others have very lean programs.

The specialists who teach and direct these activities have various titles, such as teacher, director, or supervisor. All are part of the number reported earlier.

Beginning music teachers and supervisors in all states must have a bachelor's degree. In most states a master's degree or equivalent is required for regular licensure.

The Music Educators National Conference (MENC) is the major professional association for music teachers and supervisors. About 45,000 school personnel belong to MENC.

MENC offers a selection of publications of possible interest to anyone exploring music teaching. Four in particular are helpful to those exploring music teaching in schools as a career: *Preparing to Teach Music in Today's Schools; Why Teach? Why Music? Why Me?* (a brochure); *Music Scholarship Guide*; and *Music Teacher Education: Partnership and Process.*

Physical Education Teachers

Teachers of physical education are usually considered special teachers in the elementary school. In the high school, depending on their assignment, they may or may not be designated as special teachers. Most high school physical education teachers carry the teaching load of the regular secondary school teacher. The size of the school determines more precisely how both elementary and secondary physical education teachers are designated and how they are assigned. In small districts or schools, physical education teachers may teach physical education from grades 5 through 12 in one or several schools. In systems with large schools they may have a full-time assignment in a single school.

In high schools, and usually in middle and junior high schools, physical education teachers and classes are becoming integrated by sex. In the elementary schools, men or women have always taught boys and girls together. Instruction includes exercises, games, dance of various kinds, and good sports behavior.

In the elementary school, physical education is also a kind of recreation. Young children have difficulty being confined to a desk in a classroom. Sports and games with the physical education teacher, in addition to their learning value, are a chance to let off steam.

High school physical education is more focused on physical development and sports. Tests are given to determine the students' development and fitness at particular ages.

At either level the physical education teacher also may teach classes in health. In the elementary or middle school, the physical education teacher may team-teach health with the classroom teacher, teach the subject alone, or serve as a consultant to the classroom teacher. A health class in the middle/junior high or senior high school may be an academic course and be scheduled as such.

Physical education teachers also coach intramural and interscholastic sports and dance at any level, although interscholastic sports usually do not begin until high school. Intramural sports may take place during school hours. For interscholastic sports, practice usually occurs after school, and games are in the afternoon or evening. Coaching after school is usually considered an additional duty for which physical education teachers are paid extra. Varsity coaches are often hired for their coaching ability, and teaching physical education or other classes is a secondary responsibility, or at least thought to be so. Often a varsity coach has a lighter teaching load.

To begin teaching in public schools, teachers and special teachers in physical education are required to complete a bachelor's degree and be certified by the state.

School Library Media Specialists

The number of people involved in school libraries, audiovisual centers, library/media centers, and library/media/computer centers across the country is uncertain because of the rapid change in this field, but there are over 75,000 school librarian/media professionals in the public schools. School library media specialists are a comparatively new breed, and computer specialists in this area are even newer. They work in places that keep print, recorded, photographed, audiovisual, and other materials and have names like school library, learning resource center, instructional materials center, and library/media center. The names vary so much because of the explosion in both the kinds of information and the other resources that can be stored and retrieved, and in the forms and the ways those resources are managed. What was once a library, consisting of little more than print material such as books and periodicals, has expanded with the development of multiple ways to record, preserve, and disseminate information—cassettes, tapes, microfiche, films, slides, filmstrips, videotapes, interactive videodisks, computer disks, CD-ROMs, computerized data banks, the Internet, and more. The library media field has been revolutionized by technology.

The transition is far from complete, if it ever will be. Libraries/media centers are still in the midst of change. The evolution has been under way for a number of years. As the demand for and the use of audiovisual equipment, computers, and technology resources have become greater, as their quantity and quality have increased, and as their accessibility has improved, they have been integrated into the resources of the library with other materials. For example, a book and a map depicting the life and geography of India can be supplemented by films or CD-ROMs showing the Indian people in their habitat. With the "information superhighway" becoming accessible in schools, students and teachers will have access to resources on World Wide Web sites and in databases. With E-mail they will be able to communicate with fellow students throughout the world. Some schools already have these capabilities.

The use of computers and personal computers (PCs) is progressing at a dazzling pace. For example, in only a few years, many schools have computerized their library card catalogs, and that change is inevitable for almost all schools. Databases, from which information is retrieved by telecommunication on PCs, are developing with enormous speed. When equipment becomes available in schools and students learn how to use it, they will gain access to databases and other electronic sources so quickly that finding information will no longer be a laborious process.

Books and other print materials are now also available in electronic form on the World Wide Web. It is not easy to forecast when this will become universal. Suffice it to say that librarians and media specialists are going through a period of fast and dramatic change, and their fields continue to be drawn together in school use. Despite the difficulty that personnel in the two areas are having in keeping pace with developments, and despite their reluctance to change the parameters of their work, great progress is being made.

Whereas *librarian* formerly meant strictly that, today it means library media specialist and more. The labels of state licenses in the field indicate the confusion and the difference in opinion on this specialist's role: school librarian, media generalist, librarian/media specialist, instructional media specialist, materials or media specialist, and audiovisual librarian. Anyone considering a career in this specialty should inquire about developments in the library media field, explore the curricula being offered at colleges preparing such personnel, and investigate the most enlightened programs before selecting a place to study.

Jobs as a library media specialist, therefore, vary greatly, influenced by the size of the school, the degree to which media and technology have been integrated, and the school district's concept of materials/technology support. Of course, the emphasis and the support given to the maintenance and the use of a comprehensive resource center are also important. Without a highly qualified specialist on a faculty, a library/media center is little more than a repository for learning resources.

School library media specialists perform many demanding tasks. In addition to handling all the library media management functions—selecting, ordering, and processing items—they work with teachers in finding and organizing materials, developing curricula, and preparing units for teaching. They must be well versed in the center's holdings and particularly cognizant of materials appropriate for the age level of the students they serve. If access to resources via technology is a service of the center, personnel must also have competencies in that area.

Library media specialists also orient students in the use of the center and assist individuals in finding and using materials. Some are expert in storytelling, graphics, photography, filming, videotaping, or electronic databases. Many library media specialists teach, and some team-teach with teachers.

Where computers are available, the library media specialist must not only be knowledgeable about their use but know how to help others use them. This may mean assisting people in overcoming a fear of computers, often more prevalent among teachers than students.

The work of the library media specialists is highly professional. Nearly all states require them to be licensed. Forty-nine states require a teacher's credential as well as a specialist's, particularly for the regular license (essentially a permanent license).

The master's degree in library science, media science, or library media science, historically obtainable in one year of study beyond the bachelor's degree, is increasingly demanding more time (extending beyond one year) because of the additional competencies that the position requires. In the near future, the master's degree will probably be required in most states. The American Association of School Librarians (AASL; a department of the American Library Association) and the Association for Educational Communication and Technology (AECT), in their joint standards for training and certification (last released in 1988, now being revised), recommend the master's degree as the entry-level requirement. Each association also has its own recommendations regarding the particulars of training for specialists in its area. Persons interested in library media careers in schools are advised to contact these associations for counsel and advice.

Many school library media specialists work essentially the same number of hours as teachers. However, some are classified as administrators because they oversee a large enterprise and a number of professional, technical, and nonprofessional personnel (secretaries and student and adult aides). The school year of these specialists may be a bit longer than that of teachers because there is always the need to tidy up at the end of the year and prepare for the beginning of a new year. Selecting, ordering, and processing material sometimes creates summer employment for library media specialists, particularly in larger schools where holdings are substantial. Library media administrators are often on twelve-month appointments and are classified for salary and other benefits with administrators and supervisors (see Chapter 3).

The job market for library media specialists in schools is stable and increasing as the quantity and the quality of learning resources increase. Persons with interest in the field are advised to seek part-time, work-study, or volunteer work in a library/media center. When such experience occurs before training, there is an opportunity to view firsthand the nature and the conditions of work and to gain an impression of the competence required. When such experience takes place during training, it provides the prospective specialist with an advantage over other candidates at employment time.

Salaries for library media specialists in 1995–96 ranged from a mean of minimum salaries of \$24,984 to a mean of maximum salaries of \$60,986, depending on the size of the school district, the per-pupil expenditure, and the region of the country. The mean of average salaries nationwide was \$41,761. Administrative salaries can be higher.

Computer Specialists   At this stage in the use of computers in schools, personnel involved as specialists, teachers, or consultants vary so much that it is impossible to describe the position precisely. The computer specialist is often a self-trained individual with a personal interest in computers and other technology, someone who owns his or her own computer or has access to one at school. Many specialists (and teachers) have been supported in developing their competence on computers through membership in user groups. These groups, voluntary clubs for people at all levels of sophistication on computers, exist all over the country. Although they include people of many interests from many walks of life (and all ages), the larger clubs usually have a special interest group (SIG) on the use of computers in education. Electronic bulletin boards and Web sites also provide rich resources for becoming more knowledgeable about computers and their use. People can gain access to such resources by means of modems (devices built in or external to a computer that connect to the Internet or to online services via a telephone line), provide contact with people and databases all over the world). Educators interested in computers find kindred souls with similar interests and needs via such bulletin boards and Web sites. Anyone with the equipment, the software, and access to a server can send and receive information and images with a computer.

Many of the first school specialists in computers were (and are) largely self-taught teachers, who became experts by spending hours at a computer, sharing with like-minded individuals, reading computer manuals, participating in user groups, and browsing online. Now many programs are available to help education personnel become computer experts and to assist them in remaining current in the rapidly developing field of technology in teaching. Adult education, school systems, and colleges and universities offer study in computer technology and computer literacy. The early emphasis on programming and the inner workings of the computer has shifted to a focus on computer use and facility with software. School computer specialists receive training that helps them aid teachers in using computers and in becoming proficient in the use of computers for instructional purposes. Despite this shift, some teachers still use technology in traditional ways—for drill and practice in basic skills. There is, however, major prominence today in efforts to support student-centered approaches to instruction so that students can conduct their own inquiry while the teacher serves as facilitator or coach.

Defining the place and the role of the computer specialist is complicated further because of the several approaches being tried to bring computers and other technology into use in schools, whether a computer specialist should teach or consult on computers, or whether knowledgeable teachers should tutor colleagues to become adept at using the computer in teaching. A major problem is overcoming the fear of computers among the present generation of teachers. Recently a program was initiated to recruit a cadre of computer-literate teachers to tutor colleagues. The program is already operational in a number of school districts.

Where one finds the computer specialists in the organization of a school is therefore uncertain. As yet, there is no established home base for these people. In some school districts, they are found on the staff of the library/media center, probably because the technology fits so well with materials, media, and equipment, and because the computer has a cataloging capacity. In other districts they are central office consultants who visit the schools to consult, conduct workshops, and sometimes teach students directly.

Personnel in state education departments are beginning to establish policy on the competence needed for a credential in computer technology. Most states promote technology integration in curriculum, and a little over half of the states require computer training for new teachers. However, the use and training for use of computers in schools are not far enough advanced as of this writing to find that states have established licensure in the field. Persons interested in becoming a computer specialist should seek information from the Association for Educational Communication and Technology, the American Association of School Librarians, library media departments and personal computer centers in their local community or at nearby universities, computer user groups, and electronic bulletin boards.

Guidance Counselors

There are about 165,000 professional counselors in private practice, government, and business, as well as education. Counselors in the nation's public schools represent the largest single group in this specialty. They number 104,242: 55,572 in elementary schools, 45,534 in secondary schools, and 3,136 in combined schools. All school counselors are concerned with helping individuals understand themselves better—their talents and abilities and interests, their growth and development, and their adjustment to school and the working world.

In the elementary school, counselors work with teachers, principals, other specialists, and parents to help students. The counselor may observe a youngster in the classroom to advise the teacher on possible ways to deal more effectively with the child. When the difficulty is beyond the expertise of the teacher, the specialist counsels the child, but individual counseling is less prevalent in the elementary school than in the high school.

Looking more closely at what guidance counselors do reveals a multitude of other duties. In general, guidance personnel develop and keep cumulative records on students; help students plan their school program; and collect, maintain, and share up-to-date occupational, educational, personal, and social information on students. Responsibilities also include managing individual and group testing (administering and scoring the tests, and recording and interpreting the scores), preparing case studies on individual students and holding case conferences, conducting follow-up studies on dropouts and graduates, and undertaking research and evaluation projects.

In the high school, guidance counselors arrange special programs and college and career days; help students become aware of educational and career opportunities; advise students about available loans and scholarships; stay aware of and in touch with colleges, universities, and other postsecondary institutions; and assist students in finding appropriate employment (part-time, summer, and post-school).

School counselors in some schools are still given assignments for attendance enforcement and discipline. Whether this occurs usually depends on the concept of guidance held by the administration. Most guidance experts believe that the effectiveness of the counselor is jeopardized when he or she is required to check student behavior and enforce rules. In recent years, as more principals have become sensitive to and aware of the features of effective guidance programs, they have significantly clarified both the purpose and the duties of counselors.

Counselors who serve junior highs and middle schools do more individual counseling than those in elementary schools, but they try to promote other mechanisms for guidance and advisement. Homeroom is one arrangement to serve that purpose. More and more, teachers are encouraged (and helped) to consult with youngsters on both academic and personal-social problems.

Counselors of all sorts are linked together by the American Association for Counseling and Development (AACD). This 55,000-member organization is the umbrella association for seventeen divisions serving different types of counselors and human development specialists.

AACD maintains two services of special interest to anyone exploring a career in counseling: information on approved institutions for preparation and data on employment opportunities. The AACD division that serves school personnel in counseling is the American School Counselors Association. Requirements for membership are a master's degree, with a minimum of fifteen hours of graduate credit in counseling and guidance. A student membership is available for prospective counselors.

Most school counselors work the same school year as teachers. A few have contracts of ten-and-one-half or eleven months. School counselors are on a separate salary schedule from teachers and are paid more than teachers. The rate depends on length of service, level of preparation, size of the school district, and per pupil expenditure of the district. The mean of average salaries ranges from under $41,932 to $45,983 depending on the size and the wealth of a school district. Guidance counselors on the central office staff are paid on a different salary schedule (see Chapter 4).

School Psychologists

School psychologists are viewed by the American Psychological Association (APA) as different from school counselors. In practice, though, the 20,000-plus psychologists working in educational settings provide many of the same services offered by school counselors. For example, they consult with teachers and other educators to help them develop environments that promote the intellectual, social, and emotional growth of students. They work with school faculty members to fashion programs for youngsters with disabilities and to devise strategies for dealing with disruptive students. They provide inservice education for teachers and other school personnel.

A major difference between school psychologists and school counselors is that the former can treat more serious cases of maladjustment and have more expertise in psychometrics (measurement of mental characteristics). Psychologists with a doctorate in school or clinical psychology have advanced training in counseling and superior competence in measurement and testing. School psychologists work in or out of a district's central office more often than school counselors do. Fifty percent of them work in district offices and serve students and teachers either at a student personnel center or during visits to schools.

School psychologists have slightly different preparation from school counselors, and APA, the major association of psychologists, has a higher standard than AACD regarding the level of training required to provide direct human services in schools. APA recommends that school psychologists have an earned doctorate. However, it recognizes a role for those with master's-level preparation, in supervised work within an organized setting. There is also the National Association of School Psychologists (NASP), whose standards are more in line with those of state departments of education, most of which require sixty hours of graduate study and an internship for licensure. However, requirements vary greatly. Aspirants for school psychologist positions should check the *Manual on Certification and Preparation of Educational Personnel in the U.S. and Canada*, published annually.

Hawaii is the only state that by law or regulation does not require school psychologists to be licensed. Actually, two types of licensure are available for school psychologists, one required and the other optional (in the school context). Most states require a license from the state department of education. The school psychologist with a doctorate may choose to seek a license or a certificate from the state examining board for psychology. The latter is essential only if the psychologist engages in independent, unsupervised practice. For school psychologists who have secondary employment in private practice, this license or certificate is obligatory.

Of the two professional associations to which school psychologists might belong, APA is more prestigious, includes all types of psychologists, and is larger (about 150,000 members). NASP exists exclusively for school psychologists and admits master's-level practitioners to full membership, whereas APA restricts full membership to those with an earned doctorate in psychology.

For psychologists, career opportunities in schools are numerous. In its pamphlet *Careers in Psychology*, APA describes fourteen subfields, seven of which either have practitioners in school district employment or represent specialties that serve other levels or aspects of education: clinical, counseling, developmental, educational, psychometrics and quantitative, school, and psychology of women.

A list of state examining boards for psychology is available from APA. State boards are a source of information on the status of institutions offering graduate training and on state requirements for practice. APA also disseminates a list of institutions accredited for doctoral-level study in the practice specialties of psychology, school psychology among them.

Salary, again, depends on level of preparation, experience, size of school district, and per pupil expenditure of school district. For nine to ten months of employment, the average starting salary for school psychologists is $46,844. The average salary for school psychologists with ten to fourteen years' experience is around $68,000.

School Social Workers   The role of the school social worker is less well known than the roles of most other school specialists. The visiting teacher (a respected school social-service worker of earlier times), the attendance officer, and the home-school coordinator have left behind role concepts that school social workers have had to live down because none of them are appropriate today. Definition of role is particularly important because some of the former specialties created a truant officer reputation.

School social workers are committed to providing better assurance that teachers have teachable children. Their purpose is to help students, teachers, and parents when psychosocial factors interfere with adjustment to school or when problems develop in the interaction of student characteristics and school policies and practices.

For example, a student may blatantly and persistently violate the expectations of the school by lying, stealing, threatening violence, being tardy or absent, using inappropriate or obscene language, cheating on school work, or showing gross disrespect for other students or the teacher. The student's teacher and the principal may suspect that the behavior is the result of such factors as conflict between home and school, severe social discomfort, poor mental health, or cultural differences, and they may call on the school social worker to evaluate, consult, and intervene (or take other appropriate action).

Intervention is often guided by a team of specialists, including the teacher, to bring a wide array of expertise to analyze and diagnose the problem. Frequently parents are involved in discussions of remedies. Together a plan to alter the interaction of the school, the community, and the student's characteristics is devised. The social worker may involve community-based social workers to ensure that the resources are in play to make the school, the community, and the student more compatible. The purpose is to find the most effective intervention to bring about a change in one or more of those three variables so that the student will have the opportunity to take charge of his or her own learning and development.

School social workers must have a wide array of talents, abilities, and skills. They must be able to conduct interviews, establish and maintain purposeful relationships, observe and assess circumstances, collect appropriate information, evaluate influences operating in school-community-parent relationships, determine and apply the most appropriate methods and techniques, collaborate with team members and community agencies, consult with people in the client system, maintain liaison between the student's home and the school, implement referrals to resources, identify and develop resources, coordinate interdisciplinary efforts, develop curriculum, assess intervention, and perform a host of other tasks.

The National Association of Social Workers (NASW) recommends the Master of Social Work (MSW) as the entry-level degree for school social workers. Increasingly, state boards of education are establishing minimum standards for school social work practitioners. Currently, in the states (about half of them) that regulate school social workers, most require the MSW for full licensure.

Reading Teachers

One of the popular clichés in schools is that every teacher is a teacher of reading, and that probably is true, at least to some extent. But there are teachers who specialize in reading. They are licensed to work with students from kindergarten through grade 12. Typically, they teach and tutor children in the elementary school—and sometimes in middle or junior high school—who are below grade level in reading. These are often deprived or disadvantaged children, or those with learning disabilities.

Reading teachers begin by administering a diagnostic test to determine the student's reading difficulty. Their job then is to interpret the results and prescribe remedial work to improve the youngster's reading skills. They often take children from the regular classroom during the school day to work on reading skills. This approach is called a pull-out program. The emphasis is on such skills as decoding and phonics. Reading teachers support their efforts by conferring with the regular classroom teacher (and often by consulting with parents on help and encouragement that they can give at home) to build continuity and reinforcement in the approaches used to help the youngster read. The reading teacher and the classroom teacher often work from different reading materials, so ensuring continuity and fostering the integration of classroom and special assistance are essential.

When there is time, reading teachers may also work with high-achieving kindergarten and first-grade students for enrichment purposes. Five- or six-year-olds who are advanced in reading often need special attention, support, and encouragement to stay interested because the regular pace of instruction in the classroom becomes monotonous and boring to them.

The trend in the rhetoric on reading seems to be away from a hard-driving emphasis on mechanics and basic readers toward a wider use of children's literature, development of an interest in reading, and creation of relationships between a child's writing and reading. However, practice and public pressure are still very much focused on developing reading skills, pure and simple, with a primary goal of improving test scores.

One sign of a broadening view is the development of the IBM *Write to Read* program, which emphasizes children's writing and the relationship of writing to reading (and vice versa). The computer is used as part of this program. The computer is used in other reading programs too, in what is called computer-assisted instruction (CAI). Using the computer with programs especially designed for reading, the teacher can individualize instruction. The student can proceed at his or her own pace. Programs are self-correcting and include built-in rewards.

Reading teachers are prepared at the master's level, usually after they have earned a bachelor's degree, received licensure in elementary or secondary education, and acquired teaching experience. The program for the master's degree usually includes several advanced courses (often about eighteen semester hours), among them reading and children's literature. Certification as a reading teacher is usually represented by an endorsement on a regular teaching license. An estimated 25 percent of elementary school teachers have a reading endorsement on their license, but not all of them are actually reading teachers.

The International Reading Association offers both membership and inservice education for reading teachers and other teachers who teach reading.

English-as-a-Second-Language (ESL) Teachers

The National Center for Education Statistics reports that, in the 1993–94 school year, 4 percent of the students enrolled in public school participated in English-as-a-second-language (ESL) programs. The figure continues to grow as large numbers of immigrants settle in the United States.

The main problem that the children of these immigrants face in school is acquisition of adequate language skills to catch up with their native-English-speaking classmates. Opportunities for ESL teachers exist at the elementary and secondary school levels as well as in adult education, community and four-year colleges and universities, and private language centers. Many ESL teachers also work abroad in various settings.

For the most part, the need for ESL teachers in the United States is focused in the regions tending to have the highest concentration of immigrants and refugees and other resident non-native speakers: southern California, San Francisco, Hawaii, Texas, Florida, New York, New Jersey, and other urban areas.

Throughout the United States, universities at both the undergraduate and the graduate level, and private language centers, offer intensive ESL programs to foreign students who must perfect their language skills to qualify for admission. In addition to providing English language instruction to non-English-speaking students, ESL teachers can develop curriculum, write materials, and conduct research. Several special interest sections exist within the profession, such as computer-assisted language learning (CALL), video applications, program administration, and teaching English to students with hearing impairments.

A bachelor's degree is considered the minimum qualification. Courses of study may include the grammatical, phonological, and semantic systems of the English language; methodology; second language assessment; practice teaching; and the study of another language and its culture.

Master's degrees in TESOL (teaching English to speakers of other languages) and linguistics are offered by many universities. A master's degree can pave the way for administrative responsibilities and is usually the basic requirement for teaching ESL at universities at home and abroad.

TESOL, Inc. (Teachers of English to Speakers of Other Languages) has about 18,000 members. It provides access to professional development and employment opportunities.

Special Education Teachers

There are about 311,200 teachers in the United States working with youngsters who are disabled. Around 95 percent of that number are employed in schools that serve students with disabilities from ages six through twenty-one. In a 1993–94 survey, the National Center for Education Statistics found special education teachers' assignments to be as follows:

Specific learning disability—98,125
Seriously emotionally disturbed—26,684
Mentally retarded—43,106
Speech/language impaired—41,208
Hearing impaired—6,913
Multiple disabilities—7,732
Visually impaired—2,964
Cross-categorical disabilities—73,852
Other health impaired—2,136
Orthopedically impaired—3,443
Traumatic brain injury—217
Deafness and blindness—170

More than 90 percent of elementary school special education teachers and 77 percent of secondary school special education teachers are women. Eighty-six percent are white.

In 1994, 5.4 million children were served in federally supported programs for students with disabilities. That number broke down by disability as follows:

Specific learning disabilities—2.4 million
Speech or language impairment—1.0 million
Mental retardation—554,000
Serious emotional disturbance—414,000
Hearing impairments—64,000
Orthopedic impairments—57,000
Other health impairments—83,000
Visual impairments—25,000
Multiple disabilities—110,000

Deafness and blindness—1,000

Preschool disabled—587,000

The foregoing tallies do not include teachers of youngsters who are gifted and talented, or the youngsters themselves. Youngsters who are gifted and talented and youngsters who are disabled are frequently referred to collectively as *exceptional children* or *underserved, at-risk students.*

Special education teachers work in a variety of settings in schools, including specially equipped classrooms, ordinary classrooms, resource rooms, therapy rooms, clinics, and small seminar rooms. The size of the school district often determines how students with disabilities are grouped for instruction. Age separations in special education are not as rigid as in the regular graded classroom. Also, teachers may teach a group of children with different disabilities. (Many children have more than one disability.)

Instruction is individualized as much as possible because the youngsters' abilities and disabilities are so different. In fact, there is often no other way to help a child learn. There is no set curriculum. Teachers try to discover what and how much a student is capable of learning. They are often aided by other experts in behavior and curriculum, such as the school psychologist, the school social worker, the guidance counselor, and subject-matter specialists. An individualized education program (IEP) is developed. The situation is reversed from that of the regular classroom, where curriculum and learning goals have been set for a grade or a subject and where the same textbooks are often provided to each student. In special education the challenge is to devise a program for each youngster, to find methods and materials that will achieve learning goals, to provide for the behavioral accompaniments to a particular student's disability, and, when possible, to orchestrate activities that a group can do together.

In addition to students with physical and intellectual impairment, the special education teacher is faced with students who do not or cannot understand appropriate behavior, who have not been socialized, who are hyperactive or insecure or embarrassed, who are on medication, or who have epilepsy, autism, or schizophrenia.

Worthy of special mention is the use of the personal computer in special education. Special educators have found some unique applications for the personal computer. They use it as a tool for learning (in some ways it is ideal for individualizing instruction) and to aid them in information management, record keeping, and other administrative tasks.

Federal legislation enacted in 1975 called for mainstreaming students with disabilities in the "least restrictive environment," to the extent that it contributed to their growth and learning, both academically and socially. More recently the emphasis has been on inclusion, explained earlier in the chapter. There are limits to this approach, dictated by the degree of disability, the number of students with disabilities who can be included in a particular class, and the ability of the teacher to accommodate students with special needs. Instead of students with disabilities being shifted from one setting to another, inclusion requires the special education teacher to work with classroom teachers in the classroom. The arrangement requires more individualizing of instruction for all students but also close collaboration of special education and regular teachers to ensure that students with disabilities can relate to the content of the activity under way and benefit from the experience, or engage in a modification of the activity that fits his or her needs and abilities.

Special education for gifted and talented youngsters is in many ways service to a very different type of underserved student. At first glance it may seem that teaching gifted youngsters is more different from teaching students who are disabled than it really is. Gifted students may appear to be regular students who are different only because they have above-average intelligence, greater creative abilities, or both. Gifted students may, however, be withdrawn, precocious, self-impressed, hyperactive, even obnoxious. As a consequence, the task becomes not just one of teaching students who are different but also one of contending with students whose behavior is as confounding as that of students with disabilities.

There is also the difficulty of determining what is meant by gifted and talented or underserved. Is an overachieving or culturally privileged student gifted? Is giftedness a matter of degree? Teachers and administrators must decide at what point in a continuum of giftedness a student qualifies for a special program, and then determine how to explain that decision to parents. Teaching gifted youngsters is a demanding assignment. It goes well beyond planning curriculum and instruction to challenge the capabilities of students with exceptional talents and intellects. This, again, is an area in which the teacher confers with a number of specialists, taps several opinions in assessing students' abilities, consults on the content and the strategy for teaching, seeks help in finding appropriate materials, and looks for assistance in evaluating progress and outcomes.

With the introduction of mainstreaming and inclusion, special education teachers increasingly serve less of the day as teachers of children with disabilities and more as consultants to regular teachers who are trying to cope with disabled youngsters who have been partially or completely integrated into the classroom. A system has evolved that teams the special educator with such other service personnel as the school nurse, the guidance counselor, the school psychologist, and the principal, to focus on planning and evaluating (IEPs). To the special education teacher is designated the dual tasks of documenting the student's progress and preparing the paperwork required by the administration and the government. Many special education teachers find the paperwork and the time that it takes stressful in a professional assignment that is already intense and pressure-ridden. At the same time they find it rewarding to document and report the achievements of children with disabilities.

The emotional and intellectual energy required to deal with exceptional youngsters is enormous. A reassuring note is that while special education teachers consider their work stressful, they also consider themselves able to cope.

Preparation for special education is very much like preparation for other teaching specialties except, of course, that the focus is on disability or gift-edness. In some states prospective special education teachers must first be licensed as elementary or secondary school teachers and then meet requirements for an emphasis in special education, such as teaching children who are hearing impaired or teaching children who are gifted. In other states, teachers may study and be licensed in several exceptionalities, usually related areas. Preparation takes at least four years of collegiate work, often more. Many teacher educators in special education recommend five years of training.

School Nurses

There are more than 1.7 million nurses in the country. The National Association of School Nurses (NASN) estimates that there are about 40,000 nurses in American schools. Some nurses employed by school districts are full time, others only part time. Even so, these figures are conservative because the number of public health nurses serving schools is uncertain.

School nurses perform a variety of services depending on their level of training, the size of the school district, state requirements, and other factors. Nurses are integral members of school faculties. They serve in a variety of capacities, as nurse-teachers, consultants, and practitioners treating students. Some are on "child watch," identifying children from birth to age 5 who have health problems. Most are committed to a wellness approach, promoting prevention in preference to remediation.

Since the passage of Public Law 94-142 and its successor, Public Law 101-476, school nurses have spent more time consulting with teachers and other school personnel than they did in the past. Youngsters with disabilities often have health problems as well as disabilities. In fact, a health problem often causes a disability. Nurses are members of the teams—which consist of (teachers, special education teachers, administrators, other allied health workers, school social workers, psychologists, parents, and others—that plan IEPs for youngsters who are disabled.

School nurses also consult and assist with cases of teenage pregnancy and child abuse. More than 60 percent work in classrooms with teachers. Registered nurses (RNs) with teaching credentials teach health and fitness courses and collaborate with other health professionals to promote preventive care. Currently they are heavily engaged in AIDS education, promoting better understanding of the virus and the way in which it is acquired. The school nurse-practitioner (an RN with a master's degree) is often an administrator, overseeing all the school nurses in a school district.

Preparation for school nursing varies considerably. However, all school nurses must be RNs. They are prepared in two-, three-, and four-year postsecondary programs. Twenty-two states require them to have a bachelor's degree, and twenty-two states, a nursing diploma. [The nursing diploma itself requires only an associate's (two-year) degree.] Licensure as a school nurse is required in thirty-two states. The variation in levels of preparation is due to the diversity in requirements from state to state. In a few states, a school nurse must have both a nurse's license and a teacher's license.

The American School Health Association and the American Nurses Association both serve school nurses, but NASN is the only organization concerned exclusively with school nurses.

Nurses consider work in schools attractive employment. Many move from the stress and demanding schedule of hospital work to public school nursing. Almost a third of school nurses are part-time employees. Part-time nurses have no fringe benefits. Full-time nurses have the insurance, leave, and retirement benefits of their designated category, teacher or administrator/supervisor. Salaries for nurses range from $20,000 to $60,000.

Occupational Therapists   Occupational therapy in schools is designed to enable students to function effectively in the school environment and to improve their ability to profit from the school program. It is a related service made available if needed to better enable the student to benefit from the special education program. Students with disabilities who qualify for special education may receive occupational therapy services in schools that are supported by state or federal funds.

The enactment of Public Law 94–142, the Education for All Handicapped Children Act, and subsequently Public Law 101–476, the Individuals with Disabilities Education Act (and amendments), has made schools one of the three most frequent workplaces (along with hospitals and skilled nursing facilities) for occupational therapists. In 1990 almost 70 percent of the 48,000 occupational therapists in the nation worked in one of those three settings.

The occupational therapist in schools may have one or more of three functions: assessment and evaluation, identifying a youngster's strengths and weaknesses in self-care skills and determining the skills that he or she needs to improve in order to function effectively in school; consultation, helping the IEP team plan a youngster's treatment; and intervention, directly providing occupational therapy services.

Occupational therapy is still somewhat on the fringes of the public school scene. Only about 18 percent of occupational therapists work in schools at present. However, the number is increasing with the greater attention being given to students with disabilities.

Some schools employ occupational therapists directly. Others contract with outside agencies for occupational therapy services. In such instances, children are often bused to hospitals or other facilities for treatment.

Thirty-seven states require occupational therapists to be licensed. The license is issued by a special licensure board, different in each state but usually made up of occupational therapists, medical personnel, and others.

The professional organization of occupational therapists is the American Occupational Therapy Association (AOTA). AOTA's *Guidelines for Occupational Therapy Services in School Systems* (originally published in 1989 and currently being updated) outlines the philosophical base of occupational therapy, sets forth standards for practice, states the necessary competencies, describes roles of occupational therapists in schools, and addresses several other issues of school practice.

In 1993 the average full-time salary for occupational therapists in schools was $38,100.

Physical Therapists

Physical therapists are not yet numerous in schools. But like occupational therapy, physical therapy has gained a foothold since the passage of Public Law 94–142 and subsequent disability legislation. Physical therapy is a rapidly growing profession; 80 percent of its practitioners are twenty-five to forty-nine years of age.

In schools the physical therapist offers two primary services. The first, in sports, has a long history. In that role the therapist treats the injuries and the disabilities of athletes. The second role is more general. In this capacity the therapist serves all students. Often at the request of the teacher, who recognizes a problem and calls for consultation, the physical therapist evaluates a student (patient) and identifies the difficulty. The consulting role is also a prominent service of physical therapists in serving students with disabilities under the provisions of Public Law 94–142. Physical therapists may also provide direct care (hands-on treatment) to students, but more often they consult with teachers, helping them develop a strategy to deal with the diagnosed problem and then monitor progress.

According to the Bureau of Labor Statistics, physical therapy is one of the fastest-growing health professions. There were about 99,500 physical therapists in 1997, and that number was projected to grow to over 200,000 by the year 2000. They work in a variety of institutions and settings: hospitals, nursing homes and health care facilities, health centers, rehabilitation centers, schools, industry, private practice. They also serve as athletic trainers and faculty members in colleges and universities. Across these settings a common concern is to promote optimal human health and function. Specifically, that means providing "therapeutic services and related psychosocial support to individuals of all ages with musculoskeletal, neurological, sensorimotor, cardiopulmonary, vascular, and other physiological dysfunction." The breadth of physical therapy's focus and its concern for human welfare open many employment opportunities. A physical therapy career in education in schools or colleges is just one. Consequently the physical therapist can easily make career changes within his or her profession.

Seventy percent of physical therapists are women, and 91 percent are Caucasians. To practice, a physical therapist must hold a license in the state in which he or she works. Licensure includes passing a national examination administered by the Professional Examination Service. All physical therapists currently in practice have a license.

The American Physical Therapy Association (APTA) has targeted the 1990s as the decade when the master's degree or its equivalent will be a minimum requirement for entry into the profession. Most universities have already established master's degree programs. Currently 65 percent of practicing physical therapists have a bachelor's degree, 33 percent a master's degree, and 2.4 percent a doctorate.

Preparation for physical therapy is similar to the premedical curriculum. It includes a strong emphasis on the physical and biological sciences, along with study of psychology and the humanities. Theory and its application are required in a variety of clinical settings. The average length of the bachelor's curriculum has been 4.5 years, 2.2 in professional studies and 2.3 in liberal arts. Master's degree preparation is a 6-year program.

APTA is recognized by the Council on Higher Education Accreditation and the U.S. Department of Education as the official accrediting agency for collegiate preparation programs in physical therapy. APTA describes the practice of physical therapy in *Competencies in Physical Therapy: An Analysis of Practice*. It also publishes a list of accredited institutions. Both publications are of value to individuals exploring physical therapy as a career.

A shortage exists in physical therapy. Current figures on supply and demand are not available at this writing. The results of an APTA study of supply and demand should be released before the end of 1997. Qualified personnel are in particularly short supply in higher education at the PhD level. Most teachers of physical therapy in universities hold a master's degree, and employment is available for personnel with that level of training.

Beginning salaries for physical therapists in 1996 averaged from $30,000 to $40,000. Forty-three percent of experienced physical therapists earned $45,000 to $70,000. The top 15 percent earned salaries from $70,000 to more than $100,000.

Speech-Language Pathologists and Audiologists

Speech-language and hearing personnel are closely allied. About 100,000 people in the country have training in speech-language pathology and audiology. More than 70,000 speech-language and hearing specialists hold professional certification from the American Speech-Language-Hearing Association (ASHA). Of these, about 33,000 (50 percent) work in schools, mostly elementary schools. There are about seven times as many speech-language pathologists as audiologists.

Speech-language pathologists treat two types of problems: (1) speech disorders and (2) language disorders. Speech disorders include problems with fluency (interrupted flow or rhythm of speech), articulation (difficulty in forming sounds and stringing them together), and voice (inappropriate pitch, quality, loudness, resonance, or duration). Language disorders include aphasia (the loss of speech and language abilities) and delayed language (slowness in developing language skills). Speech-language pathologists treat children individually in clinical settings, and they work with teachers in treatment. In some cases they team-teach with teachers.

Since the implementation of Public Law 94–142 and subsequent legislation on individuals with disabilities, the speech-language therapist's role has changed in a number of ways. He or she now treats a broader range of children with disabilities, including those who are severely handicapped and those who are multiply handicapped. Treatment begins earlier—down to age three—and there is more emphasis on speech and language in secondary school programs. Greater attention is given to identification and assessment, and there is more collaboration with teachers, parents, and other school personnel.

Audiologists in schools conduct programs to identify hearing impairment and to prevent such impairment from occurring. They screen and evaluate the hearing of children entering school and provide suggestions, guidance, and counseling to all students. Audiologists consult with teachers, other school personnel, and parents on dealing with hearing and communication problems and on developing IEPs for children with hearing impairments. More specifically, they test children's hearing to determine if amplification devices are needed, and they recommend the type of device or system that provides optimal listening. Some audiologists provide guidance in facing the problems that hearing impairment may cause, assist students in becoming accustomed to the use of hearing devices, and give instruction in lipreading.

Speech-language and hearing personnel are either building based, usually covering two buildings but sometimes more, or itinerant, traveling to a number of schools in a district. A small number practice in district-wide clinics.

ASHA's Certificate of Clinical Competence requires the completion of a master's degree, nine months of supervised professional experience, and a national examination. ASHA's standards are more rigorous than state licensure requirements in order to protect the public from practice that may be independent and unsupervised. Forty-six states require that a person have a master's degree to practice as a speech-language or hearing specialist. In a few states, people with bachelor's degrees in speech-language pathology or audiology may work with students who have communication problems, but they may be classified as special education teachers.

ASHA is the only professional organization recognized in every state as representing speech-language pathologists and audiologists. The association sets and applies standards for individual practitioners, for colleges and universities that offer master's degrees in speech-language pathology and audiology, and for agencies offering speech-language pathology and audiology services to the public.

In some systems, speech-language and hearing specialists are paid on a salary schedule comparable to that for teachers, and in other systems, on a schedule similar to that for school psychologists and physical and occupational therapists. In exploring employment, interested applicants should ask about the salary category in which they would be placed.

The median annual salary in 1995 was $36,159 for licensed speech-language pathologists and audiologists on nine- to ten-month contracts, $39,950 for those on twelve-month contracts.

The demand for both speech-language and hearing specialists in school is healthy. There have been many more jobs than applicants in recent years.

BECOMING A SPECIALIST

Preparation

Most specialists are required to hold a master's degree, which includes one or two years of graduate study and frequently a supervised experience or internship. Many specialists come from baccalaureate degree programs in the liberal arts and begin specialist training at the graduate level. The main exceptions are subject-matter specialists who carry the title *supervisor,* which sometimes means *special teacher.* Subject-matter supervisors have typically been teachers who began specialization in their subject at the undergraduate level. However, subject-matter supervisors are now required to hold a master's degree or higher. In fact, the master's degree is now the entry-level academic requirement for most specialties.

Specifying the requirements for education, experience, and licensure in each specialty is too extensive an undertaking for this book. There are three primary sources of requirements and standards of preparation in specialty fields: (1) the fifty state departments of education, (2) the professional boards that examine individual practitioners, and (3) the national professional associations representing each specialty. The state departments can supply information on the legal minimums for a license to practice in their respective states. The state professional standards boards provide licensure by the profession itself. For specialists in education, information is available on request from the office of teacher education and certification in the state department of education. A directory of these state offices is available from:

> Donald Hair, Executive Director
> National Association of State Directors of Teacher Education
>   and Certification (NASDTEC)
> 3600 Whitman Avenue, Suite 105
> Seattle, WA 981031

A compendium of certification requirements in the fifty states appears in the *Manual on Certification and Preparation of Educational Personnel in the United States and Canada* (3d ed., 1996–97), published by NASDTEC.

Professional association standards are usually higher than legal requirements, but they do not have legal sanction. However, professional groups are striving to make their standards (sometimes a credential) a prerequisite for practice. This is particularly so in fields in which specialists have options for employment in private or government practice as well as in schools. Considerable progress has been made by the respective professional associations in instituting professional certification. The American Speech-Language-Hearing Association, for example, has made its Certificate of Clinical Competence a requirement to practice in other than academic positions. Private practitioners must hold such a certificate to be eligible for reimbursement by Medicare and Medicaid. Counselors are certified by the National Board for Certified Counselors, an independent nonprofit organization initiated by the American Association for Counseling and Development. In physical therapy, a national examination for the professional credential is administered by the Professional Examination Service, a group independent of the American Physical Therapy Association.

Another type of professional association standard is specification of the doctorate as the profession's entry-level degree. No state requires that school psychologists hold the doctorate to be licensed for practice in schools, but the American Psychological Association has set that standard for school psychologists. The association specifies further that the doctorate be earned at a regionally accredited university or professional school.

The recommendations of the appropriate professional associations are available, usually free of charge or for a small fee, from the organizations listed with each specialty discussed in the previous section.

Another source to check in considering career preparation is accrediting agencies. They inspect and approve preparation programs in the various fields that produce practitioners in education. A discussion of accrediting appears in Chapter 9. The Council for Higher Education Accreditation (CHEA), which recognizes professional accrediting boards and councils, can verify the quality of a particular accrediting agency.

Finding Employment

Specialists find positions in much the same way that teachers and administrators do, through placement offices in universities (see Chapter 2). Because most of them become better acquainted with professors in their field in graduate study, they have some advantage over teachers. Professors have contacts with school districts and often provide leads to their advisees that are more direct and personal than the placement office's standard list of openings.

There are also networks among specialists. They get to know each other in graduate study and through professional association activities. Many a lead to employment is communicated through such informal networks.

The process of applying and interviewing is usually no different for specialists than it is for teachers, however.

Some specialists are employed in schools on a contract basis. The contract may be with an organization, such as a hospital or a clinic in the case of health service personnel, or with individuals who have the appropriate credentials and training. The latter arrangement usually requires that the professional do his or her own marketing of the service to be provided.

Fringe Benefits

Support for Professional Development and Graduate Study.

Support for advanced study and training for specialists in school districts is much like that provided for administrative personnel. It depends, of course, on whether the specialist is classified as a teacher or a supervisor and whether he or she is full time. (Part-time personnel usually do not qualify for fringe benefits.) Benefits and support provided for teachers are described in Chapter 2, and those available for personnel in supervisory or administrative categories are indicated in Chapters 3 and 4.

Insurance Benefits.

Insurance benefits for specialists are as extensive as they are for teachers and administrators. Supervisors' benefits are reported in Chapter 3. Other specialists, who clearly are teachers, may be on a teacher's salary schedule but have slightly better benefits than teachers. Because benefits for specialists are often somewhere between those for teachers and those for administrators, an individual interviewing for employment should take special care to learn what he or she will qualify for before signing a contract.

Retirement and Leave Programs.

Retirement programs for public school personnel are essentially the same for all levels of professional personnel except administrators and the superintendent of schools. The program for specialists operates in similar fashion to the programs for teachers, administrators, and supervisors. Contributions are a percentage of salary, so if specialists are paid better, they contribute a greater amount to the program. Other things being equal, they receive a larger pension when they retire because they have more equity in the program.

Like teachers and other personnel, specialists should be aware that retirement contributions are not transferable across state lines. If a change in employment involves moving to a new state, specialists should inquire about whether the contributions of the employer that they are leaving are vested and whether they can buy in to the retirement program of the new state. Vesting locks in the employer's contribution as well as the employee's, and the equity of the annuity so established can stand until retirement if the employee does not withdraw his or her contribution.

Leave provisions for specialists more often follow those for supervisors than those for teachers (see Chapter 3). The specialist is more apt to work an extended school year of ten-and-one-half or eleven months, as administrators and supervisors do.

Opportunities for Outside Employment/Income.   Many specialists have something to sell beyond their regular employment. Art and music teachers often give private lessons after school and on Saturdays. If art teachers have time to sketch or paint or sculpt, they can sell their products, provided that the products are good enough. They can also find other alternatives, for example, art therapy, museum work, gallery work, and art for the elderly. Music specialists can play or sing professionally and earn money directing church or civic choirs, the community symphony, or the town band. Physical education specialists can coach after school or in the community in recreation or health centers.

School psychologists report secondary employment in four categories: (1) independent practice, (2) health and mental health services, (3) business and government, and (4) higher education. The opportunities are in counseling, teaching, and consulting. Guidance counselors also have some of these opportunities.

Reading teachers can offer private tutoring sessions, and ESL teachers can find part-time evening employment in adult education or private language centers.

Occupational and physical therapists may engage in private practice or find part-time employment in a clinic or a hospital. Speech-language personnel typically provide therapy, and hearing personnel test and consult on hearing problems. Depending on their level of training, all four types of personnel may also teach in adjunct capacities in higher education.

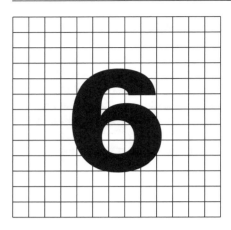

TEACHING, RESEARCH, AND ADMINISTRATION IN HIGHER EDUCATION

There is a romantic notion of higher education that comes partly from the nostalgic recollections of those who have experienced it and partly from Hollywood depictions of college life. Walls with dangling ivy, heroics on the football field, fraternity and sorority parties, a country club atmosphere, and unending opportunities for students to find mates are part of that sweet and easy view. Probably all of those conditions and events can be found on college campuses, but they are peripherals, not the main focus.

Many urban colleges and universities today do not have a campus life. Students commute, particularly at two-year colleges. Academe is much more a businesslike operation than a country club. Students are interested in credits and grades. They see college as leading to jobs and good salaries; the better the performance in college, the better the job possibilities. In the 1990s, much more so than before, accountability is the major concern of students and of faculty.

Teaching, research, and administrative careers in higher education are numerous and diverse. A few facts and figures about the people employed by, and the people studying in, colleges and universities may make the full meaning of that statement clear and convey the magnitude of higher education in the United States.

Table 6–1 presents a historical picture of higher education's dramatic growth since 1870, a year in which only one doctor's degree and no master's degrees were awarded. The total annual expenditure for higher education is around $170 billion. Almost 886,000 professionals teach upwards of 14 million students in more than 3,500 colleges and universities. These figures include all public and private two- and four-year institutions of higher education. The 1,300 or so two-year colleges account for about 254,000 faculty and 5.6 million students (public institutions about 5.34 million, private

Table 6–1 Growth in Higher Education, 1870–1995

Year	Number of States	U.S. Population	Number of Institutions[1]	Faculty	Enrollment	Earned Degrees Conferred Bachelor's[2]	Master's[3]	Doctor's	Total Expend. (in thousands)
1869–1870	37	38,558,371	563	5,553	52,286	9,371	0	1	ND
1879–1880	38	50,189,209	811	11,522	115,817	12,896	879	54	ND
1889–1890	44	62,979,766	998	15,809	156,756	15,539	1,015	149	ND
1899–1900	45	76,212,168	977	23,868	237,592	27,410	1,583	382	ND
1909–1910	46	92,228,496	951	36,480	355,213	37,199	2,113	443	ND
1919–1920	48	106,021,537	1,041	48,615	597,880	48,622	4,279	615	ND
1929–1930	48	123,202,624	1,409	82,386	1,100,737	122,484	14,969	2,299	$507,142
1939–1940	48	132,164,569	1,708	146,929	1,494,203	186,500	26,731	3,290	674,688
1949–1950	48	151,325,798	1,851	246,722	2,659,021	432,058	58,183	6,420	2,245,661
1959–1960	50	179,323,175	2,008	380,554	3,215,544	392,440	74,435	9,829	5,601,376
1969–1970	50	203,302,031	2,525	450,000	7,136,075	792,656	208,291	29,866	21,043,113
1979–1980	50	226,542,580	3,152	675,000	11,569,899	929,417	298,081	32,615	56,913,588
1989–1990	50	249,400,000	3,535	824,220	13,538,560	1,051,344	324,301	38,371	134,655,571
1994–1995	50	262,000,000	3,638	826,252	14,305,658[4]	1,192,000[5]	405,000[5]	43,000[5]	177,200,000

ND = No data.

Sources: From *Digest of Education Statistics 1995*, T. D. Snyder, Washington, DC: National Center for Education Statistics, 1995, p. 175; and *Projections of Education Statistics to 2000*, W. J. Hussar & D. E. Gerald, Washington, DC: National Center for Education Statistics, 25th ed. 1996.

[1]Prior to 1980, excludes branch campuses.

[2]From 1870 to 1960, includes first-professional degrees.

[3]Master's except first-professional degrees; beginning in 1970, includes all master's degrees.

[4]1993 figure.

[5]Projected figure.

institutions, .22 million). Around 2,000 four-year colleges and universities employ about 590,000 faculty and enroll almost 8.7 million students (public institutions 5.9 million, private institutions 2.8 million). Over 1.7 million students attend graduate and professional schools.

Nearly 70 universities enroll more than 25,000 students, whereas around 850 colleges enroll fewer than 2,500 students and 460 colleges, fewer than 500 students. About 11 percent of the colleges and universities in the United States account for 51 percent of the total enrollment. College enrollment was fairly stable in the 1980s, whereas during the 1970s it increased more than 30 percent. From the late 1980s to the early 1990s there was a 12 percent increase.

The typical age of college students has been eighteen to twenty-four years. However, in the last fifteen years the age makeup of undergraduates has changed. No longer do nearly all students come to college directly from high school. In 1993 only 54 percent of students were eighteen to twenty-four years of age. Thirty-six percent were twenty-five to forty-nine years old.

The percentages of women and minority students also have increased. Since 1979, women have accounted for more than half the total enrollment in institutions of higher education. Since 1982 they have earned more than half of the bachelor's degrees, and since 1985, more than half of the master's degrees. The increased minority enrollment is due primarily to greater numbers of Asian and Hispanic students, up from 5.4 percent in 1976 to 12.3 percent in 1993. The percentage of blacks increased from 9.6 percent in 1976 to 10.2 percent in 1993.

Educators in two- and four-year colleges and universities teach and administer in hundreds of disciplines and fields. In four-year colleges and universities they also do research. Some higher education faculty teach exclusively; this is most true of those in two-year colleges, where a large portion of the personnel are part time. Research is done mainly in the universities, where many faculty spend less than one-half of their time teaching and an average of one-third time on research.

Teaching is by far the primary function in four-year and comprehensive colleges, and it inevitably involves library research. Some four-year college faculty and many university professors also do descriptive or empirical research, which entails activities such as laboratory work or fieldwork, reviews of the literature, and searches of other databases. With publishing being a requirement for promotion, many four-year college and university faculty members write scholarly or scientific articles and books. Those in the humanities may write plays, novels, or poetry. Senior faculty often administer a department while continuing to teach. Many university professors have three or four responsibilities (teaching, research, writing, and service). Administration might be a fifth.

Sociological studies of higher education throw light on the nature of professional careers in higher education and the workings of the system. For example, Logan Wilson's *American Academics, Then and Now* provides a comprehensive description of what is, and what has been, the situation in academic life. W. Todd Furniss's *Reshaping Faculty Careers* includes vignettes of faculty careers. One must keep in mind, however, that many exceptions exist to the generalizations made in such studies and case illustrations because of the great diversity among institutions and people.

Many of the points made in Chapter 2 about teaching as an art and as a science apply to college teaching as well as K–12 teaching. Readers may want to read those parts of Chapter 2 in conjunction with this chapter in order to get a fuller picture of the generic nature of teaching.

FOUR-YEAR COLLEGES AND UNIVERSITIES

Teaching and Research The college context influences teaching in four-year colleges and universities. For example, college professors do not need to deal with disciplining students. College is voluntary. Students come expecting to conform reasonably to the protocols of college life, whatever these might entail at a particular institution. But like K–12 teaching, college teaching varies greatly in terms of the professor's beliefs about learning, the nature of the subject matter, the role of the institution in educating students, and the function of the teacher.

How a college teacher functions, of course, is controlled, at least in part, by the characteristics, policies, and practices of the institution. Higher education, as already indicated, takes place in large, middle-size, and small institutions. Most students attend large universities, many of which are urban. The combination of a large institution and an urban setting makes it difficult for students to get acquainted with their classmates and nearly impossible for professors to know their students. Large classes in an auditorium or amphitheater—often consisting of 300 to 500 students—are common, particularly for first- and second-year students. In those settings professors lecture once or twice a week, and teaching assistants, who are upper-division or graduate students, often preside over smaller group discussions that meet after the lectures. Multiple-choice tests, which are sometimes standardized, are frequently used to evaluate learning, and teaching assistants contribute a discussion grade to the composite end-of-term mark that students earn for the course. Many professors teach one such large class per term (which includes managing the work of the teaching assistants) and one smaller course at the upper-division or graduate level. In addition, they serve on committees, advise students, conduct research, and write. All these activities are figured into a professor's faculty load.

In the same universities that have such huge classes, there are also advanced undergraduate courses and graduate seminars that are much smaller in size. Sometimes they include only a handful of students. The professor in these settings has close contact with each student and probably knows many of them well. Because by this time the students have chosen a major and many of them are already specializing within it, the professor has no doubt had interactions with them in several prior courses and in other activities. Evaluation of learning is often informal and is related to actual performance, laboratory work, empirical or theoretical research, and papers prepared by the student. There is give-and-take, criticism, and feedback. The professor often serves in the role of mentor and may be the major adviser to one or two of the seminar members. The professor may teach only this one seminar, be engaged in research, work on a committee or two, advise doctoral candidates, and serve in an advisory capacity on a governor's council.

At smaller undergraduate residential colleges, a professor may teach two- or three-credit courses, maintain office hours to consult with advisees and students from his or her classes, and serve on department or college committees. Each course may be a combination of lecture and discussion. Student learning is evaluated in a variety of ways. Students prepare papers, take essay-type examinations, participate in class discussions, and have one or more individual conferences with the professor. To assess the students' abilities and knowledge, the professor reads and grades written assignments, interviews individuals, coaches them, and critiques their work.

Evening graduate courses are popular in many universities in a variety of academic areas. A professor in a large public or private university may teach two evening courses a week to a mix of students—some who are full-time students in residence at the school and others who work full time and, living at home and commuting, take one evening course. Even though the class may not be large, the professor lectures a good portion of the time because he or she wants to cover specific content. Evaluation of learning is by examination and term papers. Time and schedule often do not permit individual conferences. However, during office hours in the late afternoon, the professor is available for appointments with students who seek advice and counsel. Some of the professor's students may be his or her advisees in a master's program. In addition, the professor is involved in research and writing—often in connection with a funded project running over several years.

Professors in state colleges, often those at the assistant and associate rank, may teach twelve semester hours, consisting of four courses and often more than one section of the same course. This is considered a full undergraduate teaching load. They may lecture most of the time because it enables them to cover the syllabus and because preparation of lectures is so time consuming that planning greater diversity in method is impossible. Evaluation of learning is by frequent examination and assigned papers. Personal conferences occur when initiated by the student or the professor. Classes and office hours are scheduled during the daytime. In addition to teaching, these professors are assigned a number of advisees; the relationship with advisees often involves approving course loads at registration time. The college is committed primarily to teaching, but administrators notice those who have contributed to important journals when promotions are considered.

Preparation

Professors and administrators in colleges and universities typically have earned bachelor's, master's, and doctor's degrees. Some have skipped the middle degree and continued without interruption from the bachelor's to the doctor's degree. A doctor's degree is essential if one expects to proceed up the career ladder in four-year colleges and universities. In two-year colleges a master's degree is often adequate. (The two-year college is characterized by a different career system, which is described separately in this chapter.)

Selecting the institutions at which one prepares for a career in higher education can be very important. Where and under whom one earns degrees directly influence a career. Some undergraduate schools serve essentially as preparatory institutions for graduate schools. Anyone who aspires early in life to an academic career would be wise to select carefully a college for undergraduate study. If the information is obtainable, one should choose a college for its reputation in one's chosen field of study and for the reputations of professors in that field. Often, highly regarded college professors have connections with graduate schools and can have influence in recommending their students for admission and fellowships. In universities, professors encourage their most able students to undertake graduate study. In graduate school selecting a major adviser who is prominent in one's field is central to receiving good guidance and is often an important link to initial employment and advancement in the field after graduation.

In the course of graduate study there is time and opportunity to survey job possibilities. Making decisions about the type and the size of institution that fit one's career aspirations requires considerable thought and probably some compromise. Not infrequently, prospective professors seek to teach and do research in an institution exactly like the one at which they earned their doctorate. Some of the main questions a prospective professor should probe are: Is my major interest teaching? Am I more inclined toward research? Which institutions have the strongest faculties? ...a healthy respect for good teaching and scholarship? ...students who are challenging and able? ...provision for research and writing? ...adequate access to library and other resources? ...academic freedom and intellectual curiosity?

The job market, of course, determines how much choice the prospective college teacher or researcher has. Irrespective of the job market, however, the selection of an institution for employment is important to the candidate and to the institution. Place of employment is a major factor in a young professor's quality of life, and it often determines the extent of support and encouragement that will be forthcoming from the administration. Students of higher education use the term *fit* to describe the compatibility of a candidate and an institution. Fit has social, intellectual, and cultural dimensions. It includes issues relating to lifestyle, philosophical (and sometimes religious) persuasion, social class, devotion to intellectual pursuits, and cosmopolitanism. Fit also may have snobbish manifestations. Higher education is not immune to esoteric stodginess and stubborn tradition. A new faculty member, although freshly charged with ideas for reform and renewal, may make little difference if his or her ideas diverge too far from those of the entrenched professors. Neophytes hardly ever reform an establishment, and trying to do so is usually more punishing to them than to the veterans.

Career Patterns

On completion of the doctor's degree, a person's first college or university position is usually an assistant professorship, though it may be an instructorship. Assistant professors may be hired on a tenure track—that is, in line for promotion to permanent employment—or in a temporary position with no assurance of a job after the term of the appointment. The slower growth in enrollments of late has caused many administrators to be cautious about hiring professors on a tenure track, recognizing that tenured faculty may become excess baggage—teachers with no students. Prospective faculty should be aware that being hired on a temporary appointment often results in their jumping from job to job, and the more movement there is of this type, the more difficult it may become to find tenured employment anywhere.

The probationary period for an instructor or an assistant professor typically continues for a number of years. Often promotion to associate professor includes the granting of tenure, which is, essentially, permanent employment. The American Association of University Professors (AAUP) recommends that "beginning with appointment to the rank of full-time instructor or a higher rank, the probationary period should not exceed seven years." The Association recommends further that "notice should be given at least one year prior to the expiration of the probationary period if the teacher is not to be continued in service after the expiration of that period." If tenure is not granted, the individual has no future at the institution, and "the appointment for the following year becomes a terminal one."

The probationary period is a time of selection and self-selection. Specifically, in theory at least, it is a time when teaching, research, writing, and service are evaluated. But it is also a more amorphous process of testing fit—that is, assessing how well the professor and the institution jibe in aims, methods, and conventions. The assessment is of the professor's suitability, aptness, felicitousness, and adaptability to the goals, purposes, and style of the institution. Whether the professor has selected the right institution, and the institution the right professor, usually becomes self-evident.

The success or the failure of a professor at a particular institution may not be strictly a matter of competence. Success may occur because of congruity on the criteria just mentioned, or failure may result because of conflict on one of them. Young professors should recognize that they may be successful in one context and not in another.

The professor earns greater status as he or she moves up the academic ladder. Promotion usually also means opportunities to teach more specialized courses and upper-division or graduate students. More time is allowed for research and writing, particularly at the university level, and greater importance is placed on such activity.

The professor actually operates in two realms: that of the institution and that of his or her chosen discipline. The latter often commands the greater loyalty and holds the primary interest. As a result, it is not unusual for professors to build more networks with colleagues at other institutions who are in their field than with colleagues at their own institution who are not in their field.

With promotion, however, contacts with professors in other fields at the home institution increase. Greater participation in setting departmental, collegiate, and institutional policy is a responsibility of promotion in rank. Promotion to full professor, which comes for most after additional years of satisfactory service, increases responsibilities and privileges. The broader institutional concerns that professors develop in all-college committee work sometimes provide the motivation to move into higher education administration.

Professors who spend most or all of their time in research are a somewhat special breed. They often begin a commitment to research in the process of study for an advanced degree. They earn a research degree, the doctor of philosophy (Ph.D.), and become involved with a mentor, or major professor, in research activity. Research for the doctoral dissertation is often a segment of a larger study being directed by the major professor. Although many Ph.D. candidates take this route to meeting requirements, only a few continue with a major or full career commitment to research. Support for research professors in academe exists almost exclusively in the major universities and institutes, and most of that support comes from outside funding by government, business, and industry. The typical research professor's responsibility therefore consists, in part, of seeking contracts and grants for further study. Not infrequently a professor's research is shaped by the availability of funds for specified projects. In fact, there is considerable criticism in academic circles that too much influence on the direction and the nature of research comes from outside the university.

Promotions for teachers and researchers in higher education involve more procedural and bureaucratic steps today than in the past. One reason is affirmative action regulations. The legislation to provide equal opportunity in hiring and advancement, although admirable (most especially for women and minorities), also has brought rules and regulations that create excessive paperwork and red tape. Promotion from assistant to associate professor, at which point an institution grants tenure, perhaps involves the greatest number of hurdles. First, assistant professors must formally apply for promotion (a step not previously required). Then they must collect visible evidence of their accomplishments: publications, research reports, papers presented at professional meetings, college achievements, activities in professional associations and learned societies, and anything else that attests to fulfillment of institutional goals and objectives. Both the application and the evidence are packaged and submitted to the department head or the dean, and then review by peers and superiors takes place, culminating in recommendations to the top administrative officers.

The authors of the book *The Seasons of a Man's Life* characterize the academic life as a career with three stages. (Notice that they call it a "man's" life. Historically, most professors have been men, and that is still true, although the percentage is dropping; about one-third of full-time faculty are women.) The first stage is entry into the adult world, during which the academic finds a mentor, earns tenure, and settles into a career. The second stage, middle adulthood, begins at about age forty. In this phase the professor has more autonomy and a greater opportunity to explore. He or she becomes a mentor and takes time to broaden his or her range of interests. The third stage is late adulthood. It begins around age fifty-five and is characterized as a time of further broadening of interests, less competitiveness (because success has been achieved), and greater readiness to find new and perhaps nonacademic relationships. During this stage the professor is called on more to reflect on overall experience and offer wisdom than to provide specialized expertise. It is also a time when the professor explores career shifts, perhaps even leaving the college or university.

These stages should be considered illustrative, not absolute. To describe a pat scenario for the career of a person who starts out as an academic is misleading. There are many paths, including fairly common career changes. Some of the options for career changes that academics take are discussed later in this chapter.

One development that alters the conception of career phases just described is the extension of the compulsory retirement age. With longer life spans and continuing inflation in the economy, some professors are choosing to remain employed until age seventy and beyond. This might qualify as a fourth career stage, the senior academic.

The particulars of teaching or research careers in the standard liberal arts subjects and in the many professional and graduate schools are not explored here. That subject would call for a book in itself. Three main sources provide specific information on core undergraduate teaching fields, graduate study, and professional and specialized graduate schools. In the first two categories (undergraduate and graduate education) are the American Council of Learned Societies and the associations that represent the various disciplines, such as the American Anthropological Association and the American Institute of Biological Sciences. For professional and specialized graduate schools, the corresponding associations (for example, the American Bar Association, the American Medical Association, and the American Institute of Architects) and the respective accrediting agencies provide information on admission requirements, application procedures, academic expectations, internships or other requirements for practical experience, career opportunities and demand, accredited schools, cost of preparation, projected salary, and scholarships and fellowships.

Administration

Administration is a very different role in the college or university than it is in K–12 schools. The size, purpose, commitment, affiliation, reputation, and support/endowment of an institution are among the factors that influence what administrators the institution employs and what those administrators do.

Within the ranks of administration there are a variety of different positions, but five general groupings are recognized: executive, academic, administrative, external affairs, and student affairs. Table 6–2 lists about a hundred major positions typically found in each grouping in two- and four-year colleges and universities, public and private. No institution has all of the jobs listed in Table 6–2; some combined or alternative positions are included. For example, positions are listed for chief development officer, chief public relations officer, and chief development and public relations officer. An institution either has the first two or the third, not all three. Similarly, the table includes director of student health services, physician administrator,

Table 6–2   Types of Administrators in Two- and Four-Year Colleges and Universities, by Job Families

	Two-Year College	Four-Year College	University
Executive Office			
Chief executive officer, system			X
Chief executive officer, single institution	X	X	X
Assistant to chief executive officer, single institution	X	X	X
Academic Areas			
Chief academic officer (provost)			X
Chief health-professions officer	X	X	X
Director, library services	X	X	X
Acquisitions librarian	X	X	X
Chief technical-services librarian	X	X	X
Chief public-services librarian	X	X	X
Reference librarian	X	X	X
Catalog librarian	X	X	X
Director, institutional research	X	X	X
Director, educational media services center	X	X	X
Director, international education	X	X	X
Director, academic computing	X	X	X
Director, sponsored research and programs	X	X	X
Deans			
Architecture			X
Agriculture	X		X
Arts and sciences	X	X	X
Business	X	X	X
Communications	X	X	X
Continuing education	X	X	X
Dentistry			X
Education	X	X	X
Engineering	X	X	X
Extension	X		X
Fine arts	X	X	X
Graduate programs		X	X
Health-related professions	X	X	X
Humanities	X	X	X
Instruction	X		
Law	X	X	X
Library and information sciences	X	X	X
Medicine			X
Music		X	X
Nursing	X	X	X
Occupational and vocational education	X	X	X

**Table 6–2   Types of Administrators in Two- and Four-Year Colleges
and Universities, by Job Families—*continued***

	Two-Year College	Four-Year College	University
Pharmacy			X
Public health			X
Social sciences	X	X	X
Social work		X	X
Veterinary medicine			X
Administration			
Chief business or financial officer	X	X	X
Chief administrative officer	X	X	X
Director, environmental health and safety	X	X	X
Director, telecommunications and networking	X	X	X
Chief planning officer	X	X	X
Chief budget officer	X	X	X
General counsel	X	X	X
Staff attorney		X	X
Chief human resources officer	X	X	X
Manager, training and development	X	X	X
Manager, employee relations and benefits	X	X	X
Director, affirmative action and equal employment opportunity	X	X	X
Chief information systems officer	X	X	X
Database administrator	X	X	X
Systems analyst	X	X	X
Programmer analyst	X	X	X
Director, administrative computing	X	X	X
Chief physical-plant officer	X	X	X
Manager, landscape and grounds	X	X	X
Manager, custodial services	X	X	X
Manager, power plant	X	X	X
Comptroller	X	X	X
Manager, payroll	X	X	X
Director, accounting	X	X	X
Bursar	X	X	X
Director, purchasing	X	X	X
Director, bookstore	X	X	X
Director, internal audit	X	X	X
Director, auxiliary services	X	X	X
Manager, mail services	X	X	X
Director, campus security	X	X	X
Administrator, hospital medical center			X
Director, medical center public relations			X
Director, medical center personnel			X

Table 6–2   Types of Administrators in Two- and Four-Year Colleges and Universities, by Job Families—*continued*

	Two-Year College	Four-Year College	University
Student Services			
Student-affairs officer	X	X	X
Dean of students	X	X	X
Registrar	X	X	X
Director, admissions and student financial aid	X	X	X
Director, food services	X	X	X
Director, student housing	X	X	X
Director, student union and student activities	X	X	X
Director, foreign students	X	X	X
Director, career development and placement	X	X	X
Director, student counseling	X	X	X
Associate director, counseling	X	X	X
Director, student health services		X	X
Director, athletics	X	X	X
Director, men's athletics	X	X	X
Director, women's athletics	X	X	X
Director, sports information	X	X	X
Director, campus recreation	X	X	X
Director, minority affairs	X	X	X
External Affairs			
Chief development officer	X	X	X
Director, annual giving	X	X	X
Director, corporate and foundation relations	X	X	X
Director, planned giving	X	X	X
Chief public-relations officer	X	X	X
Director, governmental relations	X	X	X
Director, alumni affairs	X	X	X
Director, community services	X	X	X
Director, publications	X	X	X
Manager, printing services	X	X	X
Director, information office	X	X	X

Source: Adapted from "Fact File: Median Salaries of College Administrators by Type of Institution, 1996–97," *Chronicle of Higher Education*, February 21, 1997, p. A28.

director of student health services, and nurse administrator. Only one of these positions will be in evidence, probably as a function of size, perhaps also as a function of the number of students who reside on campus.

Many more positions exist that are subordinate to those listed in Table 6–2—for example, associate and assistant deans, associate directors, managers, and specialized librarians. Also, the list does not include the administrators of the individual units that make up a college or professional school, such as heads of departments or divisions.

The number of positions and the configuration of them vary primarily by size. The larger the institution is, the more positions it will have, including separate ones for such functions as development and public relations. Slight variation also exists by control of institution, most notably the presence of a position for director of church relations at private institutions.

Academic administration is basic and has the longest history. As a result, it is the most prestigious. Its practitioners emerge from the disciplines, from the ranks of professors. Department heads are usually elected or appointed from among the professors in the department; sometimes they are hired from outside.

Academic administrators, particularly department heads, often teach as well as administer. Deans and their associates and assistants may or may not teach. However, some institutions take great pride in keeping academic administrators involved in teaching. The practice helps them stay in touch with their field and with students. Also, it reduces the guilt many feel in leaving their field by enabling them to maintain a partial tie, and keeps the road back to teaching open. The latter is practical as well as idealistic because the work of administration is in most cases not akin to the academic discipline the professor labored long to master. Getting away from one's subject and losing touch with one's colleagues, even for a few years, is often irreparable. Then, too, there is among academics a measure of disdain for administrators, even though most administrators are former professors.

Executive administration is a modern phenomenon, a product of the enormous growth of the academic enterprise in the twentieth century. In earlier times, when all institutions of higher education had relatively small enrollments, the president of an institution was at least a former professor, if not an active one, and had academic responsibilities. That is still true today in small colleges. But in large colleges and universities, although most of the presidents were once academics, they are exclusively top-level managers with no academic responsibilities.

The job of executive or academic administrator does have some special requirements. Deans, provosts, and presidents, and chancellors (used here to refer to the chief executive officers of systems of higher education institutions) must rise above their discipline. They must be concerned with institutional goals and achievements (one reason former colleagues see them as lost to the discipline). Their breadth of responsibility and their place in the hierarchy determine the scope of perspective necessary. All must have a broad knowledge of higher education, including the capacity to view the relative importance of current events and trends, and a vision of direction for the future. They must have a notion of appropriate mission and be aware of how their institution ranks among and relates to comparable ones in the country. Skills in gaining support and understanding from outside groups are essential to finding resources for operating a dynamic institution. Such groups include state boards of education, state legislators, members of the college or university's board of trustees, philanthropic foundations, alumni, and the various communications media.

Academic administrators deal with the mission of their department, school, or university; curriculum content and courses; standards of student selection and retention; and the interpretation, application, and creation of policies relating to academic matters. They manage recruitment, hiring, evaluation, promotion, and dismissal of faculty. Schedules, space allocation, and budget are also in their province. They promote and facilitate the direction and support of research. Department heads represent their group at collegewide meetings and to their dean, and deans are the link to the university's top academic administrator.

The head of a unit may be a leader in name, but whether he or she can actually lead depends on whether the faculty goes along. Tenured professors have great freedom and strong, informed opinions in academic matters. When there is deep disagreement on an issue, the administrator may find it difficult to elicit any action, let alone movement, in a direction he or she would advocate.

Academic administrators do not all do the same things. For example, when an institution is large enough to have several administrators supporting deans and the president, there is inevitably a bureaucracy in which minions are delegated the details of the many tasks delineated above. In larger institutions these layers of administration create more specialties. People become experts in a phase of administration. When that happens, areas split off and become entities.

Administrative, external affairs, and student affairs positions are examples. They are more recent additions to higher education administration, functions that were separated out as institutions became larger and as the role of higher education became more complex.

Nonacademic administrators and executives in a sense relieve academic administrators of many details, most responsibilities for external and student affairs, and a large portion of the relationships with governing boards (in the case of state-supported institutions, with statewide boards, special commissions, legislators, and the executive branch). Where once an academic administrator managed all the tasks, in larger institutions the tasks have now been distributed across several domains. Academic responsibilities remain with the academic administrators, but many of the other chores are assumed by administrators or executives.

Perhaps the primary role and function of the chief executive officer is as policymaker. He or she must see the big picture—the nation and the world that the institution serves and in which it functions. Advice and opinion on policy come from faculty senates and deans and vice presidents, but the head person must make the decisions.

The chief executive officer also has taken on additional duties. For example, the national and international interests and responsibilities of the university typically flow from, or are nurtured by, the chief officer's desk. Legal matters; institutional funding; relationships with people in the state, region, and nation—all fall to the top officer. Again, subordinates are delegated much of the legwork. However, the president of a single institution or the chancellor of a system makes the final decisions and is the public spokesperson.

Although five categories of administration are identified in Table 6–2, the executive, administrative, and external affairs functions are so close in many institutions that they are organized together and managed by the executive officer.

A function that typically stands alone is the business operation, which handles tuition, endowments, taxes, grants, contracts, purchasing, payroll, and sundry other matters. Business personnel, often managed by a chief officer at the level of vice president, may not come from the ranks of academe. Their training is often in such areas as accounting, marketing, management, and finance.

Public relations is increasingly important to colleges and universities. The people who communicate to the public and the media on behalf of the institution are often trained in public affairs, journalism, or communications. In institutions with a radio or television station, the staff are media-trained people—that is, they are professionals in their field, not usually academics.

Student affairs administrators such as the dean of students, the dean of men, and the dean of women often do not come up through academic ranks. Rather, they are trained as specialists in guidance and student personnel work, dealing with such aspects of college and university life as housing, fraternities and sororities, and student activities (events and organizations). The domain of student affairs officers often overlaps with that of academic administrators—for example, in scholarships, loans, eligibility, suspensions, readmissions, and expulsions.

Preparation

There are no formal routes of preparation for administration in higher education. Some universities do have courses, internships, even programs, in the field, but any survey of college and university administrators soon demonstrates that few come to their jobs by formally preparing for administration.

Academic administrators come up through the ranks and learn most of their knowledge and skills on the job. Before their appointment, many have not had a course in the management or the administration of higher education. Some academic administrators, of course, enroll in management courses and other studies relevant to their work, and most attend conferences and workshops pertinent to their jobs.

The position of department head is usually filled by a professor elected to the post. In many cases, the position rotates among the full professors in a department. The next step, to assistant or associate dean, may come as a result of a dean's encouragement to a professor to apply, but selection is almost always from the pool of candidates who actually apply for an opening when it is advertised. Experience as a department head or other middle-level manager in a college or university is good background for an assistant or associate deanship. It is important in a résumé when applying for any collegewide administrative post.

Similarly, there is no course of study for a dean's position. A dean is selected from several applicants for a job and usually is a person with some demonstrated administrative experience.

Training for top positions in universities is almost nonexistent. Some individuals holding them are academics; others are businesspeople, professionals, military officers, or politicians. The common characteristic is administrative experience. But here, too, many have not studied or taken a degree in the administration of higher education. Business, student affairs, and external affairs officers may also not be academics and may come from a variety of backgrounds.

Career Patterns

A number of professors try administration, and many stay with it, although some return to teaching and research. When motivated, they may by chance or through initiative move up some or all of the steps in the administrative ladder—department head, assistant or associate dean, dean, provost, vice president, president, and chancellor. The promotion desired is often not available at the institution of current employment. In such instances, promotion requires finding the appropriate position at another institution. However, experience in more than one college or university broadens perspective and enlarges the contacts and the reputation of an administrator.

Tracking the careers of administrators in higher education reveals some patterns. For example, they seem to remain with the same type of institution. Administrators in private colleges and universities remain in their type of institution, and administrators in public institutions stay with their kind.

Finding Employment

Teaching and administrative positions are usually advertised, and consideration is given to all candidates who apply. Other things being equal, however, two factors prove to be influential in a candidate's gaining an edge:

1. A track record and a reputation that are personally known by the people at the employing institution who are screening applicants.
2. Ties to those same key people through work in professional associations.

Obviously, then, the knowledge that professors and administrators develop of one another over time in work and extra-institutional relationships often carries weight in who gets a job. As a consequence, specific advice on how to find employment is difficult to provide.

When a candidate maintains connections with his or her graduate school, he or she can be alerted to openings by the placement office. Advertisements of openings appear in the *Chronicle of Higher Education*, the *New York Times*, and professional journals. Personal networks are always at work in bringing news of openings. There is no prescription for getting from knowing of an available position to being one of the few under consideration. But a candidate who has had an opportunity to demonstrate abilities to the people who will be asked to make recommendations will certainly have a distinct advantage over the other applicants.

Positions as deans, provosts, presidents, and chancellors are widely advertised in newspapers and journals. The *Chronicle of Higher Education* and the *New York Times* regularly carry advertisements of open positions. Professional searchers work on contract with boards of regents and other governing bodies to find and screen candidates. Candidates may come from any place in the country. Preliminary screening may be done on the basis of credentials, résumés, telephone inquiries, and letters outlining experience, training, and interest. A committee typically conducts the search and identifies three to five candidates who best meet the standards (usually advertised) it has set. Finalists are invited to the campus for interviews, and preferences are recommended to the appropriate officer or, in the case of president or chancellor, to the appropriate board. In most cases, decisions to hire at the dean's level and above must be approved by the governing board.

The standard criteria of fit apply in this context. This is one of the reasons administrators, at least, tend to stay in the same type of institution. Selection committees pay attention to experience. They prefer the person with experience, and success, in their type of institution. For example, the dean of a state college is not apt to be the favored candidate for the presidency of a church-related liberal arts college.

Administrative jobs, particularly top positions, have been rather short stints in recent years. Hence, in initial contract negotiations, successful candidates have sought provisions to protect themselves in the event of abrupt, premature, or unexpected termination. For example, a candidate for a deanship may seek a concurrent appointment as a full professor with tenure; then if he or she resigns or is deposed, there is job security. Another provision for protection may be severance pay. Some provisions are sufficiently desirable to be labeled "golden parachutes."

Related Careers

Despite the pronouncement of Seymour Sarason that academics is a "one life—one career" profession, there are opportunities for employment outside academe that evolve from being a professor or an administrator in higher education. They do depend on one's specialty, however. For example, there is use for a professor of economics in government or business, whereas a professor of classics is seldom called on to work in other than an academic setting.

Many professors and administrators are appointed to state and federal government positions, which they occupy for part or all of a particular administration or for some other period. Employment outside the university may offer respite from academe and an opportunity to apply knowledge in the "real world." Some who take such appointments eventually return to an academic post, but others find a new career. For example, Martin Feldstein served as chairman of President Ronald Reagan's Council of Economic Advisors for two years and then returned to Harvard. Henry Kissinger and Daniel Moynihan are former professors who have spent considerable time in government.

Usually university policy limits the time a professor can take leave for outside service. When that period is up, the choice is to return or resign.

There are (unwritten) acceptable and unacceptable positions outside academe. A professor who wants to return to the campus should know this. Success in a career in higher education may be tied to selecting an acceptable or approved outside appointment, not accepting too many stints away from the campus, and not staying away too long. Professional jealousy on the part of those who remain on campus is not unheard of, particularly when the sojourn in an off-campus appointment offers special privileges, rich experience, increased financial reward, and glamour. Campus administrators may be uncomfortable when one of their professors is highly rewarded, is in great demand, and enjoys celebrity status. On the other hand, if off-campus experience supports and enhances academic pursuits, theory development, and research in the individual's field, or permits the testing of experimental models, the institution is bound to reap benefits far beyond the enhancement of the individual's reputation or bank account.

Extra and Outside Employment

Employment outside the institution is usually part time and is in addition to work for the institution and a regular teaching load. It takes place during full-time employment, not during a leave of absence. Many professors seek opportunities in their field to teach an extra course, to be a guest professor on a neighboring campus, or to consult outside the university in their specialty. In some institutions extra employment becomes so time consuming that restrictions are imposed on the amount of time spent in such activities.

In such fields as engineering, economics, political science, business administration, geology, education, computer science, and health services, professors can find operational systems that apply their discipline. They can try new ideas and test experimental constructs, assist people in improving performance, and engage their students in the real world of practice.

Extra teaching and guest teaching are popular summer and off-campus activities. Both provide work in new and different settings, and they often give a professor a chance to interact with different kinds of students. Sometimes the setting is on-site in a business, an industry, or a school, and there are opportunities to test theory and hypotheses.

Despite such positive features, some extra and outside assignments are sought mainly to earn more money. In a sense, all such employment for academics is in that category; they are not paid as well as people with equal education and experience in the business and industrial world, and money is an incentive.

Higher education personnel should be aware of the opportunities for extra and outside employment. However, they also should be wary of being exploited or deluded into expending energy and talent that will pay off in the short term but leave them little time for the study and research that are constant requirements to remain current in their field.

Salary and Fringe Benefits

Salary does not seem to be the major incentive among higher education faculty that it is in many other walks of life. Circumstances that are as important as salary in attracting and holding professors are administrative support, light teaching loads, research budgets and assistants, library and laboratory facilities, and stimulating colleagues. Tuckman says, "In college teaching, salary is not the measure of power, prestige, and success; other factors often substitute for salary in a person's decision to move or remain at an institution."

Salary, on the other hand, is not unimportant. And salaries vary, by rank, by control and type of institution, and by discipline. Table 6–3 presents supporting data on some of these variables for professors. Table 6–4 offers salary figures for selected administrative positions.

Incentives and rewards for college and university faculty are more than monetary. Many are not counted and reported in aggregate. Privileges and resources such as library holdings, laboratory facilities, computer capacity, research and teaching assistants, and secretarial help are not surveyed and reported as benefits. Perhaps they are central rather than fringe. Nevertheless, they should be assessed in seeking employment because their availability or absence fosters or detracts from effective functioning.

AAUP and the National Center for Education Statistics collect information and report on the welfare of professors. Their data include salary, fringe benefits, and tenure. Tenure is a benefit, although often not reported as such. Apparently it is an elusive benefit for some. About two-thirds of university faculty have tenure: 70 percent of men and 46 percent of women. Obviously, women need to be more inquiring about tenure practices than men, preferably before employment.

Monetary rewards are reported by the AAUP in two categories, salary and compensation. Compensation is higher than salary because it includes fringe benefits. Fringe benefits, on the average, are 25 percent of salary and are provided by the institution or the state in addition to salary. They include several kinds of insurance, contributions to retirement plans, partial payment

Table 6–3 Average Salaries of Four-Year College and University Professors by Type of Institution, Control of Institution, and Rank, 1995–96

	Assistant Professor	Associate Professor	Professor
Doctoral-Level Institutions			
Public	$42,460	$50,540	$69,750
Private Independent	49,170	58,430	88,050
Private Church-Related	44,770	54,380	75,800
Comprehensive Institutions			
Public	39,000	46,860	58,520
Private Independent	40,240	49,340	68,430
Private Church-Related	39,160	47,860	60,940
General Baccalaureate Institutions			
Public	36,400	43,390	52,480
Private Independent	37,440	45,500	59,830
Private Church-Related	33,670	39,720	48,180

Source: From *Educational Rankings Annual: 3,000 Rankings and Lists on Education Compiled from Educational and General Interest Published Sources*, edited by L. C. Hattendorf, New York: Gale, 1997, pp. 327–29.

of Social Security, and more. All these fringe benefits are specified at the time of employment. Tenured and tenure-track employees may be eligible for fringe benefits not offered to non-tenure-track employees.

In most instances both the institution and the employee make contributions to a retirement plan; to medical, dental, life, disability, and unemployment insurance; and to Social Security. Worker's compensation is another fringe benefit, the cost of which may be paid fully by the institution or shared by the institution and the employee. Many private institutions pay the college tuition of faculty members' children at either the home institution or selected other colleges and universities.

Other benefits "in kind" are provided by some institutions, including moving expenses, housing, and expenses to professional meetings and conferences. Benefits in kind may not be offered to all employees. They may accrue only to sought-after faculty, faculty in higher ranks, or those who negotiate such benefits.

Frequently there are choices among retirement plans. State college and university professors are often eligible for either a state retirement system or the Teachers Insurance and Annuity Association–College Retirement Equities Fund (TIAA–CREF). Private college and university professors may have a choice between their institution's retirement plan or TIAA–CREF. When there is a choice, the alternatives should be examined carefully. One plan may vest sooner or provide better payoff than the other. *Vest* means that both the employer's and the employee's contributions to a retirement plan lock in after a specified number of years; the total contribution becomes the

Table 6–4   Median Salaries of Selected University and Four-Year College Administrators, 1996–97

	University	Four-Year College
Chief executive officer	$174,638	$118,750
Chief academic officer	141,650	80,118
Director, library services	94,375	47,493
Director, academic computing	76,241	48,671
Dean, arts and sciences	115,012	60,376
Dean, business	131,373	57,000
Dean, education	107,067	53,084
Dean, engineering	134,900	67,695
Dean, fine arts	104,720	48,732
Dean, graduate programs	102,532	57,363
Dean, law	155,500	146,250
Dean, music	98,280	46,631
Chief business officer	122,500	78,077
Chief financial officer	103,908	63,005
Chief personnel/human resources officer	80,491	46,000
Director, administrative computing	78,147	45,000
Chief development officer	119,600	75,000
Director, corporate and foundation relations	60,860	44,350
Chief public-relations officer	81,491	45,117
Director, governmental relations	87,500	45,502
Chief student-affairs officer	106,661	63,225
Chief admissions officer	70,564	50,970
Registrar	68,468	41,000
Director, food services	65,000	48,421
Director, student housing	61,573	32,240
Director, student activities	44,761	29,574
Director, student health services, physician	98,590	84,463
Director, athletics	101,673	50,000

Source: Adapted from "Fact File: Median Salaries of College Administrators by Type of Institution, 1996–97," *Chronicle of Higher Education*, February 21, 1997, p. A28. © 1997 by the College and University Personnel Association.

property of the professor, either at retirement or upon transferring to another institution.

TIAA–CREF is transferable from one institution to another, provided both institutions participate in it. More than 1.7 million people in 5,400 education and research institutions belong to TIAA–CREF. Whether transferability is important to a professor depends in part on whether he or she expects to move to another institution at some point during his or her career. New assistant professors beginning a career may not be able to predict mobility.

State-institution retirement plans cannot be transferred across state lines, but it is often possible to buy in to the system of a new state. Usually the number of years one can purchase is limited.

The contributions of employer and employee in a state or institutional retirement plan are invested by the managers of the plan. The participants in the plan have no options as to how or where the money is invested, except perhaps through a retirement board on which a few professors may serve. Subject to the policy of the employing institution, TIAA–CREF allows each participant to allocate percentages of their retirement fund among a wide variety of investment vehicles, such as fixed-dollar obligations, common stocks and other equities, bonds, real estate, and money markets.

TWO-YEAR COLLEGES

Two-year institutions (community, technical, and junior colleges) are a giant operation, serving 5.6 million students. Less visible in American education than K–12 schools and four-year colleges and universities, they serve a multitude of functions not touched by either of these other types of institutions. The country's 1,500 or so two-year colleges (about 70 percent of them public, 30 percent private) serve full- and part-time students in the study of such areas as agriculture, architecture, business, communications, computer science, construction trades, engineering, health science, home economics, law, library science, protective services, precision production, and transportation, as well as arts and sciences. The two-year college offers vocational and preparatory programs. The latter are for study in the arts and sciences, which students usually pursue for transfer to four-year colleges and universities. (Students from vocational programs can and do transfer, though.) Over half of the 482,000 associate degrees conferred in 1991 were in occupational fields (business, engineering technologies, health sciences, protective services, and visual and performing arts). Thirty percent were in liberal/general studies and humanities. Many students attend only long enough to learn the skills necessary to qualify for a job. For others the two-year college is a second-chance institution, a place where they can try to qualify for admission to a four-year college after completing either one year of successful study or a two-year program.

One-half of two-year college students are twenty-five years of age or older, and of them, more than 63 percent are part-time students. Almost all are commuters; few two-year colleges have student housing.

A few of the private two-year colleges are exceptions to the above. These colleges are essentially finishing schools, usually for young women. The curriculum is a mix of liberal arts and business courses.

Public two-year colleges have been among the fastest-growing institutions in American education. From 1972 to 1995, their number increased by more than 60 percent, and the number of associate degrees they conferred nearly doubled (from 292,000 to 536,000). Enrollment grew from 2.8 million to 5.6 million students between 1972 and 1993. Growth continues as the 1990s progress, but at a slower rate. Hence two-year colleges are in constant need of additional faculty.

Two-year colleges are reviewed by regional accrediting agencies to ascertain general quality and by national specialty agencies in such fields as nursing, electronics, and engineering technology. Accreditation is one hallmark of quality that prospective faculty should check.

Anyone considering a career in two-year college teaching or administration should recognize the conflict that exists in two-year college circles about the purpose and the function of the institution. The differences have been alluded to above. The main bone of contention is whether two-year colleges should lean toward the model of public schools or that of senior colleges in their expectations for the academic preparation of staff, the role of faculty, tenure and rank, salary, and other matters. Obviously, the four-year college and university model has more status. Perhaps the public school model has more security and equality. Neither actually fits the two-year college, as long as it serves a diverse adult population and attends to so great a variety of educational needs.

Teaching

The primary activity of two-year college faculty is teaching. Research and writing are not often expected. There is no pressure to "publish or perish."

The mode of operation is much like that of high schools. Evaluation of full-time faculty takes place during a two- or three-year probationary period, after which tenure is granted to those who have demonstrated adequacy. The procedures and standards resemble those used in public schools. Some institutions have salary schedules that establish steps in each salary category, so that all full-time faculty with equal experience and comparable preparation earn the same salary. Categories are typically determined by levels of preparation, such as bachelor's degree, master's degree, master's degree plus thirty semester hours, and doctorate. Some two-year colleges have academic rank (that is, instructor, assistant professor, associate professor, and full professor); others do not.

Nationally, less than half of two-year college professional staff are full-time, and about a half of them have tenure. This means that less than a quarter of faculty are tenured because part-time faculty are not eligible for tenure. And because a large portion of faculty are part time, they do not become an integral part of the faculty, nor do they enjoy the fringe benefits and other advantages of full-time teachers.

Two-year colleges draw faculty from a number of sources, but primarily from high schools and vocational-technical schools. Preparation for teaching in two-year colleges is not a set pattern of courses and degrees. Core-subject teachers in arts and sciences often come from high school teaching jobs. Their initial preparation has been for high school teaching. In many cases they have graduate work in their major field. Some teachers come directly from university doctoral programs (with no preparation for teaching and no teaching experience), and their preparation has been more like that of the four-year college teacher.

Many of the occupational programs require teachers with craft, trade, and technical skills and experience. Such teachers are often drawn from the practitioners of the occupations they teach. Although the bachelor's degree is usually considered a minimum requirement and the master's is often necessary for regular or permanent employment, some of the vocational-technical staff do not have these academic credentials.

A few states have mandated minimum standards for preparation and licensure, insisting that all two-year college faculty, irrespective of teaching area, have an academic degree. Nonetheless, in those states, a good number of vocational-technical people still teach with only their expertise as a credential.

Although two-year colleges are more like high schools than colleges in their criteria for faculty, their operational procedures, and their personnel practices, they are unique in the variety of adult students they serve and in institutional function. Two-year college teachers need more breadth in their subject field than high school teachers but not as much specialization as four-year college and university professors. Preparation in the art and science of teaching is highly desired and in some places required (which is not the case for four-year college and university teachers). Since 1950, a number of four-year colleges and universities have offered preparation programs for community and junior college teachers. Internships, not unlike student teaching, are required in some of them.

Administration

It is probably safe to say that administration in a two-year college is a cross between school and college administration. Because many two-year colleges have a number of the characteristics of the schools above and below them in the education hierarchy, they inevitably reflect aspects of both types of institutions.

Two-year college administrators faces more variety in the people and the circumstances with which they must deal. Faculty teach a wide selection of courses in general education, vocational and technical education, and leisure-interest subjects. There are many part-time teachers in order to provide the necessary breadth of curriculum in business, industrial and technical areas, and crafts. A goal of one type of two-year institution, the community college, is to provide courses that people in the service area want. That is not always easy to accomplish. Departments and other college units cannot function like a cohesive faculty with so many adjunct faculty. Maintaining continuity in a curriculum sequence, for example, is often much more difficult than when all faculty are full time and when programs for students are set. There are a variety of pay scales, and faculty who are part time are usually not eligible for fringe benefits. Both those factors make payroll and budgeting more complicated. Because most students are commuters, parking is often a problem.

The staff support that a two-year college administrator receives depends on the size and the budget of the college. Many community colleges operate with just a few administrators, whereas some of the larger institutions have an array of administrators similar to four-year colleges. The tasks to be accomplished are not unlike those in any educational institution: hiring and maintaining a faculty, facilitating the development of curriculum and scheduling, overseeing plant and equipment needs, supporting a guidance and counseling service, managing support staff, planning and monitoring budget, maintaining a library/media center, operating a food service, and communicating with constituents, the community, and the press.

How all these jobs are executed by the top administrator and available staff differs from college to college. Usually there are departments and divisions, each headed by an administrator of some type.

Community, technical, and junior college administrators come largely from the public schools and two-year colleges. Many have been teachers in two-year colleges, and that is important because they understand the philosophy and purpose of the two-year institution. Some have enrolled in graduate programs in two-year college leadership. Two-year college presidents, in particular, are often specifically prepared as administrators for two-year colleges. A number of major universities offer such programs, which culminate in a doctor's degree.

Career Patterns

Career patterns for people who stay in two-year colleges are much like those of high school personnel. For example, in institutions without academic rank, teachers secure tenure in the first few years on the basis of their effectiveness as teachers. Where tenure exists, it does not depend on research and writing and does not require the doctorate.

The presence or the absence of academic rank in an institution is a factor that influences career pattern. Where there is academic rank, teachers go through evaluations for promotions in the way that four-year college people do, but with different criteria.

Whether or not they have academic rank, two-year colleges are apt to have a salary schedule, as public schools do, and to employ collective bargaining every few years to improve salary and working conditions.

The two-year college president serves at the pleasure of the board, usually on a contract, but without tenure—much like a superintendent of schools. Two-year college presidents appear, however, to have longer terms than superintendents.

Finding Employment

The advice offered in Chapter 2 on finding employment as a teacher and in Chapter 3 on finding employment as an administrator applies to two-year college job hunting. The best leads will be found in university placement offices. Positions also are advertised in journals and education newspapers.

Teachers, in particular, can inquire independently at college personnel offices and arrange to have their name placed on a list of people interested in employment. Some teachers begin as part-time instructors and are standing by when openings for full-time employment occur.

Two-year colleges have grown so much in the last twenty-five years that the demand for teachers has been constant. In fact, in the last decade, a number of candidates with earned doctorates who hoped to find positions at four-year colleges have taken jobs in two-year colleges, substantially increasing the percentage of doctorates on two-year college faculties.

Teachers and administrators in two-year colleges do not operate in a national market as senior college professors and administrators do. Hence, the market for employment is more restricted to movement within a state or region.

Salary and Fringe Benefits

Table 6–5 presents data on average salaries for two-year college faculty by control of institution, rank, and sex. Table 6–6 offers figures for selected administrative positions.

Fringe benefits in the two-year college are like those in K–12 schools (see Chapter 2). The retirement system is a mix. Many colleges are part of state retirement systems. Others participate in TIAA–CREF.

Six

Table 6–5 Average Salaries of Two-Year College Professors on Nine-Month Contracts, by Control of Institution, Rank (Where Applicable), and Sex, 1993–94

	Professor	Associate Professor	Assistant Professor	Instructor	Lecturer	No Rank	Men	Women
All institutions	$49,173	$41,534	$35,117	$30,279	$34,542	$41,040	$42,634	$38,314
Public	49,435	41,922	35,448	30,531	34,943	41,372	42,938	38,707
Private	35,540	30,200	27,901	23,813	19,933	27,978	30,783	26,142

Source: *Digest of Education Statistics 1995*, by T. D. Snyder, Washington, DC: National Center for Education Statistics, 1995, p.241.

Table 6–6 Median Salaries of Selected Two-Year College Administrators, 1996–97

Chief executive officer	$99,000
Chief academic officer	73,000
Director, library services	49,355
Director, academic computing	44,700
Dean, arts and sciences	62,041
Dean, business	58,600
Dean, continuing education	61,458
Dean, education	59,686
Dean, engineering	62,256
Dean, fine arts	54,099
Dean, occupational or vocational education	60,000
Chief business officer	69,785
Chief financial officer	58,488
Chief personnel/human resources officer	51,524
Director, administrative computing	48,539
Chief development officer	56,238
Director, corporate and foundation relations	43,435
Chief public-relations officer	45,832
Director, governmental relations	65,669
Director, community services	47,025
Chief student-affairs officer	64,620
Chief admissions officer	48,357
Registrar	43,692
Director, food services	36,751
Director, student housing	34,343
Director, student activities	40,632
Director, student health services, nurse	35,677
Director, athletics	48,000

Source: Adapted from "Fact File: Median Salaries of College Administrators by Type of Institution, 1996–97," *Chronicle of Higher Education*, February 21, 1997, p. A28. © 1997 by the College and University Personnel Association.

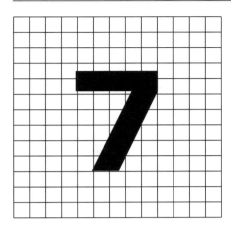

ADULT AND CONTINUING EDUCATION

In its broadest conception, adult and continuing education (hereafter referred to simply as continuing education) encompasses any program of study offered to mature people who have completed their formal education and wish to pursue further learning. In this chapter, however, the definition is limited to work-related or leisure-oriented programs that are designed to benefit individual adults, by promoting their career and profession or by enhancing their quality of life. It includes *inservice education*, a term commonly used in education to refer to individual professional development of K–12 and higher education personnel. Further, it covers *professional development* as a distinct category for individuals seeking further specialized training in law, the health professions, management, public administration, municipal and state government, and veterinary medicine. It also encompasses *staff development* for K–12 and higher education personnel because activities under this rubric, though designed to improve faculties and institutions, are client-oriented and not profit-oriented.

A broader definition of continuing education would include training that is intended first or primarily to benefit an organization for its own sake or profit—for example, training that prepares an employee to perform his or her job more efficiently in order to increase the company's profit margin, or training that teaches an employee new skills that will be applied in the workplace to improve service or productivity. That type of education is taken up in Chapter 8, under the subject of education careers in business and industry.

Over the years continuing education has had several different labels, and new ones are still being created for it. This is understandable because of the field's maverick nature. A concept of education that, according to *Adults as Learners*, "involves all people, learning all manner of subjects and skills, through all kinds of methods, from multiple providers" is bound to be in search of a name. Earlier in its history it was called nontraditional study (which it was and is) and then adult and continuing education (which is more descriptive). Recently the terms *lifelong learning* and *lifelong education and learning* have been used.

With these successive name changes, the concept has grown. Initially, the notion was to find ways of discovering what the adult learner wanted and then to provide it. As time passed and thoughtful people looked more closely at that concept, it became obvious that responding only to immediate need was haphazard and fragmentary. Gradually a more holistic concept evolved. Now, among leaders in continuing education at least, the push is for a learning society in which "men and women are the agents of their own education," in the context of a restructured traditional system and well-developed potential outside the existing system.

Despite the progress in thinking about continuing education and notwithstanding the many attempts to broaden its gestalt, continuing education can be found in the country today operating on the basis of any of the above notions. It encompasses a variety of activities. For example, some people seek basic literacy—the ability to read and write. School dropouts, realizing that a high school diploma is essential to securing a job, study to complete the General Educational Development (GED) test. Immigrants from non-English-speaking countries study English as a second language (ESL). Secretaries learn word processing on a computer to gain a promotion. Thirty-five-year-olds who have not finished—or even started—college enroll in programs that grant credit for life and work experience, and advisers help them design individualized programs of study for a bachelor's degree. People who have helplessly witnessed a relative, friend, or stranger have a heart attack take training in cardiopulmonary resuscitation (CPR).

Elder hostel programs for senior citizens might also be included. These are programs, usually a week or two long, often at a college or a university, designed for learning of all types. Participants are typically in residence during the program—in a continuing education center, at a conference center, or some other site with appropriate accomodations. The purpose of the program is to provide stimulation, challenge, and enjoyment for people in the later years of life.

At the other end of the continuum, professionals find inservice education courses to update themselves on developments in their field. For example, a physician takes a short course to learn about new medications for hypertension; a dentist enrolls in a seminar on composite bonding (a process for joining a filling to a tooth); an interior designer participates in a weeklong institute on concepts in lighting; a teacher attends a workshop on portfolio assessment.

Leisure-oriented continuing education features one-shot sessions and long-term programs on a multitude of subjects: omelet making, conversational Spanish, financial planning, computer programming, Chinese cooking, time management, parenting, picture framing, woodworking, and oil painting—to name just a few.

Somewhere between work- and leisure-related education are practical courses in coping with new tax laws, sessions on weight watching, classes in aerobics, training on new computer programs for personal accounting, and seminars on career planning.

Why is continuing education important and necessary? In a rapidly changing society, learning must be a continuous process. The education acquired in schools and colleges during childhood and youth will never again be adequate for a lifetime (if it ever was). K. P. Ross, the author of *Adults as Learners*, observes, "Margaret Mead once remarked that the world in which we are born is not the world in which we will live, nor is that the world in which we will die." People constantly need to make useful additions to knowledge, to renew perspective, to revitalize thinking. They need additional education to continue personal growth and to keep abreast of new developments and discoveries.

Radical changes have occurred since World War II. Americans have learned to use and appreciate a variety of products and devices that they never had before, including frozen foods, television, jet airplanes, air conditioning, home computers, and videotaped movies. Modems, satellites, robots, and electronic typesetting have revolutionized industry, communications, and life in general. To accommodate to, and capitalize on, these and other technological developments, people have had to acquire new knowledge, learn new skills, and adopt new attitudes. The impact of the changes has been seen in job losses, entirely new kinds of jobs and careers, changes in lifestyles, and moral and ethical conflicts. All of these developments have ignited a rethinking of general education.

The accommodations to change are far from complete. The traditional institutions of education have been slow to respond to people's needs. Often the learning involved to contend with a new development is not considered sufficiently academic to justify a place in the formal curriculum of schools and colleges. Not infrequently the people who want to enroll for study do not have the prerequisites for admission to classes in a conventional educational institution. Also, many educators have not discovered how to work with the more mature learner. The modes of instructing children, youth, and young adults in schools and colleges are not as effective with their elders. How to alter teaching for mature people is only beginning to be explored in traditional education, and by just a few institutions. Continuing education was created to fill some of the many gaps and inadequacies in the nation's formal institutions of education.

TYPES OF PROGRAMS

Continuing education takes place in all kinds of settings, with and through a variety of media. One prominent setting is the school or college campus, where continuing education is usually offered at hours when people who work have free time to attend—that is, evenings and weekends. It also is offered off campus, either with professors traveling to selected sites where instruction is given or with students studying independently at home. Community and junior colleges, in particular, provide many continuing education courses and workshops. Community schools and individual school districts are another part of the continuing education enterprise.

Independent Learning   Four independent-learning options for continuing education under school and college auspices deserve more description because they are not well known and because they appear to be increasing in importance and number. Correspondence courses, the open university, independent study, and distance learning are quite similar, yet different. A number of colleges, universities, and other education agencies offer some or all of these types of continuing education in almost any subject imaginable. Students may enroll for one or several courses over time and then terminate their involvement, or they may enroll to earn a degree, which requires a planned program of courses. The possibilities in program type and content vary with the institution.

In correspondence courses the process takes place entirely by mail. Teachers and students never meet. Students receive materials, assignments, and requirements (which are typically standardized for all students taking the same offering) from an institution and work at their own pace. They periodically send in completed written work, which is critiqued and evaluated by staff at the institution. A final examination may be required.

The open university works very much like the correspondence course in most ways. However, there is usually a closer relationship between the instructor and the student. Indeed, sometimes they may even meet. Also, assignments, course content, and requirements are not quite so standardized.

Independent study is actually either of the above two types of continuing education. However, it can be more. Students in regular graduate study may enroll for independent study with the approval of an adviser. Much doctoral study is done on an independent basis and is so tallied in registration and credits. Another type of independent study, offered by only a few colleges, is particularly intended for mature adults who seek a college degree while limiting their attendance at a campus site as much as possible. In such programs (often taken by people who have had some college in earlier years, for which they are given credit), students submit an application in which they make explicit their purpose for study. Admission is selective. Student and advisor plan a program. The student either visits with one or more professors periodically or communicates in writing or by other means about areas of study. Increasingly students are communicating with professors via E-mail. Study materials and bibliographies for courses are provided by the college. Evaluation of work is by examination, written papers, personal interview, and special projects.

Distance learning is much the same as independent study. In addition, it is supported by radio or television instruction. It is designed particularly for people in remote places and for those who must study at home. Study is guided and enhanced by print materials, audiocassettes, radio broadcasts, videocassettes, and television transmissions, which run the gamut from lectures to demonstrations, dramas, photo essays, documentaries, case studies, panel discussions, and so forth. The institution sponsoring the distance learning provides and recommends print and other materials for study and is responsible for evaluating student performance.

Professional Development Programs

Local school districts are major sponsors of the development of their staff. Some of this kind of continuing education takes place on school time, with students being given a half or a full day off. In such sessions, staff are introduced to new curricula; oriented to new federal, state, and local policies affecting instruction; and familiarized with technological developments.

Intermediate and cooperative school districts are providers of inservice and continuing education for school personnel and sometimes for parents and other citizens. These organizations are groups of public school districts banded together to provide services that single districts cannot afford.

Teacher centers and professional development centers, most commonly operating under school district auspices, are fairly recent innovations in this country (imported from England) for the continuing education of teachers and other professional school personnel. A hallmark of teacher centers is responding to the needs and requests of teachers. They serve teachers with quick help in one-shot sessions, but they also provide workshops and other activities that involve long-term, in-depth study. The site of activity is usually the professional development center, which keeps its doors open late afternoons, evenings, and Saturdays. More recently professional development center staff work on-site at the building level to facilitate school improvement. Teacher centers in many places have enlarged their role to include all school personnel. They have become professional development centers, the name change signaling accommodation of a broader school audience.

Regional Educational Laboratories, created and funded by the federal government, are another provider of continuing education, largely for elementary and secondary school teachers. Ten of them are spread across the country. They are charged with the improvement of education through special projects that articulate research findings addressing perennial and current problems in education. Typically, laboratory personnel develop materials, models, protocols, and methods that provide strategies and content to remedy a particular problem. They also provide research reports focused on best practices in schools. To foster the practical application of experience and research, they conduct related workshops and training sessions.

Professional associations and societies, including teacher unions, conduct three basic types of continuing education: (1) programs that provide instruction to further the organizational commitment of the group, (2) programs designed for the professional development of individuals belonging to the group, and (3) pilot projects with schools and colleges preparing education personnel, to promote innovation in practice. In the first category, there is direct or indirect orientation, indoctrination, and sometimes training. For example, a union may provide programs on collective bargaining and political action; a science teachers association may hold workshops on promoting the importance of science in school programs; and a language teachers' association may conduct seminars on advancing the cause of educating Americans in a second language. In the second category, associations and societies conduct conferences, workshops, and other inservice education to acquaint teachers and administrators with new content and procedures in their respective fields. In the third category, the approach has been to select a number of sites where schools or colleges (or both) engage in grassroots reform and experimentation, identifying problems and experimenting with possible solutions.

Proprietary schools most often focus on business, accounting, and secretarial training. Most of them are postsecondary institutions but are open to people of any age who seek new skills and knowledge in business, banking, and office procedures.

DANTES

The U.S. Department of Defense sponsors the Defense Activity for Non-Traditional Education Support (DANTES), a voluntary education program for active-duty military and reserve personnel. Through contracts and agreements with a variety of institutions and agencies, DANTES offers diverse programs of adult education and distance education. The military services provide tuition assistance to pay a percentage of the charges of an educational institution for the member to enroll in courses of study during off-duty time. The amount of money for support is uniform across the military services. Members of any branch of the Armed Forces are eligible.

The programs are comparable to those available to citizens outside the military and are available regardless of the service person's duty location. They are provided by accredited postsecondary vocational and technical schools, colleges, and universities.

Service members participating are provided guidance and counseling services by qualified personnel so that they can make the most efficient use of government resources and the most effective use of their own time, money, and effort.

Participants have opportunities to acquire basic educational and academic skills that are essential to successful job performance and new learning. Outside the United States, adult education programs are available to both service members and their adult family members.

Among the services and programs are (1) Examinations, (2) Professional Certification, (3) Distance Learning, (4) Military Evaluations, (5) Servicemembers Opportunity Colleges, and (6) Troops to Teachers. All take place outside the formal classroom.

The Examinations program enables service personnel, no matter where they are located—aboard ship, at remote stations, or stateside—to test for a high-school-equivalency (GED) credential or for college credit that can apply toward a college degree. Further, in the Professional Certification program, through agreements with about thirty-two professional groups, such as the American Medical Technologists, the American Nurses Association, the American Speech-Language-Hearing Association, the Institute for the Certification of Engineering Technicians, and the National Association of Social Workers, service people can take professional certification examinations to demonstrate skills learned in the military.

Through the DANTES Distance Learning program, 6,000-plus high school, undergraduate, and graduate correspondence courses are available from regionally accredited colleges and universities.

The Military Evaluations program is conducted in cooperation with the American Council on Education, which arranges for evaluations of military courses and experiences and makes recommendations regarding the acceptance of them for credit.

More than 400 colleges and universities constitute the network known as Servicemembers Opportunity Colleges. These institutions have formulated policies and implemented programs to make higher education more accessible to military personnel.

In the Troops to Teachers program, DANTES personnel compile a guide to regionally accredited institutions of higher education that offer nontraditional, off-campus learning with flexible scheduling. Counselors then use this guide to advise service personnel on suitable programs.

USDA Graduate School   The Graduate School, U.S. Department of Agriculture (USDA), is a continuing education school offering career-related courses to all adults regardless of education or place of employment. Annually the Graduate School provides more than 2,500 courses for career development and personal enrichment. Classes are designed to help individuals realize their career potential, improve their job performance, and enrich their lives. More than 1,200 instructors are drawn from government, business, and academe. As experts in their field, Graduate School instructors bring a practical focus to the classroom.

The school was created in 1921 by Secretary of Agriculture Henry C. Wallace to provide continuing education for young research scientists of the USDA. Wallace believed that a graduate school would help attract and retained qualified personnel, at a time (shortly after World War I) when the demand for them was acute. The school soon expanded to serve other government personnel. Today the name Graduate School reflects whom the school serves rather than what it does. It continues to serve adults—both government employees and the general public—who have "graduated" from full-time schooling.

Although it is affiliated with the USDA, the Graduate School is completely self-supporting; it receives no funding from the government.

CONTINUING EDUCATION STAFF

Three categories of staff are most prominent in continuing education: teachers, counselors, and administrators. The configuration of faculty in continuing education varies greatly with the type and the structure of the institution or agency. In the college or university, regular tenured faculty teach courses in continuing education as part of their normal load, or as an overload for extra pay. Also, adjunct professors—that is, people who serve part time while having full-time jobs elsewhere—are engaged to teach courses in their areas of expertise and experience. Thousands of faculty function in one or the other of these teaching categories. They serve as advisers to degree candidates and special students. The effort is to help people who work full time upgrade their skills and knowledge or earn an academic credential. Frequently an institution of higher education has a specific college or office of continuing education.

Often the full-time staff in continuing education at colleges and universities are the administrators or coordinators of the program. (The exception is community and junior colleges, where many full-time faculty may devote all of their time to continuing education and where special counselors may assess interest, ability, and aptitude to advise students in educational and career planning.) The job of administrative staff is to ascertain the training needed by particular populations, create courses, hire instructors, handle logistics (which includes place, day, and time for the courses), provide assistance in teaching methodology (some outside instructors have never taught or teach infrequently), market courses, pilot-test new courses, and evaluate the effectiveness of courses offered.

Counselors are important staff members, especially to adults returning to college after an extended time away. Senior colleges and universities are less apt to designate counselors to advise mature adults in educational and career planning. Further, they do not serve people who are looking for vocational programs or people who must first develop literacy or language skills in order to function in an educational program. Two-year colleges, evening schools, open universities, and distance learning attend to these types of students. The counselor plays an important role in guidance, admission, retention, evaluation, and other functions that facilitate the student's understanding of his or her potential and the offerings that can contribute to achieving that potential.

In professional associations and societies, the staff of the organization often serve in the capacity of teacher or manager (or both) of continuing education programs, usually for only part of their work load. Many have been teachers or professors in prior positions. Some of the most skilled planners of continuing education are organization staff. They plan and conduct innumerable workshops. The conferences they design and carry out are, in most instances, continuing education. Being privy to the thinking and the planning that organization staff give to every detail of a workshop or conference—purposes, content, participants, speakers, logistics, materials, marketing, and evaluation—is a lesson in highly sophisticated continuing education.

Teachers' Duties

Two-thirds to three-quarters of the 425,000-plus teachers in continuing education are part time. Many hold another teaching or administrative job full time or part time, or they are homemakers, craftspeople, artists, or participants in other walks of life who can contribute resources, knowledge, and skills to adult learning.

Teaching, at any level, includes: planning curriculum, assembling and preparing materials and techniques, actually instructing, demonstrating techniques, reading student assignments, preparing and giving examinations, attending to such clerical details as reporting grades, and participating in faculty meetings (see the discussion of teaching in Chapter 2). However, continuing education is different from other postsecondary teaching in some significant ways. Because participation is voluntary, continuing education is more concerned with the learner, with fashioning content and methods to fit the individual; thus it functions at the cutting edge of education. Among the goals of continuing education are making learning more self-directed, building attitudes and skills that make learning lifelong, and using multiple providers—that is, any person, institution, or organization that can contribute to learning.

In the best circumstances continuing education employs more and better techniques of teaching. There is lecturing (telling students what they ought to know is not frowned on), but teachers strive to facilitate learning rather than direct it; to engage students in problem solving, practical applications, demonstrations, discussion, and independent learning; and to give attention to the motivations and the learning styles of adults. There is more conferring with students and more time spent discovering a student's level of achievement, capability, study habits, and command of basic skills. Teachers refer students to counselors more often for assessment of abilities, capacities, and aptitudes, and for educational and career planning.

Working Conditions

Teachers in correctional, literacy, and community-based continuing education programs spend as few as three, and as many as thirty, hours a week in classes, with heavy teaching loads reaching as high as six to nine hours per day, several days per week. That situation is not true of four-year college and university professors involved in continuing education, however. They carry the traditional teaching load in higher education—generally twelve to fifteen

semester hours in colleges, six to twelve semester hours in universities—
with only part of it in continuing education.

In most situations, teaching takes place in the late afternoon, in the
evening, or on the weekend, and ranges from one-shot sessions of two to
three hours, to courses that run the full semester, meeting one to three times
a week. The *Occupational Outlook Handbook* further describes working
conditions in continuing education as follows:

> Teaching adults involves constant search and reorganization of materials, at-
> tention to needs of students, flexibility to alter lesson plans and methods as re-
> quired, and extended periods of standing and talking. Teachers may face
> frustration as a result of bureaucratic procedures within the programs, or with
> students who are challenging to teach, but they can also experience much sat-
> isfaction when students succeed.

Preparation

When the concept of continuing education is lifelong learning, involving
"learning on the part of people of all ages and from all walks of life using
the multiple learning resources of society to learn whatever they [want or
need] to know" (as phrased in *Adults as Learners*), specifying how teachers
of such learning should be prepared is difficult. Certainly, they will not all
have qualifications similar to those for teaching in traditional schools and
colleges. Many continuing education teachers are selected for their special
expertise and experience in a subject, trade, art, craft, or profession that they
practice or teach on a full-time job. As a consequence, faculty in continuing
education are a diverse group.

Most teachers have skills and knowledge developed through experience
or formal education, frequently both. The bachelor's degree is usually a minimum, except with artisans whose experience has made them experts. Many
continuing education teachers have a master's or doctor's degree. Some
states require a credential, a license, or a certificate from the appropriate professional group; other states require licensure as a teacher. Criteria are often
flexible, particularly in areas not commonly taught in academe.

Career Patterns

The path of advancement in continuing education is probably only from
teaching to administration, if that indeed is advancement. Of course, programs come in many sizes, and one form of advancement is to more responsible, more challenging jobs. Larger programs in wealthier schools, colleges,
universities, and associations have more prestige and pay better than those in
smaller, less affluent organizations. That route for advancement is more open
to administrators and coordinators than to teachers and counselors, although
becoming a professor of continuing education at a large, prestigious university represents advancement, particularly if one started out in a school district's evening studies program. Moving into university-level theoretical
work or research in continuing education also may be an advancement. The

hierarchy for advancement aside from these steps is limited (except for those who shift into or shuttle in and out of assignments in business and industry, as described in Chapter 8), partially because continuing education is less formalized than most other kinds of education and partly because it is often an adjunct operation.

Finding Employment

Because of the nature of teaching in continuing education, people often slip into it rather than prepare for it. Some teachers are sought by administrators of continuing education because their reputation has spread or their specialty is needed. In other instances teachers themselves seek out opportunities, from interest in lifelong learning, from a desire to help people who need a second chance, or from a fascination with the concept of a "blended life plan" or a "cyclic life plan." According to *Adults as Learners*, a blended life plan makes education, work, and leisure concurrent rather than linear, whereas a cyclic scheme usually involves "chunks of education and leisure time inserted into the working years and chunks of work time extended into early and late years."

For teachers wanting employment in continuing education in two-year colleges, the approach described in Chapter 2—that is, using the placement office of the college or university from which one graduated—is an effective avenue. Personnel in most state departments of education are knowledgeable about sources of inservice employment. The most obvious approach is to make direct contact with the institutions in which you hope to work. Some directors are also open to suggestions for new courses meeting the needs of the community and will consider proposals from experienced teachers or professionals proficient in their field. An understanding of the purposes and the philosophy of continuing education is essential for an individual seeking employment in the field. That understanding must be deeper and more comprehensive than can be conveyed in a chapter such as this. Courses and programs on continuing education and adult learning are offered in many universities, and the literature in the area is rich. Selected books are included in the bibliography in Appendix A. The American Association for Adult and Continuing Education (AAACE) and the National University Continuing Education Association (NUCEA) are other sources of information.

Salary and Fringe Benefits

Salary and fringe benefits in continuing education depend on whether the teacher, counselor, or administrator is part time or full time. The issue is more relevant for teachers because counselors and administrators are usually full time, if not in continuing education, then at least in another position at the institution offering the continuing education.

Because many continuing educators are also teachers, counselors, or administrators in more formal educational contexts who have part-time responsibilities in continuing education, salaries and fringe benefits for them closely resemble those described in Chapters 2, 3, 5, and 6. The salaries and fringe benefits of artisans, craftspeople, tradespeople, and other adjunct and part-time personnel who are sought out for their special expertise are so diverse as to defy description. Experience and formal education, of course, are factors in salary determinations. But so is the sponsor of a particular program. For example, a community-based continuing education program for refugees, run by a volunteer group, may pay very meager salaries because it has very few funds and because teachers feel their work is a contribution to a cause.

Adjunct personnel are rather poorly rewarded in most cases, and they do not qualify for fringe benefits. That condition exists because institutional policy usually does not provide such benefits for any but full-time employees. Few teachers complain because they are covered for insurance and retirement benefits in full-time jobs. They can afford to teach for a salary without fringe benefits. For some the motivation is extra money; for others teaching a course is just fun, a diversion from regular responsibilities or a chance to share ideas with people. Salaries for adult and continuing education teachers working a forty-week year part-time (one course) run from almost nothing to $6,000. In full-time employment the range is $30,000–$50,000. Information about salaries and fringe benefits for full-time college or university employment in adult and continuing education is contained in Chapter 6.

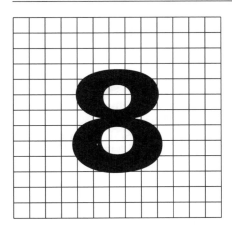

EDUCATION IN BUSINESS AND INDUSTRY

In retail business, factories, and offices such as IBM, Safeway, General Electric, and Chrysler, education—or training and development as it is called in the private sector—is a staple activity. The pace of innovation and adaptation in technical, manufacturing, and service organizations has been phenomenal. Robots, computers, lasers, and other developments in technology have brought about a critical need to retrain technical employees. Constantly changing, more sophisticated approaches to marketing have necessitated the upgrading of personnel. Experimentation and findings in personnel management, training, and ways to promote employee growth have created a wholly new field: human resource development.

Other events that have given impetus to education in the private sector are foreign competition and the emergence of the employee as a company partner. The rising industrial prowess of foreign countries, many with much cheaper labor costs (particularly East Asian nations), has devastated or emasculated some basic industries in the United States, brought about the firing of many in the workforce, and created the need to retrain thousands of employees for new jobs. The realization that employees need cultivation, involvement, nurturing, and support to function well and productively has redirected the focus of the business and industrial training effort from a concentration on skills alone to a broad concern with employee development.

Training new employees, upgrading veteran workers, and introducing new techniques, technologies, and tactics is big business. The introduction of computers alone has created myriad changes. For example, in the basic field of engineering, innumerable mechanical engineers have had to be reoriented to electrical engineering. Retraining that is less sophisticated but encompasses many more people has taken place with clerical and accounting employees. In a brief period the word processor has transformed offices, not only by replacing the typewriter, but also by radically changing the way data are aggregated, stored, duplicated, and presented.

The existence of private-sector careers in training and development is one of the best-kept secrets in American society. This is difficult to understand, given that thousands of people are teaching there and huge sums of money are being spent in the effort. In 1995, private-sector employers spent $55.3 billion on formal training, $25.2 billion on direct costs, and $27.1 billion on indirect costs (wages, salaries, and fringe benefits). The highest formal training expenditures were in transportation, communications, and public utilities. Next was mining, finance, insurance, and real estate, followed by nondurable manufacturing, wholesale trade, durable manufacturing, services, construction, and retail trades—in that order.

In 1995 about 20 million employees (16 percent) in the civilian workforce received formal employer-provided training. Workers with high levels of education, mature workers, men, and whites were more likely to receive such training than workers with low levels of education, younger workers, women, and minorities. Among support staff the greatest needs for training were skills in written communications, computer literacy, and interpersonal communication; among professional and technical staff, skills in interpersonal communication, listening, and writing.

Training in business and industry is conducted almost entirely for the benefit of the organization—that is, for what training will do to improve employee performance, productivity, service, and profit. Training runs the gamut from upgrading the skills and the work style of technicians and blue-collar workers to training supervisors and executives in better, more efficient and effective methods of management. The reasons are obvious. Competition from abroad, technological revolution, and the changing demands of consumers have modified, even eliminated, numerous business and industrial enterprises. America's move from an industrial society to an information and service society is changing the nature of work and the kinds of skills, knowledge, and relational-interactive competence required to fulfill corporate purposes.

Leaders in business and industry also recognize that pride in work and product need to be restored. That goal becomes even more important when team building—that is, learning to work cooperatively with other people—proves to be an important factor in the quality of production or service.

Education offered in the private sector is different from that offered in formal and more traditional institutions of education. Training and development in business and industry is somewhat amorphous. It has not been formalized in content or ritual. It taps many disciplines and responds continuously to changing demands and new developments. It may be for orientation, safety and health, basic skills, workplace-related matters, job skills, or apprenticeship. The delivery system for training is shifting rapidly. For example, from 1994 to 1995, classroom- and lecture-based delivery declined from 78 to 69 percent while delivery by some technology mode (technology/interactive, computer based, interactive/multimedia, TV distance learning, embedded performance support systems, and Internet/network-based distance learning) increased from 13.4 to 20 percent.

The context of education in business and industry also makes it different from education in traditional institutions. The product or service has been identified. The motive is profit. The purpose is clear. But a growing phenomenon is the awareness of executives and managers that their employees are people, not robots. This emerging recognition is not rooted in idealism. It is primarily practical. Employers and administrators are learning fast (perhaps from the Japanese) that employees are a resource, if motivated properly, involved adequately, and rewarded appropriately. They are central to the quality and quantity of an organization's product or service. Life on the job is more pleasant for employees who feel a part of the larger enterprise. When they are involved in planning, they begin to care more about their accomplishments. Workers who interact harmoniously with peers come to like their work, are less fearful of change, and cooperate more effectively. Proponents of this philosophy, such as Thomas J. Peters and Robert J. Waterman, Jr. (authors of *In Search of Excellence*), have made a reputation (and a fortune) researching and disseminating it.

The context is different too in areas influenced by technological development. Almost every year, jobs can call for different knowledge and skills. Innovation may require an accommodation and new skills. Sometimes complete retraining is necessary because an existing process or technology has become obsolete, irrelevant, or less competitive. An example is the advent of microcomputers, software for electronic typesetting, and laser printers, which together make desktop publishing possible and thus challenge conventional typesetting. The skills and the knowledge needed to operate new technologies often are completely different from those required to run former systems, even though the product may be much the same.

It is predicted that to keep pace, three-fourths of all currently employed workers will need retraining by the year 2000. According to the American Society for Training and Development (ASTD), in *Facts About Retraining America's Workforce*, "the National Alliance of Business estimates that by the end of the century between 5 and 15 million manufacturing jobs will be restructured."

The goal of the trainer of technical and service employees is to develop new skills and competencies, build attitudes of interest and acceptance, ensure healthy interrelationships, and promote improved procedures. The more progressive companies also have trainers who counsel individual employees on managing change, on future job opportunities, and (sometimes) on personal problem solving. Training for supervisors and managers includes some of these topics, but it is more often focused on tasks and authority, strategies and philosophy, management and supervision, and organization and assignment of responsibilities across an enterprise.

TRAINERS

The ASTD has described fifteen functions that the trainer performs:

1. Evaluating: Identifying the extent of the impact of a program, service, or product.
2. Facilitating a group: Managing group discussion and group process so that individuals learn and group members feel the experience is positive.
3. Counseling individual development: Helping individuals assess personal competencies, values, and goals, and identify and plan development and career actions.
4. Writing for instruction: Preparing written learning and instructional materials.
5. Instructing: Presenting information and directing structured learning experiences.
6. Managing training and development: Planning, organizing, staffing, and controlling training and development operations or projects and linking these with other organization units.
7. Marketing: Selling training and development viewpoints, learning packages, programs, and services to target audiences outside his or her own unit.
8. Producing media: Producing software and using audio, visual, computer, and other hardware-based technologies for training and development.
9. Analyzing needs: Defining gaps between ideal and actual performance and specifying the cause of the gaps.
10. Administering program: Ensuring that the facilities, equipment, materials, participants, and other components of a learning event are present and that the program logistics run smoothly.
11. Designing program: Preparing objectives, defining content, and selecting and sequencing activities for a specific program.
12. Strategizing: Developing long-range plans for what the training and development structure, organization, direction, policies, programs, services, and practices will be in order to accomplish the training and development mission.
13. Analyzing tasks: Identifying activities, tasks, subtasks, human resources, and support necessary to accomplish specific results in a job or organization.
14. Theorizing: Developing and testing theories of learning, training, and development.
15. Coaching application: Helping individuals apply their learning after the learning experience.

The trainer usually has command of a repertoire of skills and abilities, among them several that employ these fifteen functions. He or she modifies and applies technologies and approaches to satisfy the purposes of a particular training session.

Several of the fifteen functions just identified reveal a philosophy of training. The contrast with the philosophy of adult and continuing education described in Chapter 7 is striking. Philosophies are never pure, however, nor are they consistent in each camp. The philosophy of training in business and industry may be directive, reflect determined purpose, and be unequivocally for organizational benefit. But increasingly there is also concern for employee morale and welfare and a goal of involving employees in planning so that a greater commitment to company purposes is engendered. In many enterprises this is supported further by stock purchase plans, bonuses, or options that enable employees to own a piece of the company. However it is accomplished, ownership builds both commitment and loyalty, particularly in smaller companies.

There is more than a bit of glitz in this field, and it can become heady stuff for the most successful. That the trainer is flown to a session in the corporate jet and is paid a retainer of $1,800 per day leaves the educators described in other chapters envious or resentful, if not suspicious. Traditional educators in particular look askance at the gimmicks, the profit motive, and the rah-rah approach of training and development. But they rarely take a hard look, and they seldom recognize that this kind of education is part of free enterprise. Facilitating team building, helping managers analyze and solve performance problems, or transforming order takers into problem solvers translates into greater profits. No wonder top executives marvel at a good trainer's ability and pay a premium for his or her services. The results make a difference in production and service costs, employee efficiency and morale, and the quality of products or services.

One trainer confided, "School and college teachers just don't realize how much we pack into sessions. This is really a very tightly organized kind of training. And it's much more bottom-line oriented than schools. If the corporate people don't see us making a difference, we've had it."

According to *Careers in Training and Development*, trends in training and development that will probably gain momentum in the next decade are as follows:

1. "Human capital development [is] becoming a goal of more organizations as a response to the global threat [of competition]."

2. Education in organizations is being driven by needs—"strategic goals and internal organizational issues"—and is "developing different thinking styles for improving and managing performance."

3. "Corporations [are] becoming training institutions" and "job-related learning is becoming more important in determining what a person does than formal education."

4. "Organizations [are] developing new cultures for managing individual and team performance."

5. "Training [is] a growth industry" and the "key influences contributing to this growth are changing technologies and human assets being recognized for productive growth."

Preparation

There is no pat answer to the question of preparation for this career, and no one route to follow. Granted, a number of people in training and development have credentials and experience in the field of organizational development, and formal education in organizational development is available. But there is more to training and development than just organizational development. And success may depend on whether an individual seeks a job inside a company or hopes to operate freelance from outside.

People who find employment in training and development inside an organization often begin in another capacity with the company and move quite naturally into a training role. They may teach others about a job they have done or are doing, or they may informally help others learn. In this vein, experienced computer programmers induct new programmers, top salespeople share techniques and methods with other sales representatives, and veteran stockbrokers break in new members of the firm. A fairly common practice these days is for an employee to assume the role of trainer for a specified period and then rotate back into other corporate, service, or manufacturing duties. Once in the role, trainers often seek outside instruction for themselves or attend conferences and workshops to gain additional skills. Learning on the job, planning and conducting training sessions, and getting feedback from participants (and management) provide chances to further refine competence.

Becoming a freelance trainer—that is, one who works on contract with businesses and industries—happens in a number of ways. Many trainers start out as teachers in schools or colleges, often earning a post-baccalaureate degree in those roles. They also may participate in several special training sessions themselves with groups that specialize in training and development or organizational development, such as the ASTD and the National Training Laboratory. Once trainers become employees of a school system or an institution of higher education, they find opportunities for outside work as trainers, or they become consultants to university departments of industrial management, business administration, and community planning. Both avenues lead to other assignments. Reputations spread quickly and easily for quality trainers. The bottom line is results. Achieving them builds trust, which easily grows into contract renewals for the same or other types of training. Whether participants are workers or managers, when a trainer makes a difference, everyone knows it.

One critical point in training adults is recognizing that employees are mature people. They cannot be treated otherwise. Trainers who have come out of teaching in schools and colleges must be aware that adult learning has its peculiarities, its uniqueness.

Trainers also must have an awareness of the business and industrial world and be conversant with its problems and issues. For educators shifting from academe, that means becoming current with business literature and news by reading such publications as the *Wall Street Journal*, *Business Week*, and *Fortune*.

Like most professionals, trainers have networks. They know many of their counterparts inside and outside organizations. Establishing and maintaining a network is essential not only for the freelance (outside) trainer, but also for the insider, because more than employment prospects flow through a network. Networks channel ideas, information, and access to resources.

If one has something to offer, becoming part of a network of trainers is easy. But to remain in it, one must be able to interact creatively with other trainers. Networks are invisible webs connecting people who know and trust one another and among whom there is continuous give-and-take. In the give-and-take is a tender balance. One dares not give overzealously or take too much. Among trainers, particularly, reciprocity is essential. Networking may be one of the most important kinds of involvement a trainer can have.

Finding Employment

Some people are more comfortable in a salaried position. Such jobs are usually full time within an organizational setting. Other people are happier with the independence (and risk) of freelancing. Whichever one chooses, having a career means finding work and keeping it. In training and development, the route to employment is as nebulous as is a prescription for preparation. As already indicated, most trainers have a college education, but not necessarily as educators or trainers. Interest in training and development may occur well after college. Charting the way is an individual matter. That means making a careful assessment of talents, abilities, and needed skills and competencies. It means finding ways to hone existing assets and acquire new ones. Exploring the territory of colleges and universities, interviewing professionals in training and development, and becoming informed on other agencies and institutions that specialize in this area are good first steps. The labels that encompass the general area are human development, human resource development, career development, organizational development, and corporate development. The word *training* may appear with any of those titles. The ASTD gives the following advice to individuals planning a career in training and development:

1. Establish goals and keep them flexible.
2. Anticipate several careers during a lifetime.
3. Make life planning a part of career planning.
4. Write down your personal and professional values and philosophy.

5. Create an image of your desired future—look ahead three to five years.

6. Assess your present career situation and look at your preferred future.

7. Elicit feedback from your colleagues to critique, update, and revise your plan.

8. Decide in advance that you will manage your own training and development.

Salary and Fringe Benefits

The payoffs for trainers in business and industry are many. The satisfaction and the excitement of seeing people and situations change may be the two most prominent ones. Participation in an emerging field and high visibility are others.

Salaries and fees vary considerably. Top trainers, be they employees or freelancers, have incomes in the category of company executives. Internal generalists and specialists in design and development receive salaries of $200 to $350 per day. A considerably wider range is paid to contract (external) generalists. The average minimum daily salary for external consultants was around $500 in 1995, and the average maximum was considerably more than $1,000. Some specialists received $1,800 or more per day.

As for fringe benefits, trainers employed full time by an organization have the same fringe benefits as other employees. Freelancers must provide their own health insurance, retirement equity, and leave.

Employment as a trainer is high-risk work from the standpoint of job security. When corporate budgets are cut, training is often one of the first areas to see reductions. On the other hand, freelance consultants may benefit at such times because they can offer services without encumbering an organization with the expense of a full-time employee or the obligation to provide long-term employment.

CAREERS IN GOVERNANCE AND CONTROL OF EDUCATION

At the top of the education pyramid, at the state and national levels, are careers in the control and the governance of education—in state boards and departments of education, federal education agencies, professional councils and associations, membership groups, and other agencies listed in Appendix B. Most of the people in these units have come up through the ranks. They are drawn from the various schools, colleges, universities, and other agencies described in Chapters 2–7. Most are appointed; some are elected.

These positions are included as careers because that indeed is what most of them have become. In only a few positions are the holders expected to rotate in and out on a three-, four-, or five-year schedule. The rotating positions are those of elected officers of associations (for example, the president of the National Education Association) and political appointees in government (for example, the secretary of education) who either have specified terms or whose responsibilities terminate when the administration of which they are a part ends.

Perhaps the best way to suggest what careers in the top professional and government bureaucracies are like is to describe the roles of these agencies and associations and some of the duties of the professionals who staff them.

STATE BOARDS AND STATE DEPARTMENTS OF EDUCATION

The control of education rests with the states, and thus there are fifty separate systems of education. Almost every state has a state board of education that has authority to establish policies, rules, and regulations for carrying out the responsibilities delegated to it by the U.S. Constitution or state law. In some states, one board has responsibility for both elementary and secondary education, and higher education. In other states, separate boards have these responsibilities. Each state also has one or two departments that administer board policies and other regulations. The names of these departments are not uniform across the fifty states, but in all cases they are the arms of the state government entrusted with the administration and management of the system of public schooling. That system includes public elementary and secondary education (kindergarten through twelfth grade, with the exception of a few states that do not yet support kindergartens), vocational education and special schools, and public higher education.

The governance and the control of private K–12 schools vary by state. In some states private schools are monitored only for sanitation and safety; in others, curriculum, teacher competence, and other matters are regulated.

Elementary and Secondary Education

State departments of education are headed by a chief state school officer, usually called the superintendent of public instruction or the commissioner of education, though the title of secretary of education is used in a couple of states. The chief is elected by the people in fifteen states, appointed by the state board of education in twenty-two states, and appointed by the governor in thirteen states. Most chiefs are educators. Only a few are not. In several states there is no requirement that the superintendent be an educator.

The staffs of state departments of education have grown tremendously since the 1960s, partially because of federal support. Although only about 7 or 8 percent of state expenditures on education come from federal money, the federal outlay to states increased from $13 billion to almost $33 billion between 1980 and 1995. As a consequence, staff have been added to handle such programs as block grants to states for school improvement, education of individuals with disabilities, grants for the disadvantaged, bilingual programs, rehabilitation services, vocational and adult education, library programs, and Indian education.

People in state education departments implement state policies and regulations in many areas: qualifications for school teaching and administration; basic education and other curricula; teacher education; selection of textbooks; and data collection on enrollments, attendance, transportation, and special needs. Programs in special education, compensatory education, vocational education and rehabilitation (not always a responsibility of the department of education), and adult education are substantial, each with some support from the federal government.

State staff provide technical assistance in all the areas just named. They also produce reports, conduct studies, convene and consult with schoolteachers and administrators, and work with teacher educators in both public and private colleges. They coordinate and introduce state initiatives in education. Among recent ones have been standards for student achievement, mentor teachers, drug and alcohol abuse education programs, computer technology, elimination of discrimination against women and minorities, reform in teacher education, dropout prevention, science curriculum revision, sex education, AIDS prevention, and teacher evaluation. In earlier years state education department staff were primarily data collectors and inspectors. More recently the trend has been to provide technical assistance and leadership to local districts.

State education department personnel spend much of their time administering federally funded programs. The paperwork required for certain federal programs is so time consuming that many staff are in effect bound to their desks. Some think that has brought about neglect of state initiatives. State prerogatives in relation to federal programs have been increased since the advent of block grants to the states, which provide more discretion than the many categorical programs of yesteryear.

Preparation for professional jobs in state departments of education is basically that described in Chapters 2–5. That is, most state education department employees begin as public school teachers, and many then serve as public school administrators, supervisors, or specialists. A few people have been employed in colleges of education. Most personnel have at least a master's degree; many hold doctorates.

Employment is secured through application for announced openings, which must be made public to conform with affirmative action regulations. Despite the open system, some jobs may be wired—that is, the preferred choice may be in the wings waiting for the legal procedures to take their course. Getting to know state education department officials can be one of the key moves for access to notices of job openings and may be helpful in securing employment.

State education department jobs are part of the civil service, except for the top few. Employees enjoy the standard benefits in salaries and fringe benefits provided for all state employees. There is typically a salary schedule. Where a person is placed on a salary schedule depends on level of training and experience. Some states advance personnel on the salary schedule only on merit; others grant salary increases annually (usually in eight to ten steps) unless there is a budget crisis or an employee has not been performing satisfactorily. In New York state, for example, the lowest-grade professional staff member starts at $43,620 and can earn $53,711 after a series of steps (on merit). In New York's top grade for professional staff, the salary begins at $90,467 and proceeds to $107,358. Managers and directors in New York state start at $47,155 and top out at $108,518. Annual evaluations of performance by unit heads provide the evidence on which raises, merit jumps, or denial of raises is justified and authorized.

Civil service protects state employees from politically motivated harassment and discrimination. However, many veteran employees tell tales of administrations in which they (or colleagues) were essentially banned or rendered inoperative because of differences of opinion or style with the elected or appointed chief. Bureaucrats learn to survive the vicissitudes of different administrations. The staff member who concentrates on the basic educational issues of the state and faithfully carries out the goals of the state board and state superintendent can (and should) remain aloof from partisan politics. Despite gripes and criticisms of state staff, many more seem stimulated and challenged in their jobs than in former years. "There's a feeling that education is going somewhere," one perceptive leader reported.

Generalizations about state departments of education are difficult, despite the foregoing description, because the size of the staff varies so much. The more populous states, such as California, Connecticut, New York, and Pennsylvania, have several hundred full-time professional staff members, whereas states with smaller populations, such as New Hampshire, North Dakota, and Wyoming, have very few professional employees. Another illustration of the diversity is the difference in the salaries of chief state school officers, which range from $50,000 to $137,000. The spread most certainly reflects the differences in complexity and magnitude of the various state departments' responsibilities.

Higher Education

During the great expansion of public higher education in the 1950s, 1960s, and 1970s, forty-nine states (Wyoming being the exception) created one or more central commissions or boards (hereafter collectively called boards) to facilitate the administration and the governance of public colleges and universities. These boards either superseded the separate boards responsible for policy and direction of the various state-supported colleges and universities, or were put in place to coordinate the policies and functions of those separate boards. In some states universities were able to resist such consolidation. In others the flagship institution (usually the oldest and most prestigious) escaped, but other state-supported institutions did not.

The purpose of the state boards is to reduce unneeded duplication, to increase efficiency, and to allocate funds judiciously among public institutions of higher education. They also may have limited purview over private higher education. Some of the boards have direct trusteeship over state institutions. Others function largely to coordinate planning, research, data collection, and budget review; to represent the institutions to the governor, the legislature, and the public; and to promote interinstitutional communication among institutions.

The state boards of higher education also are charged with determining the tasks to be done in higher education and deciding which institutions should undertake the tasks. The early deliberations on these issues were most often undertaken with input from the administrative leadership and the faculty of the public colleges and universities—most of whom resisted in one way or another their loss of autonomy. The conflict to work out was (and is) how much autonomy is essential for the operation of a healthy, dynamic institution and how much coordination is necessary for efficient, reasonable attention to higher education in a state.

Careers as staff members of coordinating boards have developed. Persons in these roles must be capable of planning a rational system of higher education in the state, allocating roles and functions among the individual institutions, and controlling the allocation of resources appropriated by the legislature.

The staffs of coordinating boards may be large or small, depending on the size of the state and the number of institutions. In California, for example, there are three governing agencies: the Board of Governors of the California Community Colleges for more than ninety two-year colleges, the Board of Trustees of the California State University and Colleges for nineteen four-year institutions (formerly state colleges), and the Regents of the University of California for nine universities. To coordinate the three agencies, there is a Coordinating Council for Higher Education, which has an advisory role relative to the agencies and the state officials.

The staffs of state coordinating bodies (sometimes called general administration) study the various aspects of education that are relevant to their types of institutions and to the policy-making and other functions of their board. They do long- and short-range planning and projections that anticipate and respond to enrollments, educational needs, budget requirements, legal mandates, federal initiatives and funding, and other matters identified by their board. Often there is a division of duties along the lines of academic affairs, communication (public affairs and lobbying), finance, planning, research (on institutional and substantive issues), and student services. Coordinating board staff also serve as clearinghouses and conduits.

Senior staff on coordinating boards have experience in higher education and have earned advanced degrees. They are appointed and hold office at the pleasure of their board, although some have academic rank in the institution from which they were promoted (providing the institution is one of those being coordinated).

Salaries for staff of state coordinating boards are different in every state. In North Carolina the range is from the high $30,000s to more than over $100,000 for vice presidents. The president's salary is $120,200.

FEDERAL EDUCATION AGENCIES

Several federal agencies administer programs in education. The Department of Education, the National Science Foundation, the National Endowment for the Arts, the National Endowment for the Humanities, the Department of Defense, the Department of State, and the Department of Labor are among the most prominent. The Department of Education is the focus in this chapter because it administers most of the programs that affect public schools and higher education, and because careers in other agencies parallel those described for the Department of Education.

The bureaucracy in Washington is considerably maligned, and the Department of Education is no exception. Advanced to department status in 1980 (from being the Office of Education within the Department of Health, Education, and Welfare), it has been through a number of political battles since that time. The Reagan administration wanted to abolish the department, but was not successful. Criticism from conservatives continues, and threats to the department's existence remain. With the current public concern about and interest in education, though, the department will probably survive and have significant prominence in the years to come.

In the 1980 transition, the staff of the former Office of Education became the department's staff. Supporting the secretary of education are deputies for such areas as management and intergovernmental and interagency affairs. Below them are assistant secretaries for elementary and secondary education, postsecondary education, educational research and improvement, special education and rehabilitative services, legislation, civil rights, and bilingual education. The secretary, the deputies, and the assistant secretaries are political appointees, serving at the pleasure of the president.

A few political appointees and a number of career personnel (that is, regular department employees with long service) are selected to the Senior Executive Service (SES) of the department. SES members who are career personnel are protected by civil service; those who are political appointees are not. The remaining department staff, working in the divisions just named, are mostly civil servants. They have job security comparable to that of college and university professors with tenure. A few of them are political appointees and serve a specified term.

Staff duties are divided roughly into two broad areas: operations and program. The operations people attend to management, collection of information and statistics on education in the nation, planning and budget, and interagency affairs. Program personnel are (or should be) national authorities in their area. They have antennae out around the country and know what is happening and what issues policymakers need to consider. They provide advice and assistance to policymakers. They oversee the programs that the government sponsors or the work for which it contracts. They represent the federal perspective to local projects and strive to obtain the largest return for the expenditure.

Staff do research and writing, prepare requests for proposals, review and evaluate proposals, design new efforts, and draft and modify regulations. They build and maintain networks with counterparts in state departments of education, universities, and national associations. They serve in a liaison capacity for the department in meetings around Washington and across the nation. And they receive visitors and respond to inquiries.

Preparation for department staff positions usually involves experience and an advanced degree, typically the doctorate. Very few people who have just received their doctorates and have no experience in the field, are employed. The department seeks people who have credibility in the field.

Education bureaucrats have the same salary and grade levels as personnel in other government departments. Professional staff normally have General Service (GS) grades from 11 to 16. Salaries increase gradually in ten steps in each of the grades. In GS-11, the beginning salary is $38,330, which increases in ten steps to $49,831. In a career a staff member can be advanced in GS grade when openings occur. The top nonadministrative professional grade is GS-15 (although 16, 17, and 18 still exist), in which the beginning salary is $75,935 and the highest is $96,714.

Middle-level management personnel (grades GS-13, -14, -15), who supervise employees, are part of the performance management and recognition system. They advance in salary on merit (based on annual performance evaluations).

An invaluable salary and retirement provision of federal employment is indexing—that is, federal salaries are adjusted periodically to reflect changes in the Consumer Price Index, which measures cost of living. Since the introduction of that provision, changes in the index have always meant increases.

COUNCILS AND ASSOCIATIONS

The state government departments and boards discussed in the preceding sections have legal authority over the schools, colleges, and universities under their purview, and the federal agencies administering programs in education have some legal authority in those circumstances in which federal funding or legislation applies. Most of the councils and associations described under this heading only influence education. The accrediting agencies do more than influence, but only in institutions that volunteer to be inspected. Influence by any agency, of course, can be strong, especially when the image of an institution is at stake.

State Activity

National associations and unions have state affiliates or units that work at influencing decisions and public policy in such areas of education as school and college curriculum, personnel, and administration. Most of these groups represent teachers, school administrators, or professors. The 2.6 million elementary and secondary public school teachers are people in common circumstances. They coalesce easily and in all fifty states have organizations with full-time staffs (only seven states have fewer than 10,000 teachers). The 5 million full-time and .3 million part-time college and university faculty are a diverse group. In states in which they are organized, they have joined with teacher groups. State affiliates and units of both the National Education Association and the American Federation of Teachers have higher education faculty in their membership. Administrators also are organized at the state level and in several states employ full-time staff. Few other professional education groups are so formally organized and staffed at the state level.

These organizations bring demands and standards to state boards of education, state departments of education, higher education coordinating boards, state legislatures, and other state agencies and organizations. Many state teacher organizations are well staffed, their professional personnel being on a par in training and experience with government and academic staff. In fact, some move back and forth among such positions. They deal with the same topics and issues that government staff handle (as well as internal organizational agendas), except that they perform in an advocacy role for their members. For example, government bureaucrats may plan budgets that ultimately determine salaries of school and college employees. Association staff study and compare salary figures across a state and the nation to make a case with a state board, coordinating council, or legislature designed to influence an increase in appropriations and hence a boost in salaries. Staff play similar roles in attempting to influence standards of teacher preparation and certification, high school graduation requirements, specifications for testing programs, college admission standards, and innumerable other matters of concern to their members.

Association staff also work to influence decisions on salaries and working conditions at the school district and college level. Collective bargaining is a prominent tactic, but there is also research and involvement in study and advisory committees. Association representatives appear before legislative committees, make presentations at state board hearings, and confer with governors. Collectively, associations are a political force. They lobby and participate in elections, not infrequently running one or more of their own members for political office. Teachers and professors are now as well represented as other business and professional people in some state legislatures.

State association staff are mostly former teachers and administrators. A few have been college professors. They have at least a bachelor's degree, more often a master's or higher degree. Usually they have experience as the kind of educator the association serves—that is, former teachers staff teacher organizations, and administrators become staff members of administrator associations. A frequent avenue to an association staff position is through appointed and elected leadership positions in the association. Many state teacher association staff have been chairpersons of committees, local and state officers, or state presidents. Salaries for state association staff are higher than the salaries paid to the professionals they represent, but they vary greatly from one state to another.

Regional and National Activity

Regional and National Accrediting Agencies.   Accrediting at the regional and national levels is a voluntary method of quality control. Institutions apply to be reviewed. (In addition to colleges and universities, high schools, and in some regions, elementary schools, can be accredited by regional associations.) Standards for accreditation are set by professionals in a particular field with the approval of the constituencies involved. The process involves a visit to the institution seeking accreditation by a team of professionals in the field or fields under examination. An institution must be visited periodically, say, every five years, to maintain its accredited standing. The institution is evaluated on the basis of standards that have been made known to it and that serve as criteria against which the team makes an assessment.

Sometimes the institution prepares a report in advance. The report may be a self-study to inform the team how the institution measures up to criteria included in the accreditation body's standards.

The visiting team reports to a council or some other official body of the agency, and generally that body makes the decision on accreditation status. The usual actions are either approval, deferral, denial, probation, or suspension; these possibilities vary with the level of educational program being examined, the field (in higher education), and other considerations, such as whether an entire college is being reviewed or separate programs within a college. There is normally a fee for accreditation, and often the institution must pay the expenses of the visiting team. Regional accreditation, which is a review of an entire institution, usually takes the form of giving advice for needed improvement, particularly with institutions that have been accredited before. National accreditation involves inspection of various professional programs and is more often in the mode of applying standards.

There are six regional accrediting agencies—the Middle States, New England, North Central, Northwest, Southern, and Western Associations of Schools and Colleges—and about fifty national accrediting agencies that set standards and review professional programs of training in all the major professions. Information on each one can be secured from the Council on Higher Education Accreditation (CHEA).

An example in one field, teacher education, which also encompasses education of administrators and some other education personnel, may be instructive. (In this field, accrediting complements licensure.) Official agencies set standards for licensing practitioners and for accrediting institutions that prepare education personnel. In both cases the purpose is to ensure the public that standards of preparation and practice are adhered to. As indicated in earlier chapters, all colleges must receive approval from the state for their programs. Usually if an institution voluntarily seeks and receives regional accreditation, it may apply for accreditation by the National Council for Accreditation of Teacher Education (NCATE). NCATE is the sole agency authorized by the Council on Higher Education Accreditation (CHEA) to accredit institutional units preparing teachers and other professional school personnel.

Accrediting agencies do more than inspect whether the curriculum is adequate. They review institutional objectives, program quality, administrative effectiveness, financial stability, faculty and library strength, and adequacy of student personnel programs. The NCATE assesses the adequacy of curriculum design, delivery, and content; the strength of the program's relationship to the world of practice; the extent of diversity among students and the adequacy of procedures for monitoring, advising, and evaluating them; the quality and the size of faculty; and the adequacy of a program's governance and resources.

The illustration suggests some of the tasks that NCATE staff must accomplish. NCATE has several constituent organizations, representing various branches of the teaching profession. Staff are responsible for liaison with these organizations. They also manage the selection of visiting teams, arrange visitation schedules, receive reports and prepare them for presentation to the council, and carry out administrative work to support council meetings. They introduce new institutions to the standards of the council, conduct training sessions for members of visiting teams, and manage the evaluation of team members' performance. NCATE's standards are revised periodically. Staff often have a part in the arrangements for, and the process of, revision.

The staff members at NCATE are few. The president and the vice president hold doctor's degrees and are experienced in teacher education. Most were originally teachers. The president is selected by the council through a search similar to the procedure followed by universities seeking a dean. Second-line staff are appointed by the council from applicants who respond to advertised openings. Salaries are in the $40,000 to $100,000 range. Professional employees are covered for retirement by the Teachers Insurance Annuity Association–College Retirement Equities Fund (TIAA–CREF).

Educational Laboratories, Research and Development Centers, Technology Consortia, and Clearinghouses. Ten regional educational laboratories, ten research and development (R&D) centers, six Regional Technology in Education Consortia (R–TEC), and sixteen Educational Resources Information Center (ERIC) clearinghouses are funded by the federal government. A list of the locations and the specific areas of investigation of these agencies is available from the Office of Educational Research and Improvement, U.S. Department of Education.

The laboratories focus on problems and issues in education and develop models and programs for implementation in the schools in their respective regions. They are as follows:

1. The Northeast and Islands Laboratory at Brown University
2. Mid-Atlantic Laboratory for Student Success
3. Appalachia Educational Laboratory
4. Southeastern Regional Vision for Education
5. North Central Regional Educational Laboratory
6. Southwest Educational Development Laboratory
7. Mid-Continent Regional Educational Laboratory
8. WestEd (uniting the Far West Laboratory for Educational Research and Development and the Southwest Regional Laboratory)
9. Northwest Regional Educational Laboratory
10. Pacific Region Educational Laboratory

The R&D centers are what their name suggests, places where research and development on a particular topic take place. Seven of the centers are new as of fiscal year 1996. Each focuses on a particular priority, as indicated by its name:

1. National Center to Enhance Early Development and Learning
2. National Research and Development Center on Achievement in School Mathematics and Science
3. National Research Center on Improving Student Learning and Achievement in English
4. Center for Research on Evaluation, Standards, and Student Testing
5. National Center for Research on Cultural Diversity and Second Language Learning
6. National Research and Development Center on Increasing the Effectiveness of State and Local Education Reform Efforts
7. National Center for Postsecondary Improvement

Three older centers are as follows:

8. National Reading Research Center
9. Center for Research on the Education of Students Placed at Risk
10. National Research Center on the Gifted and Talented

The R–TEC program was established in 1995 to help states, school districts, adult literacy centers, and other educational institutions use technology to support improved teaching and student learning. The program supports professional development, technical assistance, and information dissemination. The six consortia attend to the needs of the various regions of the country: Northwest, North Central, Northeast, Southeast & Islands, South Central, and Pacific/Southwest. They work in a complementary and collaborative way with federally funded providers of technical assistance—such as the Comprehensive Regional Assistance Centers, the Eisenhower Regional Consortia for Mathematics and Science Education, and the Regional Educational Laboratories—and with other nationwide educational technology support efforts.

The ERIC clearinghouses index and abstract the educational literature. They also collect and store hard-to-find literature and make it available for retrieval. Each center specializes in a particular area of education, as indicated by its name: ERIC Clearinghouse on

1. Adult, Career, and Vocational Education
2. Counseling and Student Services
3. Educational Management
3. Elementary and Early Childhood Education
4. Disabilities and and Gifted Education

5. Higher Education
6. Information and Technology
7. Junior Colleges
8. Language and Linguistics
9. Reading, English, and Communications
10. Rural Education and Small Schools
11. Science, Mathematics, and Environmental Education
12. Social Studies/Social Science Education
13. Teacher Education
14. Tests, Assessment, and Evaluation
15. Community Colleges
16. Urban Education

The ERIC database is available on microfiche, via telephone line with a computer and a modem, and on compact discs (CD-ROMs) in many university libraries.

Laboratory staff are mostly people who specialize in curriculum and instruction, including the subjects of the school curriculum. Many are expert in developing materials, running workshops, and consulting on school improvement. They come largely from public school and college ranks. Their training is typically in teacher education or a specialist field with advanced study in a subject or an area of curriculum.

R&D staff include various types of researchers and a number of people with experience and expertise in policy development, curriculum development, and the specialty of a particular center. These staff are largely former college and university professors. Many have held positions in public schools.

Most professional staff of the laboratories and the R&D centers hold doctorates and have had considerable working experience. Jobs in the laboratories and the centers are secured by application for advertised positions. Most R&D centers are operated by universities on contract with the federal government. Hence, several staff are tenured university professors with a part- or full-time assignment to the center during its life at the university. Professionals hired by the R&D center who have no other ties may not have job security beyond the term of the federal support.

The professional education staffs of ERIC clearinghouses are typically very small. Often only the director is trained in the field in which the clearinghouse specializes.

National Associations and Councils.   Thousands of professional educators staff the hundreds of associations and councils at the national level. Most of these groups are located in and around the nation's capital (see Appendix B for addresses). The access to federal agencies and to Congress, and the proximity to related education associations, make metropolitan Washington a convenient location. The coming together (in housing at least) of more than twenty college and university associations in the Higher Education Center at One Dupont Circle illustrates that some organizations have chosen contiguousness.

Describing the roles and the functions of all of the education associations and councils operating at the national level is too extensive an undertaking for this book. Details about their membership, function, role, and activities can be found in the *Encyclopedia of Associations*.

National associations and councils fall into several categories, according to their unit of membership. The best known are those that offer membership to individuals, and the largest of them are teacher organizations. The two most prominent ones, the National Education Association and the American Federation of Teachers, are for teachers generally, regardless of level or subject. Other teacher groups (to which a number of college professors also belong) are the subject-matter associations, focused on the various subjects taught in schools, such as the National Council for the Social Studies, the National Council of Teachers of English, and the National Council of Teachers of Mathematics.

For college teachers there are also general membership groups. The American Association of University Professors and the American Association of University Women are examples. College teachers also participate in a number of subject-matter groups, such as the American Chemical Society, the American Sociological Association, the American Psychological Association, the Association of American Geographers, and the American Political Science Association. These organizations are more broadly based than the subject-matter associations for teachers, drawing members from all personnel educated in the subject above a certain level. So, for example, the American Chemical Society serves not only professors of chemistry, but also chemists in business and industry.

There are also associations for personnel in public schools and higher education whose jobs are alike. Some examples are the American Association of School Personnel Administrators, the National Association of Elementary School Principals, the Association for Supervision and Curriculum Development, the American Association of University Administrators, the American Association of Collegiate Registrars and Admissions Officers, and the National Association of College and University Business Officers.

In a second category are associations whose unit of membership is the institution. There are two kinds of these: associations in which an entire institution is a member, such as the National Association of State Universities and Land-Grant Colleges, the American Association of State Colleges and Universities, and the Association of American Universities; and those to which professional schools belong, such as the American Association of Colleges for Teacher Education, the Association of American Law Schools, the Association of Collegiate Schools of Architecture, and the Association of Schools of Public Health.

Still another category of organizations is the councils that have associations as members. The accrediting agencies are such groups. The governing body, the Council on Higher Education Accreditation, counts accrediting associations among its members.

In addition to the foregoing, business, commerce, military, trade, and technological associations have education officers. Whether these are indeed careers in education, or just jobs with an education component, is a matter of opinion.

The list of organizations goes on and on. Identifying some of the types, indicating various membership patterns, and illustrating some of the categories gives a flavor and suggests the comprehensiveness and complexity of the organizational effort supporting education.

The professional staff of this multitude of organizations are predominantly people who were once the type of professional whom their employing association serves or who have come from the institutions that their employing association serves. The essential background for these positions usually includes experience in the specialty of the organization. In the teacher associations, almost all have been teachers. They may or may not have earned doctorates, but most have a master's degree. In the higher education associations the common academic credential required of professional staff is the doctorate.

Although the tasks that staff perform in the associations vary, there are some activities common to most association personnel. They listen, observe, think, and talk—absorbing, reflecting, evaluating, contributing. They write—memos, newsletters, proposals, reports, monographs, letters, and more. They read continuously—research reports; newsletters, journals, and newspapers in their field; policy and position papers; proposed legislation; and government regulations. Speaking and writing and getting along with people are important skills. The flow of information across a staff member's desk is constant and voluminous. Selecting what to read is an everyday task.

They attend meetings within and outside their organization. They spend much time on the telephone answering queries, promoting the program and position of their organization, maintaining a network of contacts, learning about developments, and just making arrangements.

Many staff travel extensively—speaking, attending meetings, visiting institutions, conducting workshops and conferences, representing the organization, advising, and consulting.

Larger associations specialize the work of their staff. Some common categories are membership, publications, conference and meetings, government relations, public relations, research, educational affairs, professional affairs, scientific affairs, and continuing education. These divisions are peculiar to individual and institutional membership organizations and are not as valid for accrediting agencies.

A number of associations administer voluntary programs that examine and credential (professionally certify) practitioners in their field; candidates must usually be members of the association. The programs are a profession's own effort to ensure high standards of competence on the part of its members. Some of the bodies that apply these standards have been legally sanctioned by state legislatures. Others issue credentials in addition to, or instead of, state certification or licensure.

Many of the national associations in education participate in the National Board for Professional Teaching Standards, a comparatively new organization designed to attest to the competence of public school teachers at the level of the diplomate in other fields. Teachers must apply and qualify for this national certification.

Salaries and fringe benefits in the metropolitan Washington area must compete with those of government employees. Many organizations miss that mark. Some exceed it. Fringe benefits are generally comparable; they include hospitalization and medical insurance, retirement programs (with higher-education associations offering TIAA), life insurance, and a liberal leave policy (usually the equivalent of a month's annual leave and all legal holidays). Vision and dental care insurance are offered by more and more agencies.

ROOM AT THE TOP

Many of the staff positions described in this chapter are second or third careers for people in education. They come well after graduation from college, after successful experience and graduate study.

Moreover, once an individual secures a government, association, or council job, education continues. Every week and every year at work is a learning experience. Many individuals in these positions take advanced graduate work and complete a doctorate or some other degree in part-time study as their career moves along. There are both personal and professional benefits in such continuing education.

As in any field, people in the top jobs, often the more experienced, gradually grow older and retire. The lieutenants know the content and the procedures of the job; they understand the function and the purpose of the organization; they have built networks with constituents. They are often the heirs apparent. There is room at the top.

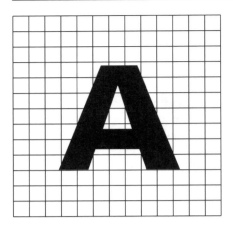

BIBLIOGRAPHY

GENERAL RESOURCES

Andrews, T. E., Andrews, L., & Pape, C., eds. *The NASDTEC Manual 1996–97: Manual on Certification and Preparation of Educational Personnel in the United States and Canada*. Seattle, WA: National Association of State Directors of Teacher Education and Certification, 1996.

Choy, S., et al. *America's Teachers: Profile of a Profession*. Washington, DC: National Center for Education Statistics, 1993.

The Condition of Education 1995. Washington, DC: National Center for Education Statistics, 1995.

The Condition of Education 1996. Washington, DC: National Center for Education Statistics, 1996.

Fringe Benefits for Administrators and Supervisors in Public Schools, 1994–95, Part 2 of *National Survey of Fringe Benefits in Public Schools*. Arlington, VA: Educational Research Service, 1995.

Fringe Benefits for Superintendents in Public Schools, 1994–95, Part 1 of *National Survey of Fringe Benefits in Public Schools*. Arlington, VA: Educational Research Service, 1995.

Fringe Benefits for Teachers in Public Schools, 1994–95, Part 3 of *National Survey of Fringe Benefits in Public Schools*. Arlington, VA: Educational Research Service, 1995.

Goodlad, J. I. *A Place Called School: Prospects for the Future*. New York: McGraw-Hill, 1984.

Haselkorn, D., & Calkins, A. *Careers in Teaching Handbook*. Belmont, MA: Recruiting New Teachers, Inc., 1993.

Haselkorn, D., & Fideler, E. *Breaking the Class Ceiling: Paraeducator Pathways to Teaching*. Belmont, MA: Recruiting New Teachers, Inc., 1996.

Hattendorf, L. C., ed. *Educational Rankings Annual: 3,000 Rankings and Lists on Education Compiled from Educational and General Interest Published Sources.* New York: Gale, 1997.

Howsam, R. B., Corrigan, D. C., & Denemark, G. W. *Educating a Profession.* Washington, DC: American Association of Colleges for Teacher Education, 1985.

Hussar, W. J., & Gerald, D. E., eds. *Projections of Education Statistics to 2006* (25th ed.). Washington, DC: National Center for Education Statistics, 1996.

Measuring Changes in Salaries and Wages in Public Schools (1996 ed.). Arlington, VA: Educational Research Service, 1995.

Occupational Outlook Handbook. Bulletin 2250. Washington, DC: U.S. Department of Labor, Bureau of Labor Statistics, 1996.

Rankings of the States, 1995. Washington, DC: National Education Association, 1995.

Requirements for Certification of Teachers, Counselors, Librarians, and Administrators for Elementary and Secondary Schools. Chicago: University of Chicago Press, 1996–97.

Rose, L. C., & Gallup, A. M. "The 28th Annual Phi Delta Kappa/Gallup Poll of the Public's Attitudes Toward the Public Schools." *Phi Delta Kappan*, 78(1), 1996, pp. 41–59.

Salaries Paid Professional Personnel in Public Schools, 1995–96, Part 2 of *National Survey of Salaries and Wages in Public Schools.* Arlington, VA: Educational Research Service, 1996.

Snyder, T. D., ed. *Digest of Education Statistics, 1995.* Washington, DC: National Center for Education Statistics, 1995.

U.S. Bureau of the Census. *Statistical Abstract of the United States 1996.* Washington, DC: Hoover Business Press, 1996.

U.S. Congress, Office of Technology Assessment. *Teachers and Technology: Making the Connection.* Washington, DC: U.S. Government Printing Office, 1995.

Wages and Salaries Paid Support Personnel in Public Schools, 1995–96, Part 3 of *National Survey of Salaries and Wages in Public Schools.* Arlington, VA: Educational Research Service, 1995.

What Matters Most: Teaching for America's Future. New York: National Commission on Teaching & America's Future, 1996.

TEACHING IN K–12 SCHOOLS

Allen, H. A., et al. *Teaching and Learning in the Middle Level School.* New York: Merrill, 1993.

America's Teachers: Profile of a Profession. Washington, DC: National Center for Education Statistics, 1993.

Bussis, A. M., Chittenden, E. A., & Amarel, M. *Beyond Surface Curriculum.* Boulder, CO: Westview Press, 1976.

A Career in Independent School Teaching. Boston: National Association of Independent Schools.

Changing Teaching: The Next Frontier. A New Vision of the Profession. Washington, DC: National Foundation for the Improvement of Education (Undated).

Characteristics of Stayers, Movers, and Leavers: Results from the Teacher Follow-up Survey, 1991–92. Washington, DC: National Center for Education Statistics, 1994.

Corwin, R. G., & Edelfelt, R. A., eds. *Perspectives on Organizations: The School as a Social Organization.* Washington, DC: American Association of Colleges for Teacher Education & Association of Teacher Educators, 1977.

Developing Career Ladders in Teaching. Reston, VA: Association of Teacher Educators, 1986.

Dickinson, T. S., & Erb, T. O. *We Gain More than We Give: Teaming in Middle Schools.* Columbus, OH: National Middle School Association, 1996.

Edelfelt, R. A. "Career Ladders: Then and Now." *Educational Leadership*, 43(3), 1985, pp. 62–66.

Estimates of School Statistics 1994–95. Washington, DC: National Education Association, Research Division, 1995.

Fringe Benefits for Teachers in Public Schools, 1994–95, Part 3 of *National Survey of Fringe Benefits in Public Schools.* Arlington, VA: Educational Research Service, 1995.

Gallagher-Polite, M. M., et al. *Turning Points in Middle Schools: Strategic Transitions for Educators.* Thousand Oaks, CA: Corwin Press, 1996.

George, P. S., & Alexander, W. M. *The Exemplary Middle School.* New York: Harcourt Brace Jovanovich, 1993.

Interstate New Teacher Assessment and Support Consortium. *Model Standards for Beginning Teacher Licensing and Development: A Resource for State Dialogue.* Washington, DC: Council of Chief State School Officers, 1992.

Kaplan, L., & Edelfelt, R. A., eds. *Teachers for the New Millennium: Aligning Teacher Development, National Goals, and High Standards for All Students.* Thousand Oaks, CA: Corwin Press, 1996.

McEwin, C. K., Dickinson, T. S., & Jenkins, D. *America's Middle Schools: Practices and Progress. A 25-year Perspective.* Columbus, OH: National Middle School Association, 1996.

Metropolitan Life Insurance Company. *The American Teacher 1984–1995: Old Problems, New Challenges.* New York: Louis Harris and Associates, 1995.

Model Standards in Mathematics for Beginning Teacher Licensing and Development: A Resource for State Dialogue. Washington, DC: Council of Chief State School Officers, 1994.

Muth, K. D., & Alvermann, D. E. *Teaching and Learning in the Middle Grades.* Boston: Allyn & Bacon, 1992.

A Nation Prepared: Teachers for the 21st Century. New York: Carnegie Forum on Education and the Economy, 1986.

Next Steps: Moving Toward Performance-based Licensing in Teaching. Washington, DC: Council of Chief State School Officers, 1994.

Private Schools in the United States: A Statistical Profile, 1990–91. Washington, DC: National Center for Education Statistics, 1995.

Sarason, S. *You are Thinking of Teaching?* San Francisco: Jossey-Bass, 1993.

Schools and Staffing in the United States: A Statistical Profile, 1993–94. Washington, DC: National Center for Education Statistics, 1996.

Standards for the English Language Arts. Newark, DE, and Urbana, IL: International Reading Association & National Council of Teachers of English, 1996.

Status of the American Public School Teacher, 1990–1991. Washington, DC: National Education Association, Research Division, 1992.

Teaching as a Career. Washington, DC: American Federation of Teachers (Undated).

Teacher Supply and Demand in the United States: 1995 Report. Evanston, IL: Association for School, College, and University Staffing, 1996.

Teacher Supply and Demand in the United States: 1996 Report. Evanston, IL: American Association for Employment in Education, 1997.

This We Believe: Developmentally Responsive Middle Level Schools. Columbus, OH: National Middle School Association, 1995.

Wood, K. E. *Interdisciplinary Instruction: A Practical Guide for Elementary and Middle School Teachers.* Upper Saddle River, NJ: Merrill, 1997.

SCHOOL ADMINISTRATION; CENTRAL OFFICE ADMINISTRATION AND SUPERVISION

The Book of the States, 1996–97. Lexington, KY: Council of State Governments, 1996.

Clark, S. N., & Clark, D. C. *Restructuring the Middle Level School: Implications for School Leaders.* Albany, NY: State University of New York Press, 1994.

An Executive Summary of Breaking Ranks: Changing an American Institution. Reston, VA: National Association of Secondary School Principals, 1996.

Farmer, R. F. *The Middle School Principal.* Thousand Oaks, CA: Corwin Press, 1995.

Fringe Benefits for Administrators and Supervisors in Public Schools, 1994–95, Part 2 of *National Survey of Fringe Benefits in Public Schools.* Arlington, VA: Educational Research Service, 1995.

Fringe Benefits for Superintendents in Public Schools, 1994–95, Part 1 of *National Survey of Fringe Benefits in Public Schools.* Arlington, VA: Educational Research Service, 1995.

George, P. *School-Based Management: Theory and Practice.* Reston, VA: National Association of Secondary School Principals, 1991.

Glass, T. E. *The 1992 Study of the American School Superintendency: America's Education Leaders in a Time of Reform*. Arlington, VA: American Association of School Administrators, 1992.

Goldberger, S., & Kazis, R. *Revitalizing High Schools: What the School-to-Career Movement Can Contribute*. Washington, DC: American Youth Policy Forum, 1995.

Jenkins, J. M., ed. *World-Class Schools: An Evolving Concept*. Reston, VA: National Association of Secondary School Principals, 1994.

Measuring Changes in Salaries and Wages in Public Schools (1996 ed.). Arlington, VA: Educational Research Service, 1995.

Principals for our Changing Schools: Preparation and Certification. Fairfax, VA: National Association of Secondary School Principals & National Association of Elementary School Principals, 1990.

Salaries Paid Professional Personnel in Public Schools, 1995–96, Part 2 of *National Survey of Salaries and Wages in Public Schools*. Arlington, VA: Educational Research Service, 1996.

Selecting a Superintendent. Arlington, VA: American Association of School Administrators & National School Boards Association, 1979.

Selecting the Administrative Team. Arlington, VA: American Association of School Administrators & National School Boards Association, 1981.

Sizer, T. R. *Horace's Compromise: The Dilemma of the American High School*. Boston: Houghton Mifflin, 1992.

Sizer, T. R. *Horace's Hope: What Works for the American High School*. Boston: Houghton Mifflin, 1996.

What Research Says About: The Role of the Principal in Effective Schools. No. 4. Washington, DC: National Education Association, Research Division, 1986.

SPECIAL SERVICES

Anderson, K., ed. *Career Education and the Art Teaching Profession*. Reston, VA: National Art Education Association.

Careers in Early Childhood Education. Washington, DC: National Association for the Education of Young Children, 1994.

Careers in Service to Exceptional Individuals. Reston, VA: ERIC Clearinghouse on Handicapped and Gifted Children & Council for Exceptional Children.

Careers in Speech-Language Pathology and Audiology. Rockville, MD: American Speech-Language-Hearing Association.

Collison, B. B., & Garfield, N. J., eds. *Careers in Counseling and Human Services (2nd. ed.)*. Largo, FL: Careers, Inc., 1996.

Compilation of Occupational Therapy State Regulatory Information. Bethesda, MD: American Occupational Therapy Association, 1997.

Directory of Physical Therapy Programs. Alexandria, VA: American Physical Therapy Association, 1997.

Doctorate Employment Survey. Washington, DC: American Psychological Association, 1995.

Excellence in School Health: The Role of the School Nurse. Scarborough, ME: National Association of School Nurses (Undated).

The Future is Information: Talented People Want It. Chicago: American Library Association, Office for Library Personnel Resources, 1993.

Guidelines for the Preparation of Early Childhood Professionals. Washington, DC: National Association for the Education of Young Children, 1996.

Music Educators National Conference. *Careers in Music Video.* Reston, VA: National Academy of Recording Arts and Sciences, 1991.

National Standards for Arts Education. *Dance, Music, Theatre, Visual Arts: What Every Young American Should Know and Be Able to Do in the Arts.* Reston, VA: Music Educators National Conference, 1996.

Occupational Therapy Careers. Bethesda, MD: American Occupational Therapy Association, 1995.

Peemo, L. N. *Status of the Arts in the States: National Visual Arts Standards Adoption/Adaptation, Alignment, and Assessment.* Reston, VA: National Art Education Association, 1996.

Preparing to Teach Music in Today's Schools. Reston, VA: Music Educators National Conference, 1993.

Psychology Careers for the Twenty-First Century. Washington, DC: American Psychological Association, 1996.

Robinson, R. L. *Preparing to Teach Music in Today's Schools: The Best of MEJ.* Reston, VA: Music Educators National Conference, 1993.

School Library Media Centers in the United States: 1990–91. Washington, DC: National Center for Education Statistics, 1994.

School Music Programs: A New Vision. Reston, VA: Music Educators National Conference, 1994.

State Licensure Reference Guide. Alexandria, VA: American Physical Therapy Association, 1997.

Status of the States: Arts Education Reports. Reston, VA: National Art Education Association, 1997.

Summary of State Directors' Reports. Scarborough, ME: National Association of School Nurses, 1996.

Teaching Art as a Career. Reston, VA: National Art Education Association (Undated.).

TEACHING, RESEARCH, AND ADMINISTRATION IN HIGHER EDUCATION

Boyer, E. L. *Scholarship Reconsidered: Priorities of the Professoriate.* Lawrenceville, NJ: Princeton University Press, 1990.

Burgen, A., ed. *Goals and Purposes of Higher Education in the 21st Century.* Bristol, PA: Jessica Kingsley Publications, 1995.

Creating a Culture of Quality and Credibility in Teacher Education. Reston, VA: Association of Teacher Educators, 1996.

"Fact File: Median salaries of college administrators by type of institution, 1996–97." *Chronicle of Higher Education*, February 21, 1997, p. A–28.

Faculty and Instructional Staff: Who Are They and What Do They Do? Washington, DC: National Center for Education Statistics, 1994.

Furniss, W. T. *Reshaping Faculty Careers.* Washington, DC: American Council on Education, 1981.

Integrating Research on Faculty: Seeking New Ways to Communicate About the Academic Life of Faculty. Washington, DC: National Center for Education Statistics, 1996.

Kerr, C., Gade, M. L., & Kawoaka, M. *Higher Education Cannot Escape History: Issues for the 21st Century. Albany, NY: State University of New York Press, 1994.*

Levinson, D., et al. *Seasons of a Man's Life.* New York: Alfred A. Knopf, 1978.

McFadden, J., Merryfield, M. M., & Barron, K. R. *Multicultural and Global/International Education: Guidelines for Programs in Teacher Education.* Washington, DC: American Association of Colleges for Teacher Education, 1997.

Merryfield, M. M., Jarchow, E., & Pickert, S. *Preparing Teachers to Teach Global Perspectives.* Thousand Oaks, CA: Corwin Press, 1997.

Readings, B. *The University in Ruins.* Cambridge, MA: Harvard University Press, 1996.

Restructuring the University Reward System. Fort Worth, TX: Sid W. Richardson Foundation, 1997.

Salaries, Tenure, and Fringe Benefits 1993–94. Washington, DC: National Center for Education Statistics, 1994.

Schon, D. A. "The New Scholarship Requires a New Epistemology." *Change* 27(6), November/December 1995, pp. 27–34.

Tuckman, H. P. *Publication, Teaching, and the Academic Reward Structure.* Lexington, MA: Lexington Books, 1976.

What Matters Most: Teaching for America's Future. New York: National Commission on Teaching & America's Future, 1996.

Wilson, L. *The Academic Man: A Study in the Sociology of a Profession.* New York: Oxford University Press, 1942.

Wilson, L. *American Academics: Then and Now.* New York: Oxford University Press, 1979.

ADULT AND CONTINUING EDUCATION

Cantor, J. A. *Delivering Instruction to Adult Learners.* Middletown, OH: Wall & Emerson, 1992.

Cavaliere, L. A., & Sgroi, A. *Learning for Personal Development.* San Francisco: Jossey-Bass, 1992.

Collins, M. *Adult Education as Vocation: A Critical Role for the Adult Educator*. New York: Routledge, 1991.

Cranton, P. *Understanding and Promoting Transformative Learning: Guide for Educators of Adults*. San Francisco: Jossey-Bass, 1994.

Hart, M. U. *Working and Educating for Life: Feminist and International Perspectives on Adult Education*. New York: Routledge, 1992.

Jackson, L., & Caffarella, R. S. *Experiential Learning: A New Approach*. San Francisco: Jossey-Bass, 1994.

Kember, D. *Open Learning Courses for Adults: A Model of Student Progress*. Englewood Cliffs, NJ: Education Technology, 1995.

Knowles, M. S. *The Adult Education Movement in the United States*. New York: Holt, Rinehart and Winston, 1962.

Knowles, M. S. *The Adult Learner: A Neglected Species*. Houston, TX: Gulf Publishing Co., 1990.

Rogers, A. *Teaching Adults*. Philadelphia: Open University Press, 1996.

Vella, J. K. *Learning to Listen, Learning to Teach: The Power of Dialogue in Educating Adults*. San Francisco: Jossey-Bass, 1994.

EDUCATION IN BUSINESS AND INDUSTRY

Bassi, L. J., & Cheney, S. *Restructuring: Results from the 1996 Benchmarking Forum*. Alexandria, VA: American Society for Training and Development, 1996.

Bassi, L. J., Gallagher, A. L., & Schroer, E. *The ASTD Training Data Book*. Alexandria, VA: American Society for Training and Development, 1996.

Bassi, L. J., et al. *Position Yourself for the Future*. Alexandria, VA: American Society for Training and Development, 1996.

Bassi, L. J., et al. *Trends that Affect Corporate Learning and Performance*. Alexandria, VA: American Society for Training and Development, 1996.

Carnevale, A. P. *Jobs for the Nation: Challenges for a Society Based on Work*. Alexandria, VA: American Society for Training and Development, 1985.

Carnevale, A. P. "The Learning Enterprise." *Training and Development Journal*. Reprint available from American Society for Training and Development, January 1986.

Chakiris, B. J., & Rolander, R. *Careers in Training and Development*, 2nd ed. Alexandria, VA: American Society for Training and Development, 1986.

Peters, T. J. *Liberation Management: Necessary Disorganization for the Nanosecond Nineties*. New York: Alfred A. Knopf, 1992.

Peters, T. J. *The Pursuit of WOW!: Every Person's Guide to Topsy-Turvy Times*. New York: Vintage Books, 1994.

Peters, T. J., & Waterman, R. H., Jr. *In Search of Excellence: Lessons from America's Best-Run Companies*. New York: Harper & Row, 1982.

Serving the New Corporation. Alexandria, VA: American Society for Training and Development, 1986.

CAREERS IN GOVERNANCE AND CONTROL OF EDUCATION

Coek, K. E., & Martin, S. B. *Encyclopedia of Associations*. Detroit, MI: Gale Research Company, 1988.

Directory of State Education Agencies, 1996. Washington, DC: Council of Chief State School Officers, 1996.

Standards, Procedures, Policies for the Accreditation of Professional Education Units. Washington, DC: National Council for Accreditation of Teacher Education, 1995.

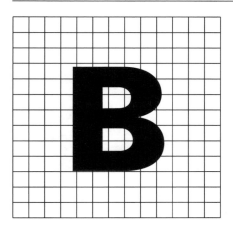

EDUCATION DIRECTORY

American Alliance for Health, Physical Education, Recreation, and Dance (AAHPERD)
1900 Association Drive
Reston, VA 20191
(703) 476-3400

American Association for Adult and Continuing Education (AAACE)
1200 Nineteenth Street N.W., Suite 300
Washington, DC 20036
(202) 429-5131

American Association for Counseling and Delevopment (AACD)
5999 Stevenson Avenue
Alexandria, VA 22304-3300
(703) 823-9800

American Association for Higher Education (AAHE)
One Dupont Circle N.W., Suite 360
Washington, DC 20036
(202) 293-6440

American Association of Christian Schools (AACS)
P.O. Box 2189
Independence, MO 64055
(816) 795-7709

American Association of Colleges for Teacher Education (AACTE)
One Dupont Circle N.W., Suite 610
Washington, DC 20036
(202) 293-2450

American Association of Collegiate Registrars and Admissions Officers (AACRAO)
One Dupont Circle N.W., Suite 330
Washington, DC 20036
(202) 293-9161

American Association of Community Colleges (AACC)
One Dupont Circle N.W., Suite 410
Washington, DC 20036
(202) 728-0200

American Association of Health Education (AAHE)
1900 Association Drive
Reston, VA 20191-1599
(703) 476-3439

American Association of School Administrators (AASA)
1801 North Moore Street
Arlington, VA 22209
(703) 528-0700

American Association of School Librarians (AASL)
Department of the American Library Association
50 East Huron Street
Chicago, IL 60611
(312) 944-6780, ext. 305

American Association of School Personnel Administrators (AASPA)
2330 Alhambra Boulevard
Sacramento, CA 95817
(916) 362-0300

American Association of State Colleges and Universities (AASCU)
One Dupont Circle N.W., Suite 700
Washington, DC 20036
(202) 293-7070

American Association of University Administrators (AAUA)
P.O. Box 2183
Tuscaloosa, AL 35403
(205) 758-0638

American Association of University Professors (AAUP)
1012 Fourteenth Street N.W., Suite 500
Washington, DC 20005
(202) 737-5900

American Association of University Women (AAUW)
1111 Sixteenth Street N.W.
Washington, DC 20036
(202) 785-7700

American Council of Learned Societies (ACLS)
228 East 45th Street
New York, NY 10017
(212) 697-1505

American Council on Education (ACE)
One Dupont Circle N.W., Suite 800
Washington, DC 20036
(202) 939-9300

American Counseling Association (ACA)
5999 Stevenson Avenue
Alexandria, VA 22304-3300
(703) 823-9800

American Educational Research Association (AERA)
1230 Seventeenth Street N.W.
Washington, DC 20036
(202) 223-9485

American Federation of Teachers (AFT)
555 New Jersey Avenue N.W.
Washington, DC 20001
(202) 879-4400

American Home Economics Association (AHEA)
1555 King Street
Alexandria, VA 22314
(703) 706-4600

American Library Association (ALA)
50 East Huron Street
Chicago, IL 60611
(312) 944-6780

American Nursing Association(ANA)
600 Maryland Avenue S.W., Suite 100W
Washington, DC 20024-2571
(202) 651-7000

American Occupational Therapy Association (AOTA)
4720 Montgomery Lane
Bethesda, MD 20824-1220
(301) 652-2682

American Physical Therapy Association (APTA)
1111 North Fairfax Street
Alexandria, VA 22314
(703) 684-2782

American Psychological Association (APA)
750 First Street N.E.
Washington, DC 20002
(202) 336-3500

American School Health Association (ASHA)
7263 State Route 43
Kent, OH 44240
(216) 678-1601

American Society for Training and Development (ASTD)
1630 Duke Street, Box 1443
Alexandria, VA 22313
(703) 683-8100

American Speech-Language-Hearing Association (ASHA)
10801 Rockville Pike
Rockville, MD 20852
(301) 897-5700

American Vocational Association (AVA)
1410 King Street
Alexandria, VA 22314
(703) 683-3111

Association for Childhood Education International (ACEI)
11501 Georgia Avenue, Suite 315
Wheaton, MD 20902
(301) 942-2443

Association for Educational Communications and Technology
(AECT)
1025 Vermont Avenue N.W., Suite 820
Washington, DC 20036
(202) 347-7834

Association for Institutional Research (AIR)
Florida State University
314 Stone Building
Tallahassee, FL 32306
(904) 644-4470

Association for Supervision and Curriculum Development
(ASCD)
1250 Pitt Street
Alexandria, VA 22314-1403
(703) 549-9110

Association for the Study of Higher Education (ASHE)
c/o D. Stanley Carpenter
Department of Educational Administration
Texas A&M University
College Station, TX 77843-4226
(409) 845-0393

Association of American Colleges (AAC)
1818 R Street N.W.
Washington, DC 20009
(202) 387-3760

Association of American Universities (AAU)
One Dupont Circle N.W., Suite 730
Washington, DC 20036
(202) 466-5030

Association of Christian Schools International (ASCI)
P.O. Box 35097
Colorado Springs, Co 80935-3509
(719) 528-6906

Association of School Business Officials, International
  (ASBO)
1760 Reston Avenue, Suite 411
Reston, VA 20191
(703) 478-0405

Association Working Group for Mustic, Art, and Design
11250 Roger Bacon Drive, Suite 21
Reston, VA 22090
(703) 437-0700

Carnegie Foundation for the Advancement of Teaching
Five Ivy Lane
Princeton, NJ 08540
(609) 452-1780

Center for Education for the Young Adolescent
University of Wisconsin-Platteville
One University Plaza
Platteville, WI 53818
(608) 341-1276

College and University Personnel Association (CUPA)
1233 Twentieth Street N.W.
Washington, DC 20036
(202) 429-0311

Council for American Private Education (CAPE)
1726 M Street, N.W. Suite 1102
Washington, DC 20036
(202) 659-0016

Council for Basic Education
1319 F Street N.W.
Washington, DC
(202) 347-4171

Council for Exceptional Childred (CEC)
1920 Association Drive
Reston, VA 20191
(703) 620-3660

Council for Social Work Education (CSWE)
1600 Duke Street, Suite 300
Alexandria, VA 22314
(703) 683-8080

Council for the Advancement and Support of Education
Eleven Dupont Circle N.W.
Washington, DC 20036
(202) 328-5900

Council of Chief State School Officers (CCSSO)
One Massachusetts Avenue N.W., Suite 700
Washington, DC 20001-1431
(202) 408-5505

Council of Graduate Schools (CGS)
One Dupont Circle N.W., Suite 430
Washington, DC 20036
(202) 223-3791

Council on Higher Education Accreditation (CHEA)
One Dupont Circle N.W., Suite 305
Washington, DC 20036
(202) 955-6126

Defense Activity for Non-Traditional Education Support
  (DANTES)
Pensacola, FL 32509-7400
(904) 452-1745

Education Research Service (ERS)
2000 Clarendon Boulevard
Arlington, VA 22201
(703) 243-2100

ERIC Clearinghouse on Higher Education
One Dupont Circle N.W., Suite 630
Washington, DC 20036
(202) 296-2597

ERIC Clearinghouse on Teacher Education
One Dupont Circle N.W., Suite 610
Washington, DC 20036-1186
(202) 293-2450

International Reading Association (IRA)
800 Barksdale Road
P.O. Box 8139
Newark, DE 19714-8139
(302) 731-1600

International Technology Education Association (ITEA)
1914 Association Drive
Reston, VA 20191
(703) 860-2100

International University Consortium
University College
University of Maryland
College Park, MD 20742-1612
(301) 985-7811

Modern Language Association (MLA)
Ten Astor Place, Fifth Floor
New York, NY 10003
(212) 475-9500

Music Educators National Conference (MENC)
1902 Association Drive
Reston, VA 20191
(703) 860-4000

National Academy of Sciences
2101 Constitution Avenue N.W.
Washington, DC 20418
(202) 334-2040

National Art Education Association (NAEA)
1916 Association Drive
Reston, VA 20191
(703) 860-8000

National Association for the Education of Young Children
    (NAEYC)
1509 Sixeenth Street N.W.
Washington, DC 20036
(202) 232-8777

National Assoication for Women in Education
1325 Eighteenth Street N.W.
Washington, DC 20036
(202) 659-9330

National Association of Administrators of Federal Programs (NAAFP)
1801 North Moore Street
Arlington, VA 22209
(703) 875-0729

National Association of Biology Teachers (NABT)
11250 Roger Bacon Drive, Unit 19
Reston, VA 22090
(703) 471-1134

National Association of Elementary School Principals (NAESP)
1615 Duke Street
Alexandria, VA 22314
(703) 684-3345

National Association of Independent Colleges and Universities (NAICU)
1620 L Street N.W.
Washington, DC 20036
(202) 785-8866

National Association of Independent Schools (NAIS)
1620 L Street N.W.
Washington, DC 20036
(202) 973-9700

National Association of Pupil Personnel Administrators (NAPPA)
3929 Old Lee Highway
Fairfax, VA 22030
(703) 549-9110

National Association of School Nurses (NASN)
P.O. Box 1300
Lamplighter Lane
Scarborough, ME 04074
(207) 883-2117

National Association of School Psychologists (NASP)
4340 East-West Highway, Suite 402
Bethesda, MD 20814-4411
(301) 657-0270

National Association of Schools of Art and Design
11250 Roger Bacon Drive, Suite 21
Reston, VA 22090
(703) 437-0700

National Association of Schools of Dance
11250 Roger Bacon Drive, Suite 21
Reston, VA 22090
(703) 437-0700

National Association of Schools of Music
11250 Roger Bacon Drive, Suite 21
Reston, VA 22090
(703) 437-0700

National Association of Schools of Theatre
11250 Roger Bacon Drive, Suite 21
Reston, VA 22090
(703) 437-0700

National Association of Secondary School Principals
    (NASSP)
1904 Association Drive
Reston, VA 20191
(703) 860-0200

National Association of Social Workers (NASW)
750 First Street N.E., Suite 700
Washington, DC 20002-4241
(202) 408-8600

National Association of State Directors of Special Education
    (NASDSE)
1800 Diagonal Road, Suite 320
Alexandria, VA 22314
(703) 519-3800

National Association of State Directors of Teacher Education
    and Certification (NASDTEC)
3600 Whitman Avenue North, #105
Seattle, WA 98103
(206) 547-0437

National Association of State Directors of Vocational-Technical Education Consortium
444 North Capitol Street N.W., Suite 830
Washington, DC 20001
(202) 737-0303

National Association of State Universities and Land-Grant Colleges (NASULGC)
One Dupont Circle N.W., Suite 710
Washington, DC 20036
(202) 778-0818

National Association of University Women (NAUW)
1501 Eleventh Street N.W.
Washington, DC 20001
(202) 547-3967

National Business Education Association (NBEA)
1914 Association Drive
Reston, VA 20191
(703) 860-8300

National Catholic Educational Association (NCEA)
1077 30th Street N.W., Suite 100
Washington, DC 20007
(202) 337-6232

National Center for Education Statistics (NCES)
U.S. Department of Education
555 New Jersey Avenue N.W.
Washington, DC 20208
(202) 219-1839

National Clearinghouse for Professions in Special Education
1800 Diagonal Road, Suite 320
Alexandria, VA 22314
(703) 296-1800

National Community Education Association (NCEA)
3929 Old Lee Highway
Fairfax, VA 22030
(703) 359-8973

National Council for Accreditation of Teacher Education
   (NCATE)
2010 Massachusetts Avenue N.W., Suite 200
Washington, DC 20036-1023
(202) 466-7496

National Council for the Social Studies (NCSS)
3501 Newark Street N.W.
Washington, DC 20016
(202) 966-7840

National Council of Teachers of English (NCTE)
1111Kenyon Road
Urbana, IL 61801
(217) 328-3870

National Council of Teachers of Mathematics (NCTM)
1906 Association Drive
Reston, VA 20191
(703) 620-9840

National Education Association (NEA)
1201 Sixteenth Street N.W.
Washington, DC 20036
(202) 833-4000

National Information Center on Children and Youth with
   Disabilities (NICCYD)
P.O. Box 1492
Washington, DC 20013
(202) 884-8200

National School Public Relations Association (NSPRA)
1501 Lee Highway, Suite 201
Arlington, VA 22209
(703) 528-5840

National Science Foundation (NSF)
4201 Wilson Boulevard
Arlington, VA 22230
(703) 306-1070

National Science Teachers Association (NSTA)
1840 Wilson Boulevard
Arlington, VA 22201
(703) 243-7100

National Staff Development Council (NSDC)
Council Business Office
P.O. Box 240
Oxford, OH 45056
(513) 523-6029

National Training Laboratories (NTL)
Institute for Applied Behavioral Science
1240 North Pitt Street, Suite 100
Alexandria, VA 22314-1403
(703) 548-1500

National University Continuing Education Association
  (NUCEA)
One Dupont Circle N.W., Suite 615
Washington, DC 20036
(202) 659-3130

Office of Educational Research and Improvement (OERI)
U.S. Department of Education
555 New Jersey Avenue N.W.
Washington, DC 20208
(202) 219-1658

Public Broadcasting System/Adult Learning Service
1320 Braddock Place
Alexandria, VA 22314
(703) 739-5000

Recruiting New Teachers, Inc. (RNT)
385 Concord Avenue
Belmont, MA 02178
(617) 489-6000

Teachers of English to Speakers of Other Languages (TESOL)
1600 Cameron Street, Suite 300
Alexandria, VA 22314-2751
(703) 836-0774

USDA Graduate School
U.S. Department of Agriculture
600 Maryland Avenue S.W.
Washington, DC 20024
(202) 401-9129

INDEX